FROM
THE
STRAIGHT
PATH
TO THE
NARROW
WAY

FROM
THE STRAIGHT PATH
TO
THE NARROW WAY

Journeys of Faith

Edited by David H. Greenlee

Associate Editors: P. I. Barnabas, Evelyne Reisacher,
Farida Saïdi, J. Dudley Woodberry

Authentic

Authentic
We welcome your comments and questions.
129 Mobilization Drive, Waynesboro, GA 30830 USA authenticusa@stl.org
9 Dolphin Avenue, Bletchley, Milton Keynes, Bucks, MK1 1QR, UK
www.authenticbooks.com
If you would like a copy of our current catalog, contact us at:
1-8MORE-BOOKS
ordersusa@stl.org

From the Straight Path to the Narrow Way

ISBN-13: 978-1-932805-42-0
ISBN-10: 1-932805-42-7

Cover design: Paul Lewis
Interior design: Angela Duerksen
Editorial team: Andy Sloan, K.J. Larson, Megan Kassebaum

Printed in the United States of America

CONTENTS

SECTION 2
UNDERSTANDING THE EXPERIENCE OF COMING TO FAITH

SECTION 3
UNDERSTANDING SOME MOVEMENTS TO FAITH

SECTION 4
CONCLUDING REFLECTIONS

ACKNOWLEDGMENTS

This book is published with thanks to the family whose generous gift made possible both this book and the consultation from which it arose.

> We thank our God every time we remember you. We pray with joy because of your partnership in the gospel from the first day until now, confident that he who began a good work in you will carry it on to completion until the day of Christ Jesus.

> (paraphrased from Philippians 1:3–6)

Thanks also to those who graciously welcomed us and hosted our gathering, to the authors who have spent long hours writing and revising these papers, to Greg who helped us get them into shape for publication, and to Volney, Angela, Andy, and the team at our publisher who have helped us make these papers available to you, the reader.

Most of all, we thank our brothers and sisters who have come to faith in Christ, whose stories we tell in these pages, and Jesus Christ in whom we share a common hope.

The Editors

CONTRIBUTORS

Hasan Abdulahugli is a Central Asian. Raised during the Soviet era, he came to faith in Christ in the early 1990s and is a leader in the growing church in his country.

P. I. Barnabas has lived and worked among an unreached people group for more than thirty-two years and speaks the indigenous language. He does direct personal evangelism and trains and equips other Christians to do likewise. He leads a monthly meeting of leaders who minister among this UPG. He received his PhD from Fuller Theological Seminary.

Lowell de Jong and his wife grew up on the mission field and as adults have worked in Africa as missionaries for thirty-two years.

Abraham Durán has served for twelve years in the Middle East. He is among the first generation of cross-cultural workers sent out from the evangelical churches of Latin America. He is associated with FRONTIERS, an interdenominational agency seeking the glory of Jesus in the Muslim world.

Since 1981 **Christel Eric** and her husband have worked among various Muslim communities in different areas in sub-Saharan Africa. Their main focus was not only to reach out themselves, but also to involve, help, and train the local Christians to share their faith with their Muslim neighbors and friends. They have developed literature and other media to equip Christians, along with helping Muslims to understand the gospel. Christel's special desire was to build close friendships with Muslim women and youth, convinced that "the hand that rocks the cradle, rules the world!" Christel and her husband are missionaries of SIM International.

Edward Evans, from England, has twenty-five years of experience with Pakistani Muslim converts in Pakistan and Britain. For more than fifteen of those years he worked in a Bible-teaching role in Pakistan. He holds a master's degree in Islamic Societies and Cultures, for which he wrote a dissertation, "Factors Affecting Attitudes to Apostasy in Pakistan." Chapter 13 is adapted from that dissertation. Edward is married and the father of three children.

David Greenlee grew up in a missionary family in South America. He has served with Operation Mobilization since 1977, currently in the role of International Research Associate. Married and the father of three children, he holds a PhD in Intercultural Studies from Trinity International University, Deerfield, Illinois, USA.

Jean-Marie Gaudeul was born in 1937. Fr. Gaudeul is a Roman Catholic priest, a member of the Missionary Society of the White Fathers. Ordained in 1963, he worked for several years in Tanzania as a parish priest. From 1975 to 1984, he taught at the Pontifical Institute of Arabic and Islamic Studies (PISAI) in Rome. Author of several books on the history of Christian-Muslim relations, he holds a PhD in Arabic and Islamic Studies from the PISAI (Rome). Currently, he is in charge of the French Bishops' Secretariat for Relations with Islam (SRI) and is a member of the Vatican Commission for Christian-Muslim Dialogue.

Paul G. Hiebert is Distinguished Professor of Mission at Trinity Evangelical Divinity School, Deerfield, Illinois, USA. Paul was a third-generation Mennonite Brethren missionary to India, the land of his birth. He holds a PhD in Anthropology from the University of Minnesota and is the author of numerous books and articles.

John Kim has been serving among a Muslim unreached people in Southeast Asia since 1994 through OMF International. He is currently working as a strategy coordinator and executive member of the Muslim ministry division of the same organization. He married Yoon in 1985 and has three children. John holds a PhD in Physics from Seoul National University in Korea.

Rick Love is International Director of FRONTIERS, serving over 800 missionaries worldwide. Prior to this appointment Rick served as US Director of FRONTIERS, and before that led a church planting team among Sundanese Muslims in Indonesia. Rick was granted a doctor of ministry degree in Urban Missions from Westminster Theological Seminary and received a PhD in Missiology from the Fuller School of World Missions. Rick, his wife Fran, and one of their daughters, Tessa, reside in High Wycombe, Buckinghamshire, England.

David E. Maranz, now retired, spent the last twenty-five years of his missionary career in Central and West Africa. He served as director of work among numerous Muslim groups in several countries. He and his wife lived for some months in a Muslim village where Sufism was dominant. For many years David has been an anthropology consultant and has written two books on Muslim and traditional societies. He holds a PhD in Islamic Studies from William Carey International University.

Andreas Maurer is married to Ruth, and they have three sons. He worked for some time as a mechanical engineer in Switzerland before studying at a Bible college in England from 1981–1984. Thereafter he enlarged his knowledge through various courses and theological studies at universities in England and South Africa. In 1999 Andreas completed his doctorate at the University of Pretoria (UNISA) on the topic: "In Search of a New Life: Conversion Motives of Christians and Muslims."

Dan McVey and his wife Brenda have worked in one West African nation for twenty-one years in church planting, leadership training, and community development. Graduate degrees in intercultural studies and Islamics have aided Dan in his work among Muslim people groups. At present, Dan is a missions coordinator for Abilene Christian University, Abilene, Texas, USA.

Since 1987, **Mary McVicker** has been a cross-cultural worker living in South Asia among Muslims. Her commitment is to find practical ways to express God's love and to help bring transformation among women and families in the community. Among her current projects is to develop the Asian Institute of Intercultural Studies, a study center and library on Islam, located in South Asia. She completed an MA in Intercultural Studies and is presently pursuing a PhD in communication studies among women in the Indian Muslim community.

David Smith has served for many years as an observer and participant in the encounter between Muslims and Christians in the Middle East.

Evelyne A. Reisacher served twenty years as codirector of L'Ami, a Christian organization serving the North African community in France and North Africa. She traveled widely in North Africa, the Middle East, and the Islamic world to lecture and meet with Christians and Muslims. She is currently assistant professor of Islamic Studies at Fuller Theological Seminary. She also travels internationally and lectures on topics including Christian-Muslim relations, gender issues in Islam, and intercultural relationships.

Farida Saïdi is the founder and codirector of L'Ami, a Christian organization that serves the North African community in France and North Africa. She is an active member of numerous Christian organizations, to which she brings her expertise on the Muslim world. She lectures and leads workshops internationally on issues relating to North African

Christianity. Farida is currently pursuing a doctorate in Islamic studies with an emphasis on church leadership issues in the Muslim world.

Helen Steadman comes from the UK and has lived in East Asia since 1968. She has served with the local church in a teaching and training ministry, taught science in several government universities, and worked with students. She also spent eleven years in a role that allowed her to travel widely in East Asia. She is currently teaching at a small theological seminary in Indonesia.

Jim Tebbe grew up in Pakistan and has worked in Pakistan, Bangladesh, Jordan, and Cyprus. He was the international director for InterServe, based in Cyprus, from 1992–2002, and is currently the vice president for Missions and director of the Urbana Mission Convention for InterVarsity. He lives with his family in Madison, Wisconsin. He has an MDiv from Gordon Conwell Seminary in Massachusetts, USA. He studied for the MA in Islamic History at the University of the Punjab, Lahore, Pakistan, has an MA in Near Eastern Studies from Princeton University, and earned a PhD in Religious Studies from St. John's, Nottingham, UK, the Open University.

Richard Tucker spent ten years in the country of "Daristan" on a church planting team.

J. Dudley Woodberry is dean emeritus and professor of Islamic Studies at the School of Intercultural Studies, Fuller Theological Seminary. He served with his family in Afghanistan, Pakistan, and Saudi Arabia. Dudley is the editor of *Muslims and Christians on the Emmaus Road* (MARC, 1989) and *Reaching the Resistant: Bridges and Barriers for Mission* (William Carey, 1998), and joint editor of *Missiological Education for the 21ˢᵗ Century: The Book, the Circle, and the Sandals* (Orbis, 1996) and *Muslim and Christian Reflections on Peace: Divine and Human Dimensions* (University Press of America, 2005).

SECTION 1
Missiological Overview

CHAPTER 1

THE "GOOD NEWS" IS GOOD NEWS!

DAVID GREENLEE

What was *good* about the good news for *you*?

Most people enjoy talking about themselves, and those who have faith in Jesus Christ seem to particularly enjoy answering this question. I ask the question often, and never tire of the answers.

In my own case, even as a six-year-old boy, the good news was *good* because it meant forgiveness for sins and the promise of heaven. And it continues to be *good* news over forty years later!

How Is the Good News *Good* for Muslims?

Recently, a group of about fifty people gathered to consider how Muslims are responding to the good news, how they are coming to faith in Jesus Christ. We represented over twenty nations, and included several who themselves had made the journey of faith from walking the "Straight Path" of Islam onto the "Narrow Way" of Jesus Christ.[1]

My own path to that consultation began in the early 1990s. In narrowing down my dissertation topic, I came across a comment by Greg Livingstone that "very little adequate research has been done, isolating the variables of how or why Muslims have been making commitments to Christ."[2] In fact, although there were numerous books of stories and testimonies, as I prepared my research proposal I found very little analytical research along the lines Livingstone had suggested. So I took up the challenge and did my field work among urban young men in a Muslim land who had come to faith in Christ.

Others were also responding to this need. Key among these studies has been Dudley Woodberry's ongoing global study, with highlights of his work presented in this volume.

But the research gap continues, as revealed in the *International Bulletin of Missionary Research* listing of English-language missiological dissertations completed between 1992–2001. Only 3 out of 925 dissertations listed fell in the category "Islam, conversion from"[3] (although the compilers missed some, including Andreas Maurer's work in South Africa, referred to in his chapter of this book).

Close to the field, my experience has been that consultations looking at Christian ministry among Muslims may touch on conversion—but the key process and event of coming to faith tends to be overlooked, with emphasis placed on issues of society, programs, ministry tools, discipleship, and church planting.

Research That Makes a Difference

Richard Peace, in his excellent book *Conversion in the New Testament*, notes, "How we conceive of conversion determines how we do evangelism."[4]

Peace and I agree that there is no simple paradigm and no single pattern of coming to faith described in the Bible. And although there are significant trends and patterns, we cannot point to any single process by which Muslims are coming to faith in Christ. Just as understanding the biblical examples of conversion is vital, research such as we present in this book is needed to help us be more fruitful in our witness.

Our work was done along the lines earlier noted, isolating the variables of how or why Muslims have been making commitments to Christ, with analysis which moves us beyond telling stories to a deeper understanding of how God is at work. When this work is done well, and applied well, it can make a significant difference in our ministry.

Let me point the finger at my own organization to illustrate the need we are trying to address. About ten years ago we produced a video promoting our work. In one scene, a young man is seen loading a suitcase with New Testaments while quoting some authority figure with words to the effect that 90 percent (or some such number) of Muslims who come to faith in Christ are impacted by literature.

The statement may well be true, and the implication is clear: invest in literature!

I wholeheartedly support appropriate literature distribution, but there is a problem. Even if it is true that 90 percent of Muslims who did come to faith were impacted by literature, what else happened? What about the 98 percent, to guess at a number, who received the same literature but did *not* come to faith?

Take your favorite tool: literature, dreams and visions, radio or satellite TV broadcasts, Bible correspondence courses—God uses them all! But far too often major investment of our resources is based on an inadequate understanding of the complex interplay of his Spirit's work in society, in the spiritual realm, and through our witness in the process of people coming to faith in Christ. (And, also far too often, some Christians scandalously claim "converts" like hunting trophies, as if they or their particular ministry or method is the only tool God uses to draw people to faith.)

But let me be more positive. The research we present here is needed because God *is* at work. There are few places in the world that we can describe as major breakthroughs, but Helen Steadman, who contributes a conclusion to this book, reminded us of the situation in 1980 when she attended another consultation: "Then we spoke of two believers here, or three there. Some said that they did not know of any [Muslim background] believers but had hopes that there were a few. But now we speak of hundreds."

She went on to say that in her country there are not many settings left where the "I am the first to hear or believe" barrier still exists. Most of us could repeat at least a few such stories of isolated followers of Christ, stories which are often best left unpublished for the sake of those new believers.

And so we do our research because *God is at work*. We want to see him do so much more.

We recognize the difficulty in applying a lesson from rural Algeria to urban South Asia. But we need to do the research and then to appropriately share it as encouragement and as instruction for one another.

A "Dirty Word" in Missions

The emphasis of this book, and of the consultation which gave it birth, is *conversion*. For some it has become a dirty word, stained by association with colonialism, extraction, culture change, and force—a word that should be eliminated from our missiological vocabulary.

We respect those concerns, especially in places where anticonversion laws are a serious threat and those who follow and serve Christ are under great pressure. Many, though, have thought long and hard in search of a better word in the English language (and other languages) to describe this process and event of coming to faith in Christ. So far, we have not found any single term that conveys the richness of meaning carried by the ten letters of *conversion*.

So, for those with concerns about the use of this word, please be patient with us. Although the contributors to this volume may ascribe a variety of nuances of meaning to the word, and we recognize the linguistic complexities associated with the word, overall we echo Andrew Walls' use of the term to refer to "the most elemental feature of the word . . . the idea of turning . . . the specifically Christian understanding of the response to God's saving activity."[5]

Join Us on This Journey

Some of those who gathered at our meeting were men and women whose names are widely recognized in the missions world. Most of us, though, are "unknowns"—many having spent years working and witnessing tirelessly, faithfully, perhaps anonymously.

Of the common factors we shared at our meeting, one was the desire to draw together excellent research and missiological reflection with significant field experience. None who came were "armchair specialists" who only knew Islam, and not Muslims. Likewise, those active in field ministry were invited both for their years of experience and their ability to interact in lively missiological discussion. While the work we did of necessity entailed a certain level of academic rigor, we hope to encourage others to pursue further research and reflection close to the field, which will help us better understand how God is at work in drawing Muslims to faith in Jesus Christ.

Dudley Woodberry opens the work with an update from his ongoing survey of global trends. Noted missiologist Paul Hiebert addresses the vital issue of transformation of worldview, while Rick Love joins me in an overview of current issues relevant to our topic. David Maranz's study points to the vital importance of Scripture in drawing Muslims to faith in Christ. Jim Tebbe draws the introductory section to a close by pointing to the theological importance and impact of changes in Christian approaches to Islam, especially regarding revelation, as exemplified by Temple Gairdner, Kenneth Cragg, and William Cantwell Smith.

A section of papers dealing with conversion motives of individuals begins with the insights of French scholar Jean-Marie Gaudeul. Andreas Maurer's work points out that "the conversion door swings both ways" as he analyzes the motives for South African Christians to convert to Islam as well as for Muslims to turn to faith in Christ. Evelyne Reisacher and Mary McVicker lead us into the world of North African and South Asian women, helping us to see and experience conversion through female eyes while Christel Eric helps us see the stages of coming to faith.

The following three chapters draw on the collective study of individuals, lending broader insights into the process of conversion in Central Asia, Pakistan, and among a large ethnic group in Asia.

We then turn our attention to movements to Christ, studies in which the research focuses more on the group as a whole than on individuals. Dudley Woodberry introduced this concept in his chapter at the beginning of the volume, referring in particular to "insider movements." Dan McVey's paper is a study of the initial growth, then plateau, of a movement in West Africa. Lowell de Jong cautions us not to move too fast in seeking to foment a movement to Christ, and in two chapters describes the long process leading to an emerging movement among Africa's Fulbe tribe. John Kim couples an interesting model from physics with missiology as he describes the spread of the gospel among clusters of Muslim villagers on "Anotoc", an Asian island. Finally, Richard Tucker points to key factors leading to a surge in the number of national believers in "Daristan" while warning that we need to look for the uniqueness of each situation since God offers us no "cookie cutter" solutions.

Drawing the chapters of case studies to a close, Abraham Durán points to seven steps that helped lead to a significant turning to Christ among a Middle Eastern people. Central to this process was an emphasis on displaying the beauty of Jesus.

Finally, Helen Steadman and David Smith, both with long years of service among Muslims but in two very different contexts, conclude the volume, reviewing the papers with personal reflections and suggesting ways to move forward in Christian ministry among Muslims.

The research presented in this book is valid—but not all of our findings will have universal application. Something may be different about *your* setting that would lead to different findings, or suggest different conclusions and applications. Our hope is that in this volume you will find challenges which cause you to reflect and reconsider, resulting in greater fruitfulness for God's glory.

As we prepare this manuscript, we still cannot refer to multitudes who have made the journey from the Straight Path onto the Narrow Way, but more and more Muslims *do* enter into the Way each day. May these papers contribute to the process of many more finding the hope of eternal life we share through faith in Jesus Christ, to whom be all the glory.

A Note on Style

The contributors to this book come from a variety of countries of origin and serve in numerous countries. Reflecting the diversity of languages they use as they serve among Muslim peoples, the authors have used a variety of spellings of names and Islamic religious terms. Rather than choosing one standard, we have intentionally allowed the authors to maintain their own chosen style. Further, we assume that readers are familiar with these terms and have only provided an English translation of the least common terms.

Some authors have chosen to write under a pseudonym while the names of some locations and ethnic groups have been changed. This has been done out of respect for the concerns of the individuals and groups described. The first use of such place or ethnic group names is generally placed within quotation marks.

CHAPTER 2

A GLOBAL PERSPECTIVE ON MUSLIMS COMING TO FAITH IN CHRIST

J. DUDLEY WOODBERRY

"It was the best of times, it was the worst of times" wrote Charles Dickens about the French Revolution in his novel *A Tale of Two Cities*. The same could be said about the state of Muslim evangelism during the current "Muslim Revolution."

"The worst of times" has been evident in the anti-Christian current that has been part of the tide of the Islamic resurgence that burst onto the world scene with the Iranian Revolution of 1978–1979 and into everyone's living room on September 11, 2001, leaving many victims and ruined churches in its wake.

"The best of times" has been evidenced in the unprecedented trickles to floods of Muslims who have followed Christ in previously evange-listically arid lands. In the late 1960s there had been a major turning to Christ in Indonesia, but now we are seeing similar major movements in sections of North Africa and South and Central Asia, along with smaller new responses in regions of Eastern Europe, South Asia, and sub-Saharan Africa and among various tribal and ethnic groups in these regions and the Middle East.

The Contexts in Which God Is Working

Avery Willis Jr. has noted how the hand of God worked in the glove of five circumstances in Indonesia in the late 1960s to draw thousands of

11

Javanese to faith in Christ.[1] We can identify a different mix of circumstances through which God has been working in the Muslim world today. This is not to say that God causes the tragedies associated with many of these circumstances, but that he works within them to draw people to himself.

The first of these circumstances has been **political**—especially the resurgence of Islam. This drew world attention with the Islamist revolution in Iran. What did not draw the same attention was the subsequently increased sale of Bibles even though the new government had closed down the offices of the United Bible Societies. Likewise, more Muslims came to churches seeking instruction for baptism. Next door, when Pakistan's martial law president Zia al-Haq tried to impose Islamic law, more Bibles were sold than before, more people signed up for Bible correspondence courses, and more accepted Christ as Savior.

In neighboring Afghanistan, after the mujahideen civil war and the rise of the Taliban who tried to enforce Islamic law, many Afghans became refugees and as refugees accepted Christ as Lord and Savior. It became evident as we studied the phenomenon that over the years secularizing trends had led to a loss of values, including religious traditional values. The result was an Islamic resurgence. When it took a militant form and/or tried to impose Islamic law and there was an attractive Christian presence, receptivity to the gospel resulted, followed by persecution.

The second finger of the glove of current events through which the hand of God is working is **catastrophes**, be they of natural or human causes. This has provided the occasion for the church to provide cups of cold water or milk in Christ's name where the Sahara Desert crept south, or bail out cups of cold water in that same name in South Asia where cyclones and tsunamis inundated their coastal lands. Both have given occasions for Christians to express God's love to victims who, by experiencing that love for their physical needs, also welcome it for their spiritual needs.

The third finger of the glove of current events is **migrations** involving refugees, new urbanites, or immigrants to the West. As such, they have new needs and often receptivity to new ideas. Many refugees from the Iranian Revolution in Turkey, and more in the West, found a new life with Christ. A majority of Muslims who followed Christ in Jordan, Syria, and Lebanon in recent years were new urban arrivals. Those who did not respond in that initial window of opportunity tended to become secularized, uninterested in spiritual matters, or disillusioned, in which case they often joined Islamist movements.

A fourth finger of the glove is the **desire for blessing (*baraka*) or power**, an important part of popular faith of large numbers of Muslims. As evangelicals have been increasingly open to ministries of healing and power—coupled with biblical teaching on the role of suffering—the gospel has been seen to meet the heart concerns of Muslim masses.

The final finger of the glove that the hand of God is using is **ethnic and cultural resurgence**. The Bengalis of East Pakistan suffered at the hands of the Punjabis and others of West Pakistan. Suppressed by their coreligionists, this ethnic group and others under similar pressure have become more receptive to the gospel. As Christian workers have understood that the gospel can be translated into various cultural forms and that all of the "Pillars of Islam" (except the references to Muhammad and Mecca) were used previously by Jews and/or Christians, they have found greater freedom to use vocabularies and forms of worship that felt indigenous. This has resulted in significant growth in the number of Muslims following Christ in many regions.

What God Is Using in Individual Conversions

An extensive questionnaire has now been filled out by 650 individual (former) Muslims who have followed Christ from 40 countries and 58 ethnic groups representing every major region of the Muslim world. Revised copies can be obtained by emailing dudley@fuller.edu. (See the Appendix for its current form.) The results have been collected on Excel spreadsheets and then transferred to an ABstat program that facilitates comparisons between different groups based on such factors as gender, age, rural or urban context, country, ethnicity, or branch of Islam. The influences God used are ranked by their importance to the individual and whether they were influential before, at the time of, or after a decision was made to follow Christ.

Only two or three groups within the total sample are represented sufficiently for somewhat reliable comparisons; nevertheless, the 650 responses do lend themselves to general observations. In these initial observations, we shall concentrate only on the relative importance of each influence toward conversion, giving twice as much weight to answers that indicated the factors had "much" influence in the conversion process in contrast to those where the respondent only indicated they had "some" influence. The relative importance thus ascribed to each factor by the respondents is indicated in each section.

Influence of Experience

The **lifestyle of Christians** (ranked first) was very influential, in part, because it contrasted with a broad perception in many Muslim societies that Christians are immoral. Instead, one North African Sufi said that there was no gap between the moral profession and practice of Christians. An Omani woman observed they treated women as equals. Others noted loving marriages. A Moroccan was welcomed by his former in-laws after a difficult divorce. A beggar was not only given a tract but all the money the woman had who gave her the tract. Many who had experienced oppression by other Muslim ethnic groups mentioned the nonracism of Christians. The poor noted that the Christian workers had a simple lifestyle and wore local clothes, while conservative Muslims observed that they did not drink alcohol or touch those of the opposite sex.

This was followed by the related cluster of **answered prayer** (second), **miracles** and the **power of God** in specific situations (third), and **healing** (fourth). North African Muslim neighbors asked Christians to pray for a very sick daughter who was healed. In Senegal, the Muslim marabout referred a patient to the Christians when he was not able to bring healing. In Pakistan, a crippled Shi`ite girl was healed through Christian prayer after a pilgrimage to Mecca did not cure her.

Dissatisfaction with the form of Islam or individual Muslims they had experienced (fifth) certainly facilitated receptivity to the gospel. This included a perceived emphasis on a punishing rather than a loving God, One who was distant, and One who did not allow enough human freedom. As for the requirement of liturgical prayer in Arabic, a Javanese man asked, "Doesn't an all-knowing God know Indonesian?" The Qur'an was seen as lacking unity and Muhammad as lacking holiness. Muslim militancy was criticized from the early conquests up to present-day Muslim violence. Most disaffection was expressed concerning Islamic law with its sexism and inability to transform hearts and society. Finally, there was disillusion with Muslim leaders, the Khomeini revolution, the fees and favors imams expected, and the writing of amulets and praying to dead saints in popular Islam.

Dreams and visions (sixth) were significant at various times in the conversion process. A young Algerian woman in France had a vision that her Muslim grandmother came into her room and said, "Jesus is not dead. . . . He is here." In Israel, an Arab dreamed that his dead father came and said, "Follow the pastor. He will show you the right way." A Nigerian had a vision of a devout Muslim in hell and a poor Christian, who could not afford to give alms, in heaven. Other dreams and visions followed. A young Turkish woman, in jail because of her conversion, had a vision that she would be released, and she was. A young man in North Africa was encouraged to persevere in prison by a vision of thousands of believers in the streets of his city proclaiming their faith.

Spiritual Needs Better Answered by Faith in Christ

Inner peace (ranked first), **assurance of forgiveness** (second), **and assurance of salvation** (tied for third) in Christian faith were attractive because, in the Qur'an, God forgives whom he wills and chastises whom he wills (al-Baqara [2]: 284). Thus there is no assurance of salvation.

One Indonesian woman was taught from the Traditions of Muhammad (hadith) that the bridge over hell to paradise was as thin as a hair. An Iranian immigrant to the United States was asked if Christ had given him freedom from fear. He responded, "Oh yes, I feel more assurance of forgiveness." An Egyptian claimed that the main attraction of Christianity for a Muslim is the assurance of salvation. A Javanese affirmed the same: "After receiving Jesus I had confidence concerning the end of my life."

The **love of God** (tied for third) is attractive because, in the Qur'an, God loves those who love him—not those who reject faith (Al 'Imran [4]: 31–32). A Gambian Muslim exclaimed, "God loves me just as I am!" A West African was surprised by God's love of all people of all races, including enemies. The Qur'an denies that God is a Father (al-Safat [37]: 152); yet the portrayal of God as a Father and friend is attractive to those who desire his love.

Muslims find this love expressed through Jesus, whom they already believe from the Qur'an to be without fault (Maryam [19]: 19), even when Muhammad is told to ask forgiveness for his sins (al-Fath [48]: 2). An Iranian Shi'a was attracted to Christ before he was attracted to

Christianity. Jesus' image as the Good Shepherd attracted a Sufi of North Africa, and his purity and demands in the Sermon on the Mount attracted a Lebanese Shi`a.

Guidance to spiritual truth in the Bible ranked fifth. A Pakistani found answers to many questions in the Bible and concluded that Muslims who charged that it had become corrupted had deceived him. Though the Gospel of John raises many problems with its focus on Jesus as the Son of God, a title denied by the Qur'an, a Bengali reading this Gospel in Japan was led to faith.

A desire for fellowship in spiritual matters (sixth) led a North African Arab to see how Christ transformed hearts and consequently Christians loved each other. Christians could be **free from fear** (seventh) and **free from loneliness** (eighth) because Christ would not leave them, they had Christians who loved them, and their future was assured.

Deliverance from demonization (ninth) was a significant influence in places where cultic practices are part of the popular expression of Muslims. In northern Nigeria, a *malam* used sorcery against a man considering Christian faith. He became insane for a time and his wives left him, along with his daughters' husbands. He asked Christ to come and take the place of two evil spirits in his life, and was delivered.

What God Is Using in Some Large Movements

Larger movements to Christ among Muslims are taking a number of different forms, some with a Christian identity and some as insider movements where they follow Christ but within the Muslim community so that they can lead their neighbors to follow him too. My colleagues and I have been studying one situation in South Asia for a number of years that I shall describe here.

Means of Expansion

The avenues of expansion were those commonly identified in church growth studies:

- The web of family and friends. When the believers focused on a new village, they sent those who had family or friends in that village. If their coming was challenged, they could respond that they were guests.

- Talking with leaders. Since the goal was to be used by God to facilitate a movement rather than just individual decisions, there was a focus on leaders as decision makers.

- Ministries of mercy. Natural disasters were occasions for new holistic ministries of transformational development.

- Jobs that facilitated belonging. Those who had or acquired needed skills like diesel engineering or fishing could become insiders, whereas others were looked at as having ulterior motives for being there.

- Structures to support ministry. Fish and vegetable farms provided structures for ministry, support, and training of personnel.

- Unplanned opportunities. On one occasion when a large group came to attack the believers, a compromise was reached that three of the believers' leaders should attend a large gathering of an Islamist revivalist group. The believers shared with the Muslim revivalist leaders about the prophets leading up to Jesus, and got the response, "What you say is true, but it is not the time to speak openly, just quietly." Subsequently, one of the believers was made a district leader in this group.

Message

The message of the expansion involved Scripture presented in various creative ways:

- They noted that the Qur'an Sharif spoke of four holy books, all of which they used, while the traditional Muslims used only one.

- They used initially the Injil Sharif (the Holy Gospel) and later the whole Bible in a Muslim-friendly translation.

- They used the Sirat al-Masih (the Life of Christ) with Muslim-friendly terms in a qur'anic style.

- They used audio cassettes and memorized Scripture because it was largely an oral society.

- Because of the felt need of an intercessor and the common Muslim belief that Muhammad was one, they demonstrated that the Qur'an does not name Muhammad as an intercessor, and that only one approved by God may intercede (Maryam [19]:87; Ta Ha [20]:109; al-Najm [53]:26). They then showed how the Injil Sharif stated that God approved of Isa (Jesus) (Matthew 3:17; Mark 1:11; Luke 3:22) and that Jesus is the only mediator (1 Timothy 2:15).

Contextualization

A number of factors influenced their forms of contextualization:

- Of the original couples that worked in the villages, only the one or two with a Muslim background were considered religious.

- The realization that Jews and/or Christians first used all of the technical religious vocabulary of the Qur'an and all of the forms of the Five Pillars of Islam (except references to Muhammad and Mecca) encouraged them to develop a liturgy using biblical content but Muslim forms.

- Almost all stopped using the Muslim form of liturgy outside the mosque because (1) of persecution, including a court case which specifically noted their use of the national language rather than Arabic in liturgical prayers; (2) it moved them away from the community.

- Those attending the mosque silently or quietly replaced the clause "Muhammad is the Apostle of God" with something like the biblical and qur'anic "Jesus is the Word (or Apostle) of God."

- They did not give the call to prayer because that would involve them proclaiming publicly that Muhammad was the Apostle of God.

- Those who did not go to the mosque previously did not begin to do so. Others were in a transition to attending the mosque only on Fridays or only on the two Ids (festivals).

- Prayer still normally was made in a Muslim style of holding one's palms upward.

- Those in Sufi contexts continued to recite/chant the names of God (dhikr) in a Sufi fashion and added the reciting/chanting of the names of Jesus.

- There is considerable variation in the styles and times of worship that normally include reading of the Bible, discussion, and prayer.

Identity

A number of questions were asked to determine how they expressed their identity and how others viewed them:

- They called themselves "Muslims," "real Muslims," "completed Muslims," "Muslim followers of Isa," *Mu'min* ("believers," a term used by both Muslims and Christians), and some "Christians," especially when they had become the majority.

- The traditional Muslims called them "Muslims if they say so" or "Christians."

• Traditional Christians are largely unaware of them.

Some support for the use of the term "Muslim" (one who submits [to God]) and "Islam" (to submit [to God]) for those who follow Christ is that in some qur'anic contexts the term refers to all who submit to God (e.g., Al 'Imran [3]:19–20, 85).

Relationships

Some questions sought to determine relationships between congregations (*jama'ats*), with traditional Christians, and with traditional Muslims:

1. Relationships between congregations were supported by the fact that

• the gospel had spread through the web of family and friends;

• they frequently married within these webs;

• they helped each other when in need;

• they knew that the others would always receive them;

• it might be a "denomination" in the making, but currently there is considerable variety in polity and style.

2. The attitude toward traditional Christians includes

• "They are brothers of the same faith;"

• "If we follow their traditions, we can't work with our own people;"

• "They eat forbidden (*haram*) food;"

• "We don't like them because of their behavior, dress, and food;"

- "We must love them 100 percent, but in our culture we must stay separate."

3. The attitude toward traditional Muslims includes

- "We try to remain within the culture;"
- "We attend the mosque, some just on Fridays, some just on Ids;"
- "We go to the mosque to stay in the community, society, and family. It's like being on a bus with TV. One person has the remote control. If you want to ride the bus, you have to watch the channel."

From the studies indicated, it is evident that the hand of God is drawing Muslims to himself in a variety of ways. The challenge for us is to see where and how his hand is at work so that our hands can cooperate with his in the great ingathering of Muslims that we are seeing in these "worst of times."

CHAPTER 3

WORLDVIEW TRANSFORMATION

PAUL G. HIEBERT

In recent years, Christian ministries among Muslims have moved center stage, and deep personal encounters with different Muslim communities have raised important missiological questions. One of these has to do with the nature of conversion when Muslims become followers of Jesus Christ. There is no simple theory that encompasses the many dimensions involved. Here we will examine one, namely the transformation of worldviews, a dimension often neglected because worldviews are largely unseen and hard to examine.

Two biblical examples can help us understand the conversion of worldviews. The first is found in Acts 1:6–7 where the disciples asked Jesus if he would now establish his kingdom on earth. Despite Christ's many teachings about the kingdom of God, they were still looking for an earthly kingdom in which Jesus would drive out the Romans and reign from Jerusalem. Only much later did Christians understand that Christ's reign is a spiritual kingdom that has invaded the earth and will be visibly manifest when he returns in glory.

The second worldview shift was experienced by Peter in Acts 10:9–33. Until then the gospel was proclaimed only to the Jews and proselytes to Judaism. Now Peter was called by the Holy Spirit to go to Cornelius, a Gentile. In his encounter in Cornelius' house, Peter learned three profound lessons. First, he came believing that God is the God of the Jews; he left realizing that God is the God of all people. Second, he thought Christianity was how he and the disciples did it; he learned that

Christianity can be done in other ways in other sociocultural contexts. Third, Peter came as an outsider, making clear that as a Jew he should not really be there; he learned that these Gentile converts were his brothers and sisters—that he was one of them.

Worldviews and Conversion

Before looking at the conversion of worldviews, we need to examine what we mean by "conversion" and "worldview."

Conversion

When we speak of conversion we refer to people who turn from other ways to become followers of God, who revealed himself to us incarnate in Jesus Christ, as the Lord of their lives. Conversion is a turning around, a moving in a new direction. This turning may be sudden or slow; as humans we do not always know when it happens. God, who sees the heart, knows. Our calling is to invite people to follow Christ and to become his disciples. Moreover, once people have turned to Christ we need to encourage them to grow in the knowledge of truth, in the love of God, and in holiness.

Conversion involves many transformations. On the social level, conversion involves changes in the ways people relate to their families, friends, and community, and to other Christians. On the psychological level, it involves new ways of seeing and feeling about themselves, and integrating their new beliefs into their personal lives. On the cultural level, it involves a new way of living in this world. This affects all three dimensions of culture: On the cognitive level, it is a new way of viewing reality. On the affective or feeling level, it brings new love and joy. On the evaluative or moral level, it leads to a new understanding of righteousness and sin, and a desire to be holy. At the core of this cultural conversion is the transformation of worldviews.

Worldview

The second concept we will use to examine Muslim conversions is worldview. To understand worldview, we need first to examine the concept of culture of which it is a part. By culture we mean the more or less integrated systems of learned beliefs, feelings, and values shared by a group of people and expressed by means of patterns of behavior, signs, and products. Cultures are the everyday worlds in which we live, shaped by nature and human creation.

Cultures have different levels. On the surface we see people's behavior and hear what they say. Beneath these are the patterns that order behavior and the linguistic and other signs they use. Humans are unique in their ability to create mental maps to think about the world around them, and to use these maps to choose courses of action. This ability to construct mental worlds that reflect the outside world is based on our ability to create symbols. A symbol is anything that stands for something else in the minds of a person or a group of people. For example, we see real trees and have a mental image of them. We create the spoken word *tree* to represent them. Thereafter, when we hear the word *tree* we retrieve the mental images of real trees we have seen. Because symbols link thoughts to external realities that can be experienced by other humans, we are able to communicate our thoughts to them.

Each culture organizes its symbolic world in different ways. For example, in English we speak of six colors in the rainbow. Telugu speakers in South India use two: hot and cold colors. They see as many colors we do, but use adjectives to note the differences.

In culture we use signs to create belief systems that organize our thoughts. In the West these systems include beliefs about medicine, physics, car repair, cooking, child rearing, and theology. Belief systems are what we think about and discuss. They are essential for human life.

25

Beneath symbols and belief systems are basic assumptions about the way the world is put together. These are what people take for granted about the nature of things and the categories and logic they use to form a coherent understanding of reality. Taken together these assumptions make up a "worldview," a way of looking at reality.

Worldviews make cognitive assumptions about the nature of reality. In the West these include the reality of atoms, viruses, and gravity. In Arabia they include jinn, baraka, and evil eye. Modern people see time as a straight line from a beginning to an end that can be divided into uniform intervals such as years, days, and minutes. It does not repeat itself. Other cultures see time as cyclical, a never-ending repetition of summers and winters, days and nights.

Worldviews have affective assumptions that underlie notions of beauty and style and influence people's tastes in music, art, dress, and food, as well as the ways they feel about themselves and life in general. For example, in cultures influenced by Theravada Buddhism, life is equated with suffering. By contrast, in the United States after World War II many people were optimistic and believed that by hard work and planning they could achieve a happy, comfortable life.

Worldviews also have evaluative assumptions regarding the nature of right and wrong. For instance, North Americans assume that honesty means telling people the way things are, even if doing so hurts their feelings. In other countries one must tell others what they want to hear, because it is more important that they be encouraged than that they know the facts.

Taken together these assumptions provide people with a way of looking at the world that makes sense out of it, a worldview that gives them the assurance that they understand the world and that their understanding is right. Those who disagree with us are not wrong;

they are not crazy and out of touch with reality. If our worldview is shaken, we are deeply disturbed because the world no longer makes sense to us.

Worldviews are largely implicit. Like glasses, they shape how we see the world around us. They are what we look *with*, not what we look *at*. Like glasses, it is hard for us to see our own worldview; others often see it better than we do.

Worldviews serve several important functions. On the cognitive level, our worldview gives us a rational justification for our beliefs and integrates them into a more or less unified view of reality. On the level of feelings, it provides us with emotional security. On the evaluative level, it validates our deepest cultural norms. In short, our worldview is our basic map of reality and the map we use for living our lives. Finally, our worldview monitors our responses to culture change. We are constantly confronted with new ideas, behavior, and products that come from within our society and from without. Our worldview helps us select those that fit our culture and reject those that do not. It also helps us reinterpret those things we adopt so that they fit into our overall cultural pattern.

Worldviews change over time. New ideas may challenge our fundamental assumptions, and internal inconsistencies in our beliefs create tensions. To reduce the stress, we modify or drop some of our assumptions. The result is a gradual worldview transformation of which we ourselves may not even be aware. At times our worldview no longer makes sense of our world. If another, more adequate one is presented to us, we may reject the old and adopt the new. For example, Muslims may decide that Christianity offers better answers to their questions than does their old religion. Such worldview shifts are at the heart of what we call conversion and transformation.

Contextualization

Before we look at converting worldviews, we need to look at the relationship between the gospel and the human social, cultural, and historical contexts in which we communicate it. Our initial thought is to separate the gospel from human contexts. We see it as something apart from these, an acultural message unaffected by the culture and history of the hearers. While it is true that the gospel is divine revelation and therefore, in one sense, unchanging, it must be communicated in terms of their language, culture, and worldview for humans to understand it.

On further thought, we realize the need to communicate the gospel in the cultural systems of the people, but tend to see their old culture as evil and in need of radical transformation. Since we are Christians, we assume that converts in other cultures should become like us in their theology, worship forms, ecclesiology, and lifestyle. But then Christianity is seen as a foreign religion, and the old religious ways do not disappear but go underground and are practiced in secret.

As we study other cultures deeply, we begin to see the good in them and to call for a radical, uncritical contextualization of the gospel. We also realize that our own form of Christianity is culturally bound and often unbiblical. The result is theological relativism, a loss of absolutes, and a loss of unity in the church.

As we relate to churches in different cultures, we come to see that the gospel came to all of us from without and that our theologies and ecclesiologies are our attempts to understand it in our contexts. There are absolutes and universals in divine revelation, and these speak to all humans in all their contexts. We realize, too, that God's revelation was given to humans through humans who lived in particular historical and sociocultural contexts.

In short, we affirm the truth of Scripture as divine revelation, given in human contexts but communicating God's Word to us. We must not equate that gospel with any human culture, but we must also communicate it in human cultural forms so that people may hear and believe. The gospel is not simply information to be accepted as truth; it is a call to follow God who revealed himself in Jesus Christ. For most followers this involves a transformation not only of their beliefs and practices, but also of their worldviews.

Converting Worldviews

Conversion on the cultural level should involve all three dimensions: beliefs, feelings, and judgments. There must be some minimum knowledge of Jesus and a desire to follow him. These must lead to a decision to follow him. Conversion is not simply holding an orthodox knowledge of Christ, or a love of him, but choosing to follow him. Often conversion has a minimum of knowledge or even desire and decision, but through careful discipling these can grow to maturity.

To be complete, conversion must involve all levels of culture. As outsiders, when we see people who say they have become followers of Jesus, we tend to first look at their behavior. Do they enjoy fellowship with fellow Christians? Do they study their Bibles and participate in worship? In short, do they act like Christians? Transformed behavior is important in the process of conversion because it is a sign of inner transformation and a testimony to the world of that transformation. But behavior can also be falsified. People may act like Christians and yet not have experienced a fundamental transformation of their allegiance. Or people may have truly turned to God through Jesus Christ, but our evaluation of their behavior is biased.

On another level we often look for transformation in rituals. Are the new followers of Jesus willing to be baptized and to take the Lord's Supper? Rituals are times when we give expression to our deepest beliefs, feelings, and values, and participation in rituals is an even more public witness to inner transformation. But people can take part in rituals for wrong reasons: they may want to remain part of a community that converts, or seek favor with the missionary.

Underlying behavior and rituals is the conversion of beliefs. Can and do the new followers of Jesus express their new faith in basic, simple terms? Do they affirm the Lordship of Christ, the authority of Scriptures as divine revelation, and their asking God for his salvation? Here we may make the list long or short, but we seek to know what the seekers truly believe. Yet people can publicly affirm their faith without truly experiencing a conversion in their inner being. We cannot assume that their belief systems are complete when they become followers of Jesus.

At its deepest level, complete and lasting conversion must transform worldviews. It is possible for a person to become a "Christian" at all the higher levels and still retain a sub-Christian worldview. This is the case of Simon in Acts (Acts 8:9–24). He was converted and baptized, but still saw God's manifestations of power in terms of his old magical worldview—a power to be bought, learned, and controlled by magicians who understood its formulas. He saw Peter as a super magician. Peter rebuked him, and he repented. He had to experience not only a change in beliefs, but also a transformation in his worldview.

How can we help those who are coming to faith as they wrestle with their encounter with Scriptures and the challenges it poses to their world-views? This takes time and patience and is a lifelong process, both for the new believers and for the missionaries—who are often more shaped by their modern worldviews than by a biblical worldview.

Phenomenology

The first step is to help new believers study their local culture and worldview phenomenologically.[1] Here the local church leaders and missionary lead the congregation in gathering and analyzing traditional beliefs and practices associated with issues that arise in the life of the church. It is important not to pass judgment on the findings. If the leaders criticize the customary beliefs and practices, the people will not talk about them for fear of being condemned.

Premature judgments often focus on the orthodoxy of the beliefs rather than the struggles the believers face. The result is a deep cognitive dissonance that remains unresolved in the minds of the believers between what they are expected to believe and their old beliefs and practices which cannot simply be displaced. Old ways must be consciously dealt with and owned by the new believers themselves or the new ways become meaningless. Moreover, because the old ways are not adequately dealt with, they often go underground.

Ontology

The second step in converting worldviews is to help new believers study the Scriptures related to the question at hand, evaluate their own past beliefs in the light of their new biblical understanding, and formulate new, more biblical ways of looking at reality. The gospel is not simply information to be communicated and accepted as truth. It is an invitation to which people must respond. In the process it is not enough that the leaders be convinced about changes they think must be made. They may share their personal convictions and provide leadership, but they must allow the people to make the final decisions in evaluating their past worldviews. If the leaders make the decisions, they must become policemen who enforce them. If the people make the decisions corporately, there is more accountability and less likelihood that the customs they reject will go underground.

To involve people in evaluating their own culture and worldview in the light of new truth draws upon their strength. They know their old culture better than the missionary and are in a better position to critique it once they have biblical instruction. Moreover, to involve them is to help them grow spiritually by teaching them how to apply scriptural teachings to their own lives. It puts into practice the priesthood of all believers in a hermeneutical community.

It is also important for missionaries from outside the culture to study their own worldviews, for they use these in studying the Bible, and their interpretations are often shaped more by their culture than by the Scriptures.

A Christian community may respond to old worldview assumptions in different ways. Many they will keep, for they are not unbiblical. Others they will explicitly reject as unbecoming for Christians. The reasons for such rejection may not be apparent to outsiders who see little difference, but the people know the hidden meanings and associations of their old beliefs. On the other hand, at some points the missionary may need to raise questions that the people have overlooked, for they may fail to see clearly their own worldview assumptions until they are pointed out. New Christians will also replace old assumptions with those drawn from Christian communities elsewhere, and so join the historical and international church.

What helps check this process of critical contextualization from leading us astray? First, the process takes the Bible seriously as divine revelation and as the rule of life and faith. Second, it recognizes the work of the Holy Spirit in the lives of all believers open to God's leading. Third, the church acts as a hermeneutical community, checking against individual interpretations of the Scriptures. This corporate nature of the church as a community of interpretation extends not only to the local gatherings of believers in every culture, but also to the church around the world and in all ages. In a hermeneutical community the role of the leaders is to mobilize all members in the community to participate in the study and decision making, not to make and enforce decisions by themselves. The leaders have expertise in some aspects of the process, but other members of the community do in other areas of life

Missiology

The final step in worldview transformation is to help new believers live out the choices arising from their faith. Often challenges arise when they face critical decisions, forcing them to think about their new beliefs. Such situations call for immediate decision and response. It is important that these also be used as times to reflect deeply on the worldview issues that underlie the problem at hand and to stimulate long-term discussions in the Christian community regarding its response to similar situations.

In this third step we must begin where people are and lead them to maturity in Christ through a careful discipling of their worldviews. This is a long process, and we must be patient and encouraging, slow to judge and quick to pick up the weak and faltering. People cannot jump from one worldview to another. There are times of radical worldview shifts, but most often worldview transformations are processes of thinking and rethinking key worldview themes. People begin with the worldviews they have. Over time they need to examine and transform them. Moreover, it is important not only that the worldviews of individuals be converted, but also that the worldview shared by the community also be transformed.

Worldviews and Muslim Ministries

There are many worldview issues involved in Muslim ministries. These vary from country to country and from religious community to religious community. Current discussions often touch on worldview transformations, particularly as these relate to orthodox Islam, such as the nature of God, of Jesus, of human relationships to God, of the cross and salvation, and of eternal destiny. We need also to examine the worldview assumptions of folk Muslims, such as their beliefs in spirits, dreams, baraka, jinn, and evil eye. A systematic analysis of the world-views underlying these beliefs can help us understand many of the issues we wrestle with.

We also need to examine worldview assumptions we bring with us when we debate critical issues in Muslim ministries, such as what it means to become a believer, how believers relate to one another and the society around them, and the nature of the church. We need to examine our assumptions underlying issues such as "holistic ministries," "spiritual warfare," "people movements," and "the kingdom of God."

Finally, we need to seek to embody the gospel in new social and cultural contexts without losing its message and power. If we overcontextualize the gospel, we lose it. If we undercontextualize it, we fail to communicate the gospel and make it captive to foreign contexts, and in so doing, also lose it. Effective long-term ministries among Muslims need to take into account not only the personal and social dimensions of becoming a follower of Jesus Christ, but also the cultural and worldview transformations that need to take place as individual believers and entire churches grow in Christian faith.

CHAPTER 4

CONVERSION THROUGH THE LOOKING GLASS: MUSLIMS AND THE MULTIPLE FACETS OF CONVERSION

DAVID GREENLEE AND RICK LOVE

"The most wicked woman I ever knew is now my closest friend."

The couple serving in the Southeast Asian village has paid a great price. Life is simple, health problems are frequent, and their children go to boarding school in another country. Yet to hear the missionary wife succinctly describe the transformed life of a Muslim village sorceress explains why it is worthwhile.

This new follower of Jesus might not pass a basic Bible school theology course. (Perhaps she cannot even read.) She never "went forward" and probably never "prayed the sinner's prayer." She may have seen the *Jesus* film in a trade language, but neither the Scriptures, nor the film, nor any other Christian materials have ever been published in her mother tongue.

From outward appearances you would probably assume she is just another village woman, although not as rough and fearful as in the past, normally going about her business with a gentle smile on her face. Villagers who know her would certainly be aware of the change, but it is not because she started going to church (there is none), or reading the Bible, or displaying other "religious" behavior. This dear woman knows that, like Mary Magdalene, Jesus delivered her, and she loves him with all her heart.

Meanwhile, in a European city, Iranian immigrants gather every Sunday in the facilities of a Christian church. They overlap with the international English-language congregation but enjoy fellowship, worship, and teaching in a separate service held in their mother tongue. Some of the group are professionals; the leader is a medical doctor; most are refugees. Their children go to the public schools, and some of the teenagers discuss changing their Islamic birth name to something with a more Western or Christian flavor.

Although they are believers from a Muslim background, these followers of Christ are openly baptized, churchgoing Christians and might be puzzled if we referred to them as "MBBs" (Muslim background believers). People around town would have no doubt of their Middle Eastern origin, but beyond any presuppositions their physical appearance produces, they are clearly Christian.

No Simple Descriptions

When we consider how Muslims are coming to faith in Christ, simple, universal descriptions fail. As these two stories illustrate, there is incredible diversity among the world's 1.2 billion Muslims, and a corresponding diversity in how some have come to faith in Jesus Christ and how they live out that faith.

Clifford Geertz observed in his classic work on Islam in Indonesia and Morocco that "their most obvious likeness is, as I say, their religious affiliation; but [it] is also, culturally speaking at least, their most obvious unlikeness. . . . They both incline toward Mecca but, the antipodes of the Muslim world, they bow in opposite directions."[1]

Failure to recognize this diversity can lead to misunderstanding and unnecessary disagreement between those trying to understand Muslims, including those who have turned to faith in Jesus Christ. Too often we talk past each other in discussions on contextualization because we fail to recognize, or at least are unfamiliar with, each other's contexts. Further confusion arises over the location of the boundaries between acceptable variation between our different cultures in the practice of our faith and what the Bible prescribes as normative and universal.

The words we use to describe our faith and those who follow Jesus can also lead to confusion and controversy. *Christian* may carry the meaning it held in first-century Antioch (Acts 11:26), but today in many settings that word refers more to issues of diet, culture, and ethnicity than to believing in and following Jesus Christ. *Convert* and related words are similarly loaded, resulting in the preferred use by many of the descriptive phrase "Muslim background believer." In its most blatant form, the thought of Muslims *converting* to Christianity implies a rejection of their cultural heritage and an acceptance of Western culture and Christian traditions, many of which are *un*biblical but not necessarily *anti*biblical. This misunderstanding of conversion is not what the Bible teaches nor what we ought to communicate.

Exploring the Facets of Conversion

The concept of conversion is multifaceted and complex. We suggest that there are at least seven lenses to help us understand what it means to come to faith in Christ, seven sets of questions or modes of analysis that may guide our research and reflection. These are the lenses of psychology, behavior, sociology, culture, spiritual warfare, the human communicator, and God's role. None of these lenses gives us the full picture, but each highlights aspects filtered out or overlooked when we study conversion from other perspectives alone. We recognize some overlap in the categories; our concern is not to defend the categories as such, but to point to the importance of the issues we raise.

The Psychological Lens

The psychological dimensions of conversion must be understood if we are to communicate Christ effectively. The *Engel Scale*[2] and its two-dimensional development by Viggo Søgaard[3] describe a step-by-step process whereby a person who knows nothing about God is led to a true knowledge of God. These scales highlight the fact that conversion is a process, not simply a crisis. While the process leads to an event, which many report as a climactic turning to Christ, it also usually involves a gradual change in the thinking of the person being converted.

The psychological dimension of conversion is implicit in the Gospels. The conversion of the monotheistic apostles took place gradually as they lived and interacted with Jesus. First, they understood him as an authoritative teacher, one who cast out demons with a mere command (Mark 1:27). Next, they saw him as a healer, as one who had authority over sickness (Mark 2:1–12). Then, they wrestled with the fact that he had authority over creation. "Who is this? Even the wind and the waves obey him!" (Mark 4:41). Finally, after considerable time, Peter made his famous confession: "You are the Christ" (Mark 8:29).

People repent and believe in the gospel after hearing and understanding crucial truths about God, sin, and salvation. While the essence of the gospel is unchanging, we proclaim Christ in radically different contexts. Certain dimensions of the gospel are more relevant in particular contexts, and the process of conversion varies with the people being converted. Therefore, we must study the people we are called to reach, so that we can speak to their unique needs and address their particular problems.

Linking the study of psychology to Christian conversion has the potential of controversy, the danger that we seek to explain religious reality merely in the terms of psychological theory. Paul Vitz points to the strength of "psychology as religion" which is "deeply anti-Christian.

Indeed, it is hostile to most religions."[4] Psychology may help us understand people and their needs; misused, we may employ it as a tool of
manipulation or control.

And yet psychology can grant us significant insights as we consider
how people come to and grow in faith in Christ. Much, for example, has
been reported in Christian circles on God's use of dreams in drawing
Muslims to faith in Christ. In reports of such divine intervention, rare is
the Christian writer who carefully analyzes the events and interacts with
the helpful work of scholars such as Gustave von Grunebaum.[5] Dreams
are such complex psychological phenomena that, even recognizing God
as the source, a touch of humility is in order before broad claims are
made in analyzing just how he is at work.

Our sense of shame and guilt are also linked to psychology. How does
the Holy Spirit cause us to know we have fallen short of God's standard?
Hannes Wiher, drawing on scholarship and his many years of service
among Muslims in Guinea, has developed a helpful understanding of the
conscience based on an analysis of shame and guilt orientations. Making
excellent missiological application of psychological theory, he points to
the continuity and discontinuity between the indigenous conscience, the
missionary's conscience, and biblical norms. For example, Wiher states
that

> The content of every conscience is close enough to God's norms
> in order to be an initial reference point (Romans 2:1–16). In
> initial evangelism, the missionary should therefore speak of sin
> with reference to the indigenous conscience, particularly [the
> aspect] of their conscience that is in agreement with Scripture.
> . . . Other areas should not be approached in evangelism, but
> only after conversion in teaching and counseling. These are
> of great concern to missionaries but of little concern to the
> indigenous. Therefore, the message causes misunderstanding in
> the audience and represents a call to accept the culture of the

missionary. People may refuse, because conversion would lead from their "familiar, successful, and good" culture to an alien, perhaps even seemingly immoral culture. Or they may choose to convert exactly because it is a conversion to another culture that seems preferable. A conversion would in this case not be based on conviction, but on opportunism. Conversion, which bypasses the indigenous conscience, may lead to superficial conformity or to compartmentalized conformity, that is, syncretism. The missionary would have to take the role of permanent policeman with the misunderstood new culture.[6]

The Behavioral Lens

Biblically, the term *conversion* centers on a number of words. *Epistrepho* (turn) and *metanoia* (repentance) are two of the most frequently used terms to describe conversion. The Bible speaks about conversion as turning away from wickedness (2 Timothy 2:19), turning to God from idols (1 Thessalonians 1:9), or turning from darkness to light and from the dominion of Satan to God (Acts 26:18). Thus, conversion is most fundamentally about "turning." It speaks of change at a heart level, a reorientation of life around Christ.

An experienced observer of Christian witness among Muslims in Southeast Asia recently commented about the conflicting sets of questions Western Christians and Asian Muslims ask regarding religious commitment. A Western theologian asks questions about faith, the nature of God, and the atonement. If the right answers are given, the Westerner may say, "Well, these people are evangelicals theologically, but they have funny eating habits and strange postures for prayer." Meanwhile, concerned about apostasy and too much talk about *Isa al Masih*, the local religious leaders quiz the same subjects. Their conclusion is that "they were born in our community, pray in the right way, keep the fast, and don't eat pork; they must be Muslims."

Of course the diet and behavior question is not new. Andrew Walls points out that, had the Jerusalem council turned out differently, "whole stretches of Paul's letters would have been unnecessary. . . . But Paul envisages a new sort of Christian lifestyle, where believers do join pagans at the dinner table and have to face the implications of acting, thinking, and speaking as Christians in that situation, speaking of Christ, perhaps at a pagan friend's table."[7]

As we encounter such questions of behavior we must avoid the dangers of what Paul Hiebert has termed "bounded set Christianity."[8] Too often we wrongly focus on meeting norms of behavior without looking at the direction of the heart—centered on Jesus or turned toward other gods? A converse danger is that we ignore behavior and define a follower of Christ in terms of answers given to a theological quiz, such as those polls in the United States that show no significant difference in social behavior between so-called evangelicals and the general population.

We as outsiders are usually not in the best position to determine which behavior and practices the new believers should change. We may be unduly concerned about a practice we do not understand, or overly lenient because we fail to perceive underlying sinful background and meaning. Cultural insiders should listen to the wisdom of loving, well-informed outside Christians and to the historic voice of the church, but generally they must play the leading role in evaluating the complexities of meaning of current behavior and formulating any changes.

Changed behavior, or, as in the Galatian controversy, keeping the Law, is not what makes someone a follower of Christ. But the process of conversion involves change in behavior: not in order to *become* a Christian; but *because of who I am in Christ*, enabled by the Spirit, I keep this "law" which is not just written on tablets or in a book but on my heart (Jeremiah 31:33). The universals of behavior that should define the followers of Christ are found in Paul's exposition of the works of the flesh and the fruit of the Spirit (Galatians 5)—the former, specific actions; the latter, qualities of character and the heart.

The Sociological Lens

The Bible describes the conversion both of individuals and of groups. The baptisms of extended households in the New Testament highlight the more community-oriented nature of Greco-Roman culture (Acts 10:44–48; 16:15, 34; 18:8). Similar to that first-century Mediterranean culture, most Muslims do not make decisions as individuals but as groups. In ministry among Muslims, Westerners from cultures usually characterized by individualism should heed the wise advice of Harvie Conn:

> Continue to stress the necessity for a personal relationship to Christ as an essential part of conversion. But it must also be recognized that in the world's cultures such personal relationships are entered into not always by isolated "individual" decisions in abstraction from the group, but more frequently, in multipersonal, infra-group judgments. "Personal" cannot be equated with "individual."[9]

This suggests that it is often wise to evangelize people in groups, through the natural social networks rather than just isolated individuals. We should consider touching entire families and clusters of friends in our evangelism. We might ask why there seem to be so few oldest brothers among those who have come to faith, and how we might be more fruitful among men and women of influence. Whenever possible our goal should be to reach groups that will lead ultimately to the establishment of new churches. This is especially important among Muslims where the conversion of an isolated individual can lead to severe social ostracism or even death.

The final section of this book focuses on movements and points to group aspects of coming to faith in Christ in a variety of Islamic settings. John Kim's paper describes an Asian village setting and is particularly insightful in its description of clusters, existing social groups who have corporately turned to faith in Christ.

The Cultural Lens

The first great crisis of the early church centered on the relationship between conversion and culture (Acts 15). Jewish believers, not yet understanding the fullness of God's mystery (Ephesians 3:6), sought to impose their own religious culture upon new Gentile believers. They wanted the Gentiles to be circumcised and follow the Torah. But the apostles and elders in the church of Jerusalem rejected this external view of conversion.

Paul's message to the Ephesians and Galatians and the conclusions of the Jerusalem council (Acts 15) affirm that conversion to Christ does not require abandoning one culture for another. Gentile believers did not have to adopt Jewish culture to be saved. The decision made by the Jerusalem council remains foundational for our understanding of the relationship between conversion and culture.

We can better understand the radical nature of the decision reached by the Jerusalem council when we interpret Acts 15 in light of Jesus' warning recorded in Matthew 23:15: "Woe to you, teachers of the law and Pharisees, you hypocrites! You travel over land and sea to win a single convert, and when he becomes one, you make him twice as much a son of hell as you are."

Some Jews were actively engaged in missions prior to the coming of Christ. They used two terms to describe the fruit of their missionary labors. *God-fearers* were those Gentiles who worshiped Yahweh and followed his ethical teachings but did not receive circumcision. *Proselytes*, by contrast, were those Gentiles who not only believed in Yahweh but also embraced the culture of the Jews, including the painful rite of circumcision.[10]

The decision of the Jerusalem council made it clear that Gentile believers were not to be like Jewish proselytes. Instead they were Gentile converts to Christ. Andrew Walls draws astute missiological deductions from Acts 15, wise guidance for those engaged in ministry among Muslims.

> The distinction between proselyte and convert is vital to Christian mission. It springs out of the very origins of that mission, demonstrated in the first great crisis of the early church. The later church has seen many heresies come and go, but the earliest of them has been by far the most persistent. The essence of the "Judaizing" tendency is the insistence on imposing our own religious culture, our own Torah and circumcision. Christian conversion as demonstrated in the New Testament is not about substituting something new for something old—that is to move back to the proselyte model, which the apostolic church could have adopted but decided to abandon.[11]

In most settings of ministry among Muslims there is still a great need for outsiders, those from other cultures, to be engaged in service and witness. Whether cultural insiders or missionaries from a distant land, are there principles that can help increase our fruitfulness? The concept of cultural congruence may be of value: the idea of significant overlap, contact, or match but not, like the milk we drink, homogeneously blended into one substance.

Referring to the cultures of messenger and receiver of the message, Lewis Rambo notes, "The more consonant the cultural systems—in the context of cultural contact—the more likely it is that conversion will transpire. The more dissonant, the less likely it is that conversion will occur."[12]

Expressing another aspect of this issue, David Britt observed that "congruence is similar to homogeneity in that congruence also assumes that most of us are attracted to others who share like values. Congruence differs, however, from homogeneity in that it refers not only to a characteristic of the congregation, but also to a relationship between the congregation and its community context."[13]

Studies of those who had come to faith in a North African context suggest a principle of "Congruence of Cultural Values" confirmed among North Africans in a European setting[14] that "people are more likely to come to faith when their own cultural values are significantly congruent with the cultural values of the witnessing Christian community and the means of communicating the gospel."[15]

What some refer to as *insider movements* of those who maintain many outward Islamic[16] practices could also be described as *congruent communities* of followers of Jesus Christ.

We often refer to certain movements in Southeast Asia as "contextualized" approaches, while avoiding that term to describe the Iranians referred to at the start of this chapter or the Kabyle Berber movement of North Africa. In one sense all of these movements are contextualized—but the contexts are different, so the outworking in the lives of the believing community is different. One reason for growth is that in each setting the principle of congruence of cultural values is fulfilled.

On the other hand, we might say that certain movements are more contextualized than others because they do not borrow outside cultural forms to express their faith in and worship of Jesus Christ. The appropriateness of approach may be indicated by the community's level of satisfaction and desire for change: content and secure, as might be the case among many Muslim peoples of Southeast Asia, or in crisis and seeking change, as among certain non-Arabic minorities of the Middle East who see other Muslims as the oppressors.[17]

The Spiritual Warfare Lens

The Bible also describes conversion in terms of spiritual warfare: a great deliverance. The one true, triune God has created spiritual beings and human beings (who, of course, have body *and* spirit). We humans corporately form an inanimate world system, the society in which we live. Our own sinful human nature, the system of the world, and the spiritual forces of evil are all in rebellion against God. Human sinful nature is reinforced and energized by the impersonal "ways of this world" and the personal "ruler of the kingdom of the air" and the spiritual beings who serve him (Ephesians 2:1–3). One aspect of conversion involves recognition at the worldview level of these biblical, cosmological truths; another has to do with effectively dealing with them.

To be converted is to be rescued from the domain of darkness and transferred to the kingdom of Christ (Colossians 1:13). It involves the human spirit, and is part of our struggle that is "not against flesh and blood, but against the rulers, against the authorities, against the powers of this dark world and against the spiritual forces of evil in the heavenly realms" (Ephesians 6:12). Paul's calling was to turn people from darkness to light and from the dominion of Satan to God (Acts 26:18).

This lens is especially relevant in Muslim ministry because more than three-quarters of Muslims participate in occult practices.[18] Several chapters which follow in this book document cases of conversion involving some kind of healing, exorcism, or supernatural manifestation that demonstrate God's power, drawing Muslims to faith in Jesus Christ.

In some cases, there are overt demonic influences that must be overcome as a person comes to or grows in faith in Christ, such as Mary

Magdalene (Luke 8:2). At other times, the personal forces of evil are less present and it is the sometimes dazzling but more often subtle light show (2 Corinthians 11:13–15) of deception we must counter. In one setting with which we are familiar, the influence of Jehovah's Witnesses among new Muslim background believers was a more persistent problem than issues of demonic deliverance. False teachers who slip in among God's people (Jude 4) and secretly deny the "Lord who bought them" (2 Peter 2:1) are no less diabolical (1 John 2:22) than Simon the sorcerer (Acts 8:9–24) and the Philippian fortunetelling slave girl (Acts 16:16).

Although we must live out this conflict, Jesus has won the battle (1 John 3:8) from the wilderness temptation to his crucifixion, burial, resurrection, ascension, and glorification (Colossians 2:15; Ephesians 1:20–22; 1 Corinthians 15:1–8). He will complete the victory at his return (2 Thessalonians 2:8; Revelation 19:19–21; 20:7–10) when Satan and his allies will be permanently vanquished.

The Human Communicator Lens

As numerous texts on communication theory confirm, the human messengers of the gospel play a vital role in the conversion process. Although we may choose a variety of media, it is we who preach the good news of Christ's death and resurrection and seek, graciously and appropriately, to persuade nonbelievers to repent and believe in the gospel. John the Baptist, Jesus, Peter, and Paul all include repentance in their preaching (Mark 1:4, 15; Acts 2:38; 3:19; 20:21; 26:20). Moreover, the church is commissioned to preach "repentance and forgiveness of sins . . . to all nations" (Luke 24:47; cf. Acts 17:30).

The means by which we communicate the gospel and make this call to conversion is of vital importance. An appropriate choice of media, in an appropriate language, presented at the appropriate time, and used in synergy with other media may increase the likelihood that our message is understood, but of course cannot guarantee that anyone will come to faith in Christ. Writers such as Viggo Søgaard[19] help us understand how differing audiences respond in various ways to media at different stages in the process of conversion. A new emphasis on "storying the gospel" and sensitivity to the needs of the world's majority population of "oral learners" are long-needed applications of communication theory to Christian witness.

Communication *by* the new believer is also an important aspect of the ongoing process of conversion. Donald Smith points to the importance of communicating a new belief in order to foster deepened commitment. Public witness, he found, was far more important than teaching in developing a lasting commitment to Christ.

> Belief is reinforced when it is communicated, allowing it to involve emotions and relationships actively. Failure to communicate a new belief will weaken commitment to it. Lacking emotional and relational involvement, the belief becomes increasingly irrelevant and may eventually be given up. On the other hand, active participation in communication can lead to change of attitude and acceptance of new beliefs.[20]

In settings with significant religious freedom Smith refers to, such as Brazil and the Philippines, it is usually socially, legally, and culturally acceptable for a recent convert to publicly profess faith in Christ. Public testimony may yield some ridicule, but not the level of social ostracism, even death, experienced by Muslims.

How do Smith's findings apply in Islamic settings? Whereas wisdom normally suggests that Muslims who have come to faith in Christ be discrete in public witness, Smith's communication theory points to the erosion of the ongoing conversion process caused by muting the voice of the new believer. Those we know who have found the courage to appropriately make their faith known may face increased difficulties, but they often find both greater freedom and commitment to Christ.

The Divine Lens, Perceiving God's Role

As missiologists we rightly focus on the role we Christians play in the conversion of others. We constantly evaluate how we can more effectively share the gospel. Although we gain valid and vital insights by looking at conversion through the lenses of human behavior and response, we must also be sure that we look at how God himself is at work.

We preach the gospel to people who are dead in their sins (Ephesians 2:1–3). Because of this, God's Spirit must bring people to life. This is God's part in conversion, described as "regeneration" or "rebirth" (Titus 3:5) or, more popularly, being "born again" (John 3:1–8). In the words of Donald Bloesch, conversion "represents the incursion of divine grace into human life, the resurrection from spiritual death to eternal life. . . . Conversion is the sign but not the condition of our justification, whose sole source is the free, unconditional grace of God."[21]

We affirm that conversion is ultimately a divine act, a supernatural, and in this sense, an instantaneous work of the triune God (Titus 3:4–7). As the Jewish believers in Jerusalem responded when they heard Peter's report of the first Gentile converts, "God has granted even the Gentiles repentance unto life" (Acts 11:18). Luke's description of Lydia's conversion also underscores the priority of God's gracious initiative in conversion: "The Lord opened her heart to respond to Paul's message" (Acts 16:14).

Conversion seen as a process is equally a *divine* process, led and enabled by God. It is impossible to come to Jesus unless the Father draws us (John 6:44). Once having initially come to faith, "We, who with unveiled faces all reflect the Lord's glory, are being transformed into his likeness with ever-increasing glory, which comes from the Lord, who is the Spirit" (2 Corinthians 3:18).

Implications for Ministry among Muslims

Insights gained while looking through each of these seven lenses contribute to our missiology of conversion. They help us integrate our understanding of the underlying principles of how people come to faith in Christ, as described in the Bible and observed in our ministry.

Missiology, however, is not just theory; it points to application. Rather than attempt ourselves to further illustrate and apply the insights of this chapter, we invite you to read the rest of this book with your vision enhanced as you and the authors employ some or all of these seven lenses. We trust that this "looking glass" will help clarify your understanding of conversion, experienced and lived out by real men, women, youth, and children coming to faith in Jesus Christ.

FIGURE 4.1 CONVERSION THROUGH SEVEN LENSES

CHAPTER 5

THE ROLE OF THE SCRIPTURES IN MUSLIMS COMING TO FAITH IN JESUS

DAVID MARANZ

My interest in this paper rests specifically on the role of the Christian Scriptures in the process of turning from allegiance to the Muslim belief system to faith in Jesus and into vital, conscious fellowship with God through him. That process may be linked to a sudden crisis or to the climax of a prolonged conflict; regardless, it results in the conscious acceptance of Jesus Christ as personal Savior and in the consecration of life to his service.[1]

Almost all the data are first-person testimonies. Most were obtained from Internet sites,[2] while a few came from my personal contacts. There are hundreds of testimonies of Muslims who came to faith in Jesus on the Internet. Searches yield hundreds of thousands of hits, using criteria such as: <the Bible and Muslims>, <Muslims leave Islam>, <Muslims for Christ>, <Muslim testimonies>, and <testimonies ex-Muslims>. Testimonies from the Internet were primarily chosen on the basis of the reliability of the site where they appeared. From these, autobiographical accounts were chosen that were detailed enough to give a real sense of the process of conversion. About 120 testimonies, from both men and women, were reviewed.

In the first section of my findings, I will provide sample testimonies to illustrate specific points; in the later section, space limits me to an outline listing of the factors.

This, then, is a survey of the ways God uses to bring Muslims to the Scriptures, which he then uses to bring them to faith in himself. It confirms the words of Robert Brow, "When Muslims actually get to read the Bible, they find it presents a vast compelling picture. Getting people to read the Bible for themselves is a high priority for us."[3]

The Preconversion Role of the Scriptures

We will examine the varied ways the Scriptures have influenced Muslims to put their faith in Jesus, as revealed through personal testimonies. Excerpts are arranged by what appear to be repeated patterns.

Circumstances that Led to Reading or Hearing the Scriptures

There is some overlap between circumstances and motivations (discussed in the next section), but the differences are sufficient to justify separate consideration.

Problems of Life. God often uses difficult circumstances of life to bring Muslims to himself, as he does with individuals everywhere. Personal problems are commonly cited in testimonies that led Muslims to search for truth. An example by a Saudi:

> My circumstances became very difficult for me. . . . After one
> year of reading the Bible in an honest way, I understand now
> what happened to me: I found my way to God, the real God, the
> Lord Jesus Christ.

Initiated through Dreams. Many recount the fact of dreams as important to their coming to faith—in many instances, not just one significant dream, but also a sequence of dreams or wonders. We also find testimonies of visions, which involve supernatural appearances while the individual is conscious, and signs, which refer to miracles or supernatural events separate from, or not involving, dreams or visions.

These ex-Muslims believe that God directly intervened in their lives, sometimes several times, while leading them to saving faith. An example from Sudan of two multiple dreams, separated by three years:

> One night M. had a dream in which he saw a stranger. The man told him he should go to another city for three years. At the end of those years, something wonderful would happen to him. . . . One night near the end of his three years in this city, M. had another dream [in which] another stranger appeared to him and showed him a big book opened [to] Psalm 51, but he could not read the text below. . . . [Upon hearing Psalm 51] M. wanted to follow this God immediately and to know more about his salvation.

Doubts about Islam or the Qur'an. Testimonies often describe the doubts that arise in Muslim minds about problems they discover in their religion, such as its rituals, the violence preached by some Muslims, or even historical accounts found in Muslim literature.

> My own belief in Islam was severely tested by the empty formality and unconcealed hypocrisy I witnessed in virtually every aspect of its social and institutional life. I finally came to the place where I cried out to God, "If you exist, show yourself to me; prove yourself." (Algerian woman)

Fortuitous Events. There are many examples of Muslims being led to the Scriptures who do not seem to have been seeking for spiritual answers. Here is an example from Morocco:

> In high school a boyfriend spoke to me about Jesus Christ and gave me a Gospel of John to read. . . . I was very suspicious and reluctant, but started to read it in secret out of sentiment for the boy.

Unique Circumstances. The majority of circumstances that have led to Muslim conversions are unique, personal, and made-to-order by a loving God. One example was an Egyptian finding a pen pal in the United States in order to evangelize on behalf of Islam. Another was a merchant sailor from Senegal stuck on a broken-down ship in Abidjan, Ivory Coast:

> Our [ship's] reducer needed repairs. . . . During this time I met an Ivorian man who spoke to me for the first time about Christ . . . [hearing me] talking about the Qur'an, he wanted me to also know the Bible.

Motivations for Muslims Reading the Scriptures

Some Muslims come to Jesus because they have been searching for truth and find it in him. At the opposite end of the motivational scale, Jesus makes himself known in spite of what appears to be a lack of spiritual motivation or indifference to spiritual matters.

Searching for Truth. Many testify to having long searched for truth, some since childhood. A Palestinian provides an example:

> Vowing to make a decision for "the truth," I stayed up late many nights comparing many details between the Qur'an and the Bible. At some point during my study, I prayed, saying: "God . . . I want to do your will in my life; I long for your love and in the name of 'the truth' I ask. Amen!"

Setting Out to Attack, Refute, or Oppose Christianity. With some, motivations are insincere; yet God can use even impure motives to bring Muslims to faith in Jesus. A Turkish woman testifies to her own false motives for studying the Bible:

If you are going to fight against something, you need to know it
well, so I asked [my Christian friends] to give me a Bible. Knowing that I would find contradictions and inconsistencies, I started
to read it. However, a miracle happened! Each day, the words
brought more and more peace to my heart and hope for my life.

Attempts to Relieve Inner Conflict or Spiritual Void. Spiritual or
familial turmoil has led Muslims to find solace or peace in the Bible. An
Egyptian relates:

The Lord [woke] me up in the middle of the night as I had
no sleep or rest. Inner conflict reached its zenith. Restless, I
reached out to my Bible and opened it at random.

Nonspiritual or Superficial Motivations. Motivations can be as
many as there are converts, yet God can bring about spiritual results even
from nonspiritual motives. An example from Bangladesh:

One book [about Jesus] . . . in Bengali . . . attracted me because
of the colorful cover. I bought one copy.

The Claims of Jesus or the Bible. What Muslims hear or read
about the claims of Jesus can stimulate them to find out more by going
directly to the Bible.

The question came to my mind: Can one have confidence in
this extraordinary claim of Christ? I concluded that . . . in the
first place, Christ is accepted by Muslims as sinless, glorious
. . . descriptions which are applied to Jesus . . . At this thought,
I fell into a state of ecstasy. (An Afghani struggling with the
claims of Jesus)

Obeying or Following Up a Dream. A man from Saudi Arabia
writes:

One night, I had this horrible dream of me being taken into hell.
. . . Suddenly one day, Jesus appeared to me and said, "Son, I
am the way, the truth, and the life. And if you would . . . follow
me, I would save you from the hell that you have seen." . . . So I
started looking for a Christian who could give me advice about
this Jesus I have seen and possibly get one of the Christian Holy
Books, which I now know is the Bible.

Doubts about Islam, Muhammad, or the Qur'an. From a Somali
believer:

I believed in the God of Muhammad. Then I began to doubt
the credibility of Islam. . . . Through [a friend] I discovered
Christianity, and I began to compare the two religions. This
man also gave me a Bible and I started to read it.

The Role of the Bible Versus the Qur'an

Many testified that the Qur'an itself awakened interest in exploring
the Bible, or in otherwise finding out more than the little written in the
Qur'an.

Passages in the Qur'an Led to Jesus or the Bible. Sometimes
what is written in the Qur'an repels the Muslim, pushing him or her
away from Islam. A number of qur'anic passages are cited repeatedly as
an influence that eventually led to faith in Jesus. God has left himself a
witness in the Qur'an. An Iraqi recounts:

Through reading the Qur'an I discovered the greatness and
uniqueness of our Lord Isa (Jesus) the Christ. . . . That very day,
I hurriedly bought a copy of the Holy Bible. I started reading it
. . . in it I felt that the words of our Lord Isa (Jesus) cannot be
the words of men; for no man or prophet dare say that he is the
way, truth, and life.

After despairing over what he found in the Qur'an, an Afghani turned to the Traditions (hadith), which brought an even greater sense of hopelessness in attaining salvation.

> In this desperate and depressed state of mind, I began to read the Holy Injil [New Testament] to correct any possible defects in my investigations. As I opened the Holy Injil, my eyes fell on these words: "Come to me, all who labor and are heavy-laden, and I will give you rest." . . . For a sinner like me, it was indeed the supreme proclamation of good news. This life-giving verse had a tremendous effect upon me.

Statements in the Qur'an Justified Consulting Christians or the Bible. From Egypt:

> Muhammad himself is claimed in the Qur'an to have been urged, by God, to refer to the People of the Book (the Jews and the Christians) if in doubt concerning the Qur'an (Surah Yunus 10:95). For the first time in my life, I began asking why and challenged everything I took for granted.

Comparisons of the Qur'an and the Bible Led to Doubts about the Former. From Malaysia:

> I tried to get correct answers by asking learned and devout Muslims in Islam about Isa Al-Masih [Jesus Christ] and the Christian teachings. . . . After making a comparison between the two, only then did I obtain some answers as to who Isa Al-Masih actually is in the Al-Qur'an and Injil. . . . I began to have doubts about my previous confidence.

Beyond these factors, below I outline without great detail many of the other ways the Scriptures impact Muslims, derived from generalizations or patterns seen in many testimonies.

The Impact and Influence of, or Reaction to, the Scriptures

- The love or voice of God or Jesus was especially meaningful or convincing.

- Scripture brought an immediate response.

- Specific Scripture verses spoke to a particular need or very personally.

- The Bible was convincing.

- Assurance of forgiveness or salvation was a major influence.

- Reading the Bible raised doubts or disbelief about Islam or the Qur'an.

- Reading the Qur'an or other Muslim sources stirred up doubts about Islam.

Biblical Passages or Teaching Were of Special Importance

- Holiness and righteousness had great appeal.

- The prophet Jesus was of special interest.

- The offer of knowing God was a major attraction.

- The authority and power of the Bible were convincing.

Preconversion Attitude toward the Bible or the Christian Faith

- Originally they had little or no knowledge of the Bible.

- They had been opposed to the Christian faith.

- They believed that the Bible had been the ancient revelation of Allah.

- They had only known of Jesus through what is written in the Qur'an.

Preconversion Influences Other than the Scriptures

Although the impact of the Bible is vital, it is coupled with other factors in leading to Christian faith.

The Role of Dreams or Other Supernatural Events Versus the Bible

- Dreams where Jesus appeared or spoke (some pointing to the Bible)

- Dreams giving instructions (also pointing to the Bible)

- Signs (supernatural events without dreams)

- Dreams involving healing (some pointing to the Bible)

- Dreams involving dialog

- Visions (supernatural appearances while conscious, some pointing to the Bible)

- Dreams brought assurance.

The Role of Christian Witness, Using the Scriptures or Other Means

- Scriptures were a gift.

- Selling Bibles and Christian literature

- Muslims took the initiative in obtaining a Bible.

- Hearing or reading the Bible was significant or decisive.

- Nonverbal witness was important.

- Bible reading events, debates, or competitions led to faith

- Witness through study of the Bible

- Witness aside from direct use of the Scriptures

Personal or Spiritual Aspirations or Concerns Expressed, While a Muslim

- Desiring closeness with God/Allah

- Searching for truth

- Conscious of sin and wanting deliverance

- An innate desire for learning which led to Christian faith

- A sense of emptiness that needed to be filled

Problems, Questions, or Doubts about Islam Had Been Experienced

- The refusal of Muslims to examine the claims of Islam was a problem.

- The use of a language not understood (especially Arabic) was a problem.

The Roles of the Scriptures that Led to Christian Faith

Finally, God used the Scriptures to address diverse concerns of those who eventually came to faith in Christ, and provided access to the Scriptures in a variety of ways.

Initial Doubts about, Resistance to, or Problems with the Bible

- The Christian concept of God as Father

- Muslim objections to consideration of Christian matters

How the Scriptures Were Accessed

- Bible correspondence course

- Books, Christian or secular, that include passages from the Bible

- Calendars containing Scripture verses

- Gift of a Bible

- Hearing the Scriptures read

- The Internet

- Listening to or overhearing a radio

- Nonprint media (includes radio, videos, tapes, CDs, DVDs, television, etc.)

- Reading in a major language

- Reading in a vernacular (minority) language

- Through invitations to study the Bible

The Language of Bible Translation Used

Few mention the language of the Bible that they used. Consequently, no lessons or conclusions can be drawn from this missing evidence.

Missiological Implications

I examined testimonies written by ex-Muslims born in at least thirty-three different countries. An exact count is not possible because, for security reasons, names and countries of origin are often omitted or specified only by region. In those more than a half page in length, only two did not include references to the importance of the Bible, the New Testament (Injil), a comparison of the Qur'an with the Bible, or similar citations. In most, the role of the Bible or some passages of Scripture were central to conversion. How could it be otherwise? Might we think that there are conversions in which the Scriptures are important and others in which they are not?

So in a sense, the examination of this topic is superfluous. There is no way to faith except through the Word of God. Scripture tells us that "faith comes from hearing the message, and the message is heard through the word of Christ" (Romans 10:17). Apart from hearing (or reading) there is no message of salvation. Although the Scriptures are primary, there are many ways to disseminate them: from a dream pointing a Muslim to the truth (in the sovereignty of God), to the inclusion of a Bible verse in a secular publication, to the organization of a Bible-reading contest, and in countless other ways.

Because dreams, visions, and/or wonders are frequently a subject of interest, I examined their incidence. Out of approximately one hundred converts, twenty-two wrote of having visions or dreams.

How an Examination of the Ways God Uses Scripture in Bringing Muslims to Faith Helps Sharpen Evangelization Strategies

First, it should encourage us to point Muslims to the Scriptures as early as possible in our relationships, since the message of the Bible grips and convinces Muslims of its truth.

Flowing from that, the Bible needs to be in a language that best speaks to the heart of the Muslim reading or hearing it. This is one area where Christianity has a great advantage over Islam, in that our sacred text can be presented in the language of the people receiving it. The Islamic use of Arabic text even for non-Arabs was a key point in many testimonies.

Thus, good translations of the Scriptures are sharp instruments that God will use to bring Muslims to himself. Good translation means being faithful to the original texts while being sensitive to the culture and vocabulary of the speakers of each particular language.

Cultural Sensitivity

A great deal of healthy attention is currently given to cultural factors in evangelism, Bible translation, and gospel presentation. In a recent article on the life and work of the very effective Syrian Christian, Mazhar Mallouhi, cultural factors are clearly evidenced:

> Mallouhi now spends most of his time and energy working to present the Christian Holy Scriptures in ways that Muslims can respect. . . . By presenting the Scriptures as culturally Middle Eastern, Mallouhi has gained unprecedented access and acceptance for God's Word. At a recent Arab book fair in a North African country with very few local Christians, *An Oriental Reading of the Gospel of Luke* was the bestseller. (The book was prepared under Mallouhi's guidance. It includes the biblical text, and "Muslim-focused commentary that effectively explains the Scriptures and presents Christ as the Middle Easterner that he was.") After reading it, a Muslim professor commented, "This is the first time we've seen that Christ has Middle Eastern roots, related to our own culture! Historically, we've only received Christianity through the imposed view of Western colonialists. But we want everyone and every student in our Department of Islamic Studies to read this." It has since become a required textbook in his university.[4]

This is well and good and certainly biblical. Yet during my reading of the many testimonies used in this survey, I was struck by the fact that God, through the Holy Spirit, speaks directly and powerfully through his Scriptures—sometimes even before they are available and in spite of cultural, linguistic, and other barriers. Cultural factors matter, yet God works in spite of cultural barriers; nonetheless we should strive to lower as much as possible the barriers we have so far come to recognize with the tools currently at our disposal.

A significant number of testimonies reviewed relate how they were positively influenced to become Christians while away from home. Although few specifically wrote that while out of their Muslim country they had the freedom to consider the claims of Jesus, this was doubtless an important element in their coming to faith. Very often while in the West, they came in contact with outgoing Christians and the Bible, which led to faith in Jesus.

Let us make it a high priority to point our Muslim friends to the Scriptures, whatever other specific ways we are engaged in sharing our faith.

CHAPTER 6

THEOLOGICAL IMPLICATIONS OF CHANGES IN CHRISTIAN APPROACHES TO ISLAM

JIM TEBBE

Good theology does not always produce good mission, but no theology or bad theology will certainly produce bad mission. I would like to reflect on one theological aspect of Christian engagement with Islam that perhaps can help ministry to Muslims be good mission.

In 1987, the Presbyterian Geneva Press clarified the nature of revelation:

> What people believe about God is directly related to what they understand to be revelation. In Christianity and Islam, God's self-revealing word is the form and substance of revelation. For Muslims, that word is the Qur'an; for Christians, Jesus Christ.[1]

In 1995, a book published by InterVarsity used the same comparison:

> It is essential for Christians to realize that *the Qur'an is to Muslims what Jesus is to Christians.* It is a mistake to make a direct comparison between the role of Jesus in Christianity and the role of Muhammad in Islam, or between the place of the Bible in Christianity and the place of the Qur'an in Islam.[2]

Comparing Christ to the Qur'an (as opposed to comparing the Bible to the Qur'an and Jesus to the Prophet Muhammad) is a phenomenon not even sixty years old in Christian engagement with Islam. Despite its relative lateness onto the theological scene, it has come to be broadly accepted. Most recently it has become commonplace among evangelicals—a paradigm shift in theological as well as in cultural understanding and worldview.

Why did this change occur recently? Are there longer-term theological implications/consequences? This paper explores both questions separately.

Part 1 – Models for Understanding How Christian Engagement with Islam Has Changed over Time

Others have analyzed why the nature of Christian engagement with Islam may have changed over the centuries. Arne Rudvin and Wilfred Cantwell Smith, though coming from different perspectives, give roughly the same assessment on developments in Christian-Muslim encounter.

Bishop Arne Rudvin	Wilfred Cantwell Smith
Mutual refutation between Islam and Christianity	Heresy/Scripture corruption charges
Confrontation	Recognition of Islam and Christianity as members of different faiths
Dialogue	"A question not yet answered"

Undoubtedly, changes have occurred and any analysis of change can best be understood in models. I would like to suggest an alternative to Rudvin's and Smith's categories: the model of premodern, modern, and postmodern approaches as characterized by the interactions of three people with Muslims: Temple Gairdner, Kenneth Cragg, and Wilfred Cantwell Smith.

From Premodernity to Modernity

By premodernity, we mean the approach to knowledge largely based on belief in revealed truth—*God said*; *God showed*—as opposed to skeptical questioning, leading to empiricism and reason as the foundation blocks of truth (modernity).

William Henry Temple Gairdner (1873–1928) was a noted Christian missionary in the Muslim world (Cairo). Gairdner's "call" to the mission field grew out of his enthusiastic participation in the Oxford Inter-Collegiate Christian Union (OICCU). During his time it was marked by a zealous commitment to prayer, evangelism, and a simple lifestyle where the group avoided personal expenditure wherever possible with every penny saved being given to missions. Throughout his life he remained positive about his involvement in the OICCU, recognizing that zeal provides a motivation which can later be tempered by wisdom. His fundamental motivation in mission remained constant. "All 'debate' or 'dialogue' was with intent to save, not crudely to score, nor idly to compare, nor cosily to converse."[3]

By modernity, we mean the underlying assumptions of modern thought and life which arose out of the eighteenth century Enlightenment but continue to find expression in the nineteenth to twenty-first centuries. Morality and truth are no longer rooted in traditional concepts such as the character of God as understood in the Bible. Rather, there is an emphasis on reason and the "universal ideal."

Thirty-five years after Gairdner, Kenneth Cragg was an active participant in the same movement in Oxford, including being the representative of his college and engaging in public evangelism. Yet Cragg's motivation in ministry later differed from that of his college years and consequently that of Gairdner. Cragg came to see his mission as speaking to the mind of Islam (not so much to Muslims), showing the relevance of Christ and the New Testament to Islam *on its own terms*. In contrast, to the end of his life Gairdner saw his ministry as being to Muslims, intending their conversion.

Given similar backgrounds, motivation, and tasks, had Cragg lived some fifty years earlier, there are many ways in which he could have been a Temple Gairdner. Separated as they are by a half-century, they had significantly diverging perspectives. Gairdner maintained a largely premodern outlook on faith issues, while Cragg's contribution was made through a synthesis of his faith and a worldview influenced heavily by modernity. Cragg is not a modernist in the sense of seeing reason in place of God. But the influence of modernity is seen in his finding common ground between Christianity and Islam.

Although Gairdner was a learner *about* Islam, he would not have seen it as his vocation to be a learner *from* Islam and its Qur'an as Cragg came to be. For Gairdner there remained an uncritical acceptance of the Bible as Scripture. His approach was premodern with a continued reliance on propositional truth as conveyed through the Bible.

There is no evidence, despite his softening stance towards Islam over the years, that Gairdner ever accepted the Qur'an in quite the same way as Cragg did. For Gairdner the Qur'an remained part of a non-Christian system that could only be construed as error. Cragg on the other hand looked for a commonality between the faiths and tried to build reasonable argument for it—a characteristic of modernity.

Modernity's mindset had touched Christianity as well as the rest of culture and needed someone who could reconcile it to faith questions. It was for this reason that Cragg's early book, *The Call of the Minaret* (1956), was so well received and acclaimed by the Christian mission world, including evangelicals. It was, however, more than a compassionate understanding of Islam from a Christian faith position; it marked the beginning of a philosophical change influenced by modernity in its search for universal, common truth, which became clearer in Cragg's later writings.

From Modernity to Postmodernity

By postmodernity we mean a move away from *common* values to individualized (either small cultural groupings or personal) cultures/beliefs, each with no more "value" than another. One outcome of postmodernity is that the pressure to conform that came with modernity is gone. In its place is an acceptance of differences bordering on what would have been deemed as bizarre in earlier generations. Postmodernity is a reaction to modernity and its naïve assumption that common global values can be achieved.

Wilfred Cantwell Smith (b. 1916) was active in the Student Volunteer Movement for Foreign Missions in Canada. He too went out as a missionary, to Lahore, Pakistan (then India), and throughout his life maintained his Presbyterian Church ties. Smith founded (in 1951) and for fifteen years headed McGill University's Graduate Institute of Islamic Studies in Canada. He moved from there to Harvard to become professor of World Religions and also the director of the Center for the Study of World Religions.

Although there are many ways in which Smith's background can be compared to that of Gairdner and Cragg, the shore on which he landed is quite different from either of them. The colonial mindset can be clearly seen in the premodern approaches to Islam of Samuel Zwemer and Gairdner. We have seen how Cragg's writings have been influenced by modernism. Similarly, postmodernity is clearly identifiable in Smith's later work.

Smith does not seek common ground of understanding; rather, what is important to him are faith-transcending belief systems, which are actually only cumulative traditions that tell something about the faith. "With

Christianity no longer at the center of the religious world, each religion can be recognized as having a partial perspective on the divine."[4]

In his move towards a "world theology," Smith has given up the quest for a rational common ground. He even goes so far as to note that it would not be irreverent or facetious to say, "It is only by becoming in part Hindu that a Westerner is enabled to be both Christian and Muslim at the same time."[5]

Both Muslim and Christian critics charge Cragg with reinterpreting Christianity in Islam. This, in essence, is an argument against the modernity seen in Cragg's worldview. But in reverse there is an argument against Smith which Cragg brings. According to Smith, there can be no outside possessing and interpreting of Islam by Christians or any other non-Muslims. Cragg would argue that surely people of other faiths have the right to critique and even "possess" another's scriptures and faith traditions. This critique that Cragg brings against Smith is in essence a rejection of postmodernity.

Revelation, not Scripture, is the issue for Cragg. For Smith neither is the issue, but both are pointers to a world theology in which personal faith is at the core. The kind of careful study Cragg does of the Qur'an would be invalid if we take Smith's position. Similarly, Cragg's efforts at holding to Christian basics and seeing many of them in one form or another in Islam could be construed as nothing short of religious imperialism by Smith.

Summary

In Gairdner there is some theological movement that could be construed as an attempt to come to grips with Western modernism. Yet his perspective on the world remained largely premodern and at the same time very biblical. To the end, he had a passion to see Muslims become Christians.

Cragg's popularity in some Christian circles grows out of his attempt to remain faithful to Christianity but at the same time to accommodate modernity by finding common ground with an alternative system of thought—i.e., Islam.

Smith addresses shortcomings in modernity's approach to questions of faith with many useful insights. But in so doing he embraces aspects of postmodernism which would be hard for many Christians sincerely engaged with Muslims to accept.

Part 2 – How Changes in Approach to Islam Might Have Affected Christian Evangelical Theology

For dialogue to take place there must be common ground. The nature of encounter between Christianity and Islam in the nineteenth century was such that there was no need to find that common ground. Consequently, the implications of whether the comparison of Christ to the Qur'an was an acceptable theological framework were not considered. The comparison of revelation to revelation, rather than book to book, assumes an openness to another faith not present in the stages of refutation and confrontation. Previous to the twentieth century, the logical coherence of the Muslim belief system was not recognized as possibly being valid. This change, coupled with the move back to the pre-Reformation theology of seeing revelation as housed primarily in Christ rather than Scriptures, opened the door for this comparison to be seen through the dual lenses of a changed worldview and changed relations between the two faiths.

Changes in Christian Understanding of Revelation

Roman Catholic theologian René Latourelle notes that in patristic times revelation was primarily seen to be housed in Christ, about whom Scripture gives testimony. It was not until the Middle Ages that this began to change. Latourelle attributes the major change to Thomas Aquinas. Pannenberg supports this, noting that the change was pivotal for Reformation theology.[6]

A modern illustration of this point is the Presbyterian Church USA, where, through its confessions, there is documentary evidence of change. The Westminster Confession of 1643 reflected "the exaggerated concern for the authority of Scripture that characterized the orthodox theology of that time."[7] It referred to Christian Scriptures as the Word of God many times but never used that expression for Jesus. This position of "an authoritative canon of Scripture . . . as just the Word of God written"[8] grew out of the Reformation's concern for the authority of Christian Scriptures over the church.

Orthodox Presbyterianism continued to maintain a similar position on Christian Scriptures well into the time of Zwemer and Gairdner. B. B. Warfield (1851–1921), from his leading role at Princeton Theological Seminary, held a position formally similar to that of the Westminster Confession.

> What is important to recognize is that the Scriptures themselves represent the Scriptures as not merely containing here and there the record of revelations—"words of God" . . . given by God, but as themselves, in all their extent, a revelation, an authoritative body of gracious instructions from God; or, since they alone, of all the revelations which God may have given, are extant—rather as the Revelation, the only "Word of God" accessible to men, in all their parts "law," that is, authoritative instruction from God.[9]

This is contrasted with the Presbyterian Confession of 1967. According to this view, Christ is God's supreme revelation. Christian Scriptures bear witness to that. Although this concept was initially rejected by many evangelicals in the Presbyterian Church and was not incorporated immediately into the wide range of popular theologies, today it has gained a widespread acceptance.

What is of significance is that, for those who have engaged with Islam, the need for this distinction articulated in the Confession of 1967 was perhaps more immediately apparent and so found expression rather earlier. Hints of the view that revelation is housed in the person of Christ rather than generally in the Bible are discernible in both Zwemer's and Gairdner's writings as they grappled with quranic issues. This was still in the days of B. B. Warfield, and yet their hints predate Barth's theology of revelation. It was Barth who was largely responsible for moving this view of God's revelation primarily being housed in Christ into mainstream Protestantism.

Two Potential Liabilities for Christian Engagement with Islam

The comparison of Christ to the Qur'an has benefited Christian understanding of how Muslims view their Qur'an and may help Muslims' understanding of the Christian belief in the incarnation as God's supreme revelation. It also has served the useful function of helping Christians articulate and better understand the nature of revelation. There are, however, at least two potential liabilities to this comparison. They are the risk of sidestepping scriptural issues and excluding the atonement from our theology.

Overlooking Scriptural Issues. One of the great divides in Christianity has been over the nature of the Christian Scriptures and their place in the Christian faith. The Reformation called the church back to Scripture as the authoritative basis for belief and practice. *Sola Scriptura* ("Scripture alone") is arguably the best-known of Martin Luther's five *solas*. It represents the most fundamental of the theological insights he offered but also continues to be a dividing point among Christians. Engagement with Islam planted seeds for new theological insights into understanding the nature of revelation in Christianity, but has not done the same for the nature of Scripture. One could argue that it has created a tendency among those engaged with Islam to sidestep theological questions on Scripture altogether.

The issue is as follows: To the outsider, the Christian doctrine of Scripture seems tepid when compared to the lofty claim of a Qur'an dictated by God. R. C. Zaehner challenged the Western world with the question "Why not Islam?"—basing his arguments on his perception of the relatively straightforward nature of revelation in the Qur'an versus the complexity of the same in Christianity and other religions. "There has never been any dispute as to what is Koran. . . . For once, then, God had spoken plainly in the full light of history . . . his revelation in the Koran makes some sense. And free from theology as the Koran is, it even makes simple sense to simple men."[10]

The place of the Bible as the revealed Word of God can easily be overlooked in the rush to Christ as revelation. At a time when Protestant doctrine of Scripture is in genuine need of a theology for today's issues, Christian engagement with Islam is in danger of overlooking this vital question. The emphasis on revelation in engagement with Islam seems to mask rather than highlight the need for new theological insights into Christian Scripture. One would expect that engagement with Islam would be a catalyst to challenge our theological understanding of the nature of Scripture. Instead, the issue is ignored in our haste to move to Christ as God's revelation.

Excluding the Atonement. By communicating to Muslims a primary understanding of Jesus Christ as revelation—similar to how Muslims view their Qur'an—we run the risk of reducing the person and work of Christ to only that of revelation. The kingly (Jesus as divine) and priestly (the atonement) roles can all too easily be overlooked. Kenneth Cragg's theology on the subject of Christ as revelation is but one illustration of how this can happen.[11]

For Cragg, what is important is the way prophethood and revelation comes through the person of the prophet. It is not that biblical prophecies are untrue or inaccurate, but rather they are, if not actually revisionist, highly interpretative. The Messiah could be fulfilled because "[Jesus] had only been Messiah by first redrawing all the criteria."[12] It is not the word or propositions but the person which is the key to revelation. There are different propositions between Christianity and Islam, but there is shared ground in the area of prophethood.

It is in these assertions that we can see the influence of modernity on Cragg. Traditional Protestants would have little quarrel with Cragg's high view of the New Testament and its interpretation. Yet Cragg's approach diverges from the traditional in his heavy emphasis on the single theological strand which constantly comes back to the true nature of revelation. "It cannot be overemphasised that the Christian understanding of Christ is the Christian understanding of revelation."[13] It is primarily upon the single strand of prophethood that Cragg builds his Christology. "We can say that Christian theology reads Christology from prophethood because it saw prophethood in suffering as the clue to Christology."[14]

Cragg's emphasis on revelation as suffering prophethood masks other aspects of who Christ is in Christian theology, almost to the point of exclusion. For Cragg, the priestly identity of Jesus has come to be intrinsically linked to the prophet's role. "Prophethood was God's agency inside human history. Suffering was inherent in it. Suffering could be taken redemptively and be properly associated with God Himself, seeing that prophethood and all it entailed was His devising."[15]

The continuity from Old Testament sacrifice to the cross as the atonement is an interpretation Cragg actually rejects. Instead, he sees the link as a tieback to the suffering prophets who called Israel away from an exclusive ethnic identity to an internal and more universal faith. He explains the New Testament references which easily lend themselves to the concept of a substitutionary atonement as "metaphors of oblation borrowed to describe [Jesus] from the sheepfolds that fed the Temple altars." Thus it was "instinctive for the disciples to tell of him in the same idiom of sacrifice and innocence for sin."[16]

According to Cragg, the priestly role of Jesus is virtually indistinguishable from his true prophetic role. To stop the march of evil, this vicarious suffering must be assumed by true believers who are followers of Jesus. Vicarious suffering prophethood offers continuity between Christianity, Islam, and the Old Testament and is seen in Jesus on the cross in its perfection. This has the effect of lessening the strong traditional Christian understanding of the priestly role of Jesus and has come to take the place of a traditional understanding of the atonement for Cragg.

Summary

While the analogy or model of comparing revelation to revelation and so Christ to the Qur'an is useful, it also has potential pitfalls. Christ is so much more than the perfect revelation of God to humanity. He is Lord of the universe as well as our lives (King), and he paid the price for our sins on the cross (Priest). It is not enough that Jesus suffered; it is critically important that he died on the cross and rose again from the dead. Kenneth Cragg's writing is but one example of how the comparison of Christ to the Qur'an can lead to a position where the work of Christ is seen as no more (or less) than the revelation of God. Many theological approaches to Islam today, including evangelical, emphasize the incarnation to the exclusion of the atonement.

There is a second potential liability in using this comparison. We are tempted to gloss over important questions about our own Scriptures. What is inspiration, and what does it mean? There are very strong, positive assertions that can be made in contrast to the Qur'an about how God communicates to us within and through the diversity of our own cultures which can be overlooked when we rush too quickly to answer our Muslim friends with the comparison of Christ to the Qur'an.

SECTION 2
Understanding the Experience of Coming to Faith

CHAPTER 7

LEARNING FROM GOD'S WAYS

JEAN-MARIE GAUDEUL

In this contribution I draw from two sources: the first is a survey of personal accounts where people explained how they came to faith in Christ. This survey led to a book, which tried to discern the trains of thought which led a number of Muslims to Christ.[1] The second is the collective experience of my missionary institute, which has been working among Muslims for almost 150 years.

My first thought is a sense of wonder at God's ways of leading people towards a real, live encounter with himself. We are treading on holy ground as we examine the extraordinary variety of personal experiences through which God revealed his tenderness and love to so many millions of human beings. Each human conscience is a holy temple where the Lord meets his children and draws them to himself.

We find it normal that people be led to Christ through means that are familiar to us: Christian witness, the Bible, good books, and charitable works. But we are somewhat surprised and bewildered when God seems to lead people through events—good or bad—circumstances or doctrines that have apparently little or nothing to do with church personnel or the Christian message.

"Nothing can keep us apart from God's love manifested in Christ Jesus" (Romans 8:39) and "everything works for good for those who love God" (Romans 8:28). Open-minded though we certainly are, we may be surprised to discover that many have been led to Christ through doctrines, rituals, and beliefs that belong to Islam and are, in some cases, theoretically incompatible with the Christian message. This needs explanation.

Five Common Patterns

As I tried to make sense of the testimonies of new Christians, it dawned on me that even though each person was unique and followed a different path, one could discern similarities among them. Gradually a number of common patterns emerged, as if these people belonged to different "families":

Some came to faith through an encounter with the **person of Christ**.

Others were drawn by thirst for **truth** and certainty.

Others had looked for a **community** of believers.

A number looked for an experience of **forgiveness** and redemption.

Many were drawn by their hunger for a personal **encounter with God** through prayer.

These "families" were not exclusive of each other. All these elements can be found in all authentic experiences of faith in Christ; what differed was the degree of centrality of a particular element in the overall picture. Some focused their attention on one of these ideas; others kept their heart set on another theme.

Whatever the "family," their way to Christ began from an Islamic perspective, and some elements of Islamic faith and life were used by God to "send them on their way." Let us examine each of these "families" of prospective believers as they bear witness to their own evolution.

Drawn by the Person of Christ

Many Muslims coming to faith in Christ began their spiritual journey with the Qur'an and the way it describes Isa. In the Qur'an, Jesus is presented as a simple prophet who would never have allowed Christians to honor him and his mother as if they were two gods in place of the one and only God. At the same time, the Qur'an gives him mysterious titles like *Word of God* and *Spirit coming from God*. Other passages insist on his "elevation" to God at the end of his prophetic career, thus apparently casting doubt on the reality of his death on the cross.

Muslim mystics present Jesus as "the seal of sanctity," describing him as a wandering monk preaching perfect poverty and urging people to search for God. Theologians, zealous for orthodoxy and anxious to protect the faithful from the influence of Christian neighbors, insist that Jesus was only a prophet and that his mission was restricted to the Jewish people, while Muhammad was sent to the whole world with the superior message of the Qur'an. Muslim controversialists have built up a body of polemical anti-Christian literature, sometimes making fun of Jesus as the Gospels present him.

The fact remains, however, that many Muslims find Jesus a strangely fascinating figure. One in four Muslim converts to Christianity speaks of the role which Jesus played in his or her religious development. Jesus has attracted them, fascinated them, spoken to them—even in a very direct fashion. A decisive step is taken when one stops speaking about Jesus and begins talking to him, even though one may still consider him as a mere prophet. One's ideas may not be quite clear, but Jesus is met as a very real person, a master, a friend, someone who listens and helps.

This cannot surprise us; Jesus is not a set of ideas. He is alive and draws people to himself, as he did with his disciples who followed him, loved him, and only slowly came to an awareness of his mysterious identity. We know of many Muslim believers who follow the same path.

Drawn by Thirst for Truth and Certainty

For better or worse, Islam has the reputation of being a religion of simple dogmas and strong convictions. Its adversaries use these characteristics to accuse it of fanaticism, while its defenders see in them the proof that it is the religion of pure reason and of evident truth. Many converts from Islam testify that it was in their family or in the course of a classical Muslim education that they received this passionate desire to know the truth which God has revealed to people.

What then are we to say of the substantial number of Muslims who explain their faith in Christ as the fruit of a search for the truth? Why can they not be satisfied with this "luminous" Islam?

It is public knowledge that present-day Islam is torn by quarrels and violence. Conflicting interpretations of their religion divide Muslims among themselves. On all sides, people fight in the name of "true Islam." Some, however, keep looking for an answer to their doubts, which none of the conflicting parties seems to offer. Their thirst for truth, begun in Islam, eventually leads them to Christ.

Looking for Community

It is quite true that Islam proposes an ideal of fraternity and equality. The Qur'an wished to replace old Arab tribal ties by a solidarity based on faith: "Believers are only brothers" (Surah 49:10).

Muslim tradition expands this vision. Believers are as equal as the teeth of a comb; an Arab is not superior to a non-Arab and vice versa, nor a black person to a red person and vice versa. Individuals differ only in their degree of piety.

The ideal is clear. Yet the actual organization of Muslim society creates institutionalized inequalities between men and women, slaves and freemen, Muslims and non-Muslims.[2] In practice, furthermore, Muslim believers have been unfaithful to their ideal, just as Christians have been to theirs.

Some Muslims become profoundly dissatisfied with their experience of community. This may be due to some aspects of the ideal or to a failure to put this ideal into practice. Islamic education instills the ideal of a society which is the expression of faith in God and of the worship due to him. Naturally, religious aspirations often take the form of a search for the ideal community in which the religious dimension can find full expression.

At the present time, many people are aware that their community does not correspond to this ideal, and they may therefore cast their eyes on the wider world to see what the situation is in other communities. Their need for community may lead them to Christian groups. The encounter is not always a happy one. In many cases, however, it is: quite often, in spite of its weaknesses, the Christian family lets Christ's presence show through "earthen vessels."

It is striking, however, that no matter how important the community may have been as the starting point of their journey, for many newcomers the irresistible personality of Jesus eventually takes over as incomparably more important than the community. The church has meaning only as the people of Jesus.

Here again, Christ fills a need that Islamic education had aroused.

Looking for Forgiveness

At the heart of Islam is the clear and trenchant affirmation of the existence and grandeur of God. The God presented in the Qur'an is also the Compassionate and Merciful One, the one who always forgives, who is patient and generous.[3]

At the same time, the God of Islam is just. He is present everywhere; he sees all things, knows all things, and is the Judge before whom we shall all have to appear. He keeps an exact record of all our actions. The God of Islam is also the Avenger God.[4]

It is in the name of this strictly just God that Muslim theology rejects the idea of a redeemer or savior. Each human being is responsible and will have to account to the Judge for the smallest actions: "He who has done an atom of good will see it, and likewise he who has done an atom of evil" (Surah 99:7–8). The outcome of the judgment will be either paradise or hell, each of which the Qur'an describes in some detail.

The basic message of the Qur'an is therefore a call to conversion to the virtuous life, with the assurance of a strictly proportionate reward and punishment after death; for the mercy of God cannot interfere with his essential justice. Divine forgiveness can only be given when divine justice has been satisfied and sins have been expiated.

Christianity also uses the terms "justice" and "mercy," but in quite different proportions. God offers an unmerited forgiveness which heals and transforms the sinner, pouring into his or her weakness the strength of the Holy Spirit. We may remember here the encounter between Jesus and the adulterous woman as described in the eighth chapter of John's Gospel.

The promises and threats contained in the Qur'an educate in a sense of sin and tend to form a delicate conscience, sensitive to the sins of daily life. This in turn can lead to a longing for perfection, which nothing can satisfy. For other Muslims, it has been not so much the need for perfection as the experience of their personal sin, which has sent them in search of a Savior who forgives.

These are the two main reasons why some of those brought up in Islam may feel the need to search for salvation and, having failed to find it in their religion, look for it elsewhere. Here again, their encounter with Jesus brings them peace at last.

Hungering for God

It cannot be repeated too often that at the heart of Islam is the religious experience of the Prophet Muhammad, the founder of the Muslim community. Born and brought up in the paganism of sixth-century Arabia, he sought and found a truth obscured by the pagan cults of his milieu. Beyond all the tumult of the world, infinitely above the illusory goals of ambition, profit, and idols, there is God—the Unique, the True, and the Creator of all things.

One can understand that the Qur'an formulated this discovery of God by Muhammad in negative terms. All else had to be rejected: false gods, idols, human-made divinities. God, the All Highest, has no equal or rival or associate; nothing in heaven or on earth can compare with him. Both the Old and New Testaments of the Christian Bible are full of similar expressions. To bring out the greatness of God, one insists upon the littleness of the creature. To express his majesty and transcendence, one insists that he cannot be contained within the limits of our finite and contingent condition.

Later, theologians declared that since God is the Wholly Other, he must be radically unknowable. He does not reveal himself, but only manifests his will and his commandments in the Qur'an. Since he is the Most High, he is infinitely above his creatures, and any attempt at intimacy with him would be an act of disrespect towards his majesty. There can therefore be no question of union with God, either in prayer or in life.

In the Qur'an, Muhammad is presented as the "Seal of the Prophets." Theologians concluded from this image not only that the teaching of Muhammad confirmed that of his prophetic predecessors, but also that he was the end of the series, the last Prophet. It was not to be thought that any later believer could have an experience of divine revelation, since this would make him a prophet later than the last Prophet.

For many Muslims, this teaching first arouses in people a great sense of God's majesty and a desire to get closer to him. At the same time, many experience a growing desire to meet this merciful God. We know that Muslim mystics developed a spirituality which led to a certain experience of union with God. When this ideal was made public, it led to persecution: some of the Sufi were executed, among them Mansûr al-Hallâj, in 922. During the following centuries books were written in an attempt to contain the Sufi mystics within the limits of orthodoxy. They were obliged to bridle their burning desire to meet God directly and content themselves with formal prayer. To this day the conflict between Islamic orthodoxy and mysticism has not been resolved, and there are numerous local confrontations between them.

This conflict is in fact mirrored in the heart of every Muslim believer. It may be no more than a fruitful dialectic, a tension between love for God and the respect which is due to him. At the same time, a narrow religious training, or particular circumstances, can bring certain Muslims to feel that they are in an impossible situation: torn between an irresistible desire for a personal encounter with God and a loyal desire to respect the official veto on any such encounter.

It is not therefore surprising that some Muslims find in Christianity the reconciliation between these two aspirations. They find that Christianity fulfils the aspirations which Islam had aroused. In various ways, they come to experience an encounter with God as someone who responds to their desire, intervenes in this world, reveals his care for each person, manifests his fatherly love to people, and listens to their prayers.

It was the thirst for prayer that drove these Muslims out onto the pilgrim road. What, we may ask, have they found which they could not have found elsewhere? Their reply is simple: a personal God who is interested in everyone and who wishes to be known and loved in himself; a God who is *Father*, to whom one can speak *like a son or daughter*. They have found liberation and the rapture of being finally able to *understand* the words of their dialogue with God and to hope for a reply.

All had the same fundamental experience which puts them at the heart of the Christian tradition, reflected in the prayer which Jesus left to his own: "When you pray, pray like this . . . " (Matthew 6:9).

Possible Conclusions

From these observations, I suggest a number of indications for a better service of God's designs in this world.

Doctrinal Controversies

It is quite true that Islam and Christianity offer teachings that are opposed to each other on a number of important issues. More than fourteen centuries of controversies have produced in both religions a number of books where theologians explain at length the truth of their own religion and the error present in the other.

The topics treated in those controversies can be listed: God's uniqueness and Trinity, Christ's nature and salvific mission (Are we saved by grace or by the practice of the Law?), his death and resurrection, the authenticity of the Scriptures (Bible or Qur'an), rituals and practices, and finally communities and their way of life. All these points are essential and cannot be swept under the carpet.

But it is just as true that, when people indulge in such controversies, they tend to forget all else and focus on the task of proving the other wrong at whatever cost. The danger is that they forget that religion is not about the triumph of one community over another, but about turning ourselves over to God. Is not that the definition of *metanoia* (conversion) and *islam* (submission)? This is why mystics—both Christian and Muslim—avoid indulging in controversies.

My own experience is that arguing and bickering mobilize minds and hearts, harden people, and prevent them from paying attention to God's voice in their innermost being.

Spiritual Experience

As shown above, God seems to guide people to faith in Christ through all sorts of means, including their own religious background. Whatever the doctrinal differences, he calls all people and draws them to himself, making use of anything that could arouse an attitude of surrender to his love.

As we hear the witness of many new Christians, we discover that elements of Islam which may contain teachings contrary to Christian doctrine seem to have been used by God's grace insofar as they contain the potential to arouse a sense of God's majesty, a feeling of trust in him, and surrender to his will. This fits with Jesus' approach as we discover it in the Gospels. His teaching does not deal with doctrines or rituals but with the way in which each person faces God's presence in truth. "When you pray, go into your room, close the door and pray to your Father" (Matthew 6:6); "Not everyone who says to me, 'Lord, Lord,' will enter the kingdom of heaven, but only he who does the will of my Father who is in heaven" (Matthew 7:21).

I am convinced that anyone who surrenders to God in this way will be gently molded by God in the image of his beloved Son and drawn to him across the borders traced by doctrinal differences.

Mutual Witness

This belief leads me to another approach of my ministry. The people I meet may be Muslims or people of other religious convictions. My mission as a Christian seems to be that of witnessing, not arguing. "You will receive power when the Holy Spirit comes upon you, and you will be my witnesses in Jerusalem, throughout Judea and Samaria, and to the ends of the earth." (Acts 1:8).

A witness can only talk of things experienced. Teachers develop ideas and doctrines; witnesses speak of the impact of these ideas and doctrines on their lives—a spiritual experience. Instead of disputing about Trinitarian dogma, we can bear witness to the fact that it is "Christ who lives in us" (Galatians 2:20) and prays in us through his Spirit, "a spirit of adoption, through which we cry, 'Abba, Father!'" (Romans 8:15). Our witness is about our experience of the Spirit who puts us in touch with God's Trinity. An experience cannot be denied: it belongs to the realm of fact. All Christian doctrines stem from spiritual experience and lead to spiritual experience.

As we focus on that level of spiritual witness, we are led to discern in our friends another spiritual experience, and we may ask them to share it with us. If they are Muslim, Islam is seen from the point of view of spiritual experience: What did they find in it that led them to love God better?

Some dimensions of their experience may help me surrender to God in a deeper way, and vice versa. Far from being adversaries in a theological dispute, we discover that we stand side by side before the same loving Lord, even if our ideas about him differ.

Our part is to focus on that joyful and loving relation with God so that people may sense they are called to the same kind of encounter. If we have to talk about things Islamic, our concern might be to stress in it what leads to a truer and deeper surrender to God, letting God's Spirit speak to their spirits and draw them further on.

The New Testament word for "conversion"—*metanoia*—literally signifies that sort of deep turning to God in words and in deeds that allows God to guide and direct each one of us till we reach the whole truth.

People coming to faith in Christ have been led to him in that *metanoia* climate. It was true when John the Baptist preached in the desert, when Jesus began his ministry: "Repent and believe the good news!" (Mark 1:15). Insofar as we can judge from the many examples we meet nowadays, it is still as true as ever.

Praise God who draws all human beings to himself, making use of everything—even our sins, our strengths, and our weaknesses. In him do we trust.

CHAPTER 8

IN SEARCH OF A NEW LIFE: CONVERSION MOTIVES OF CHRISTIANS AND MUSLIMS[1]

ANDREAS MAURER

During the nineteenth and twentieth centuries, both Islam and Christianity have increased their adherents worldwide. As a result, Christians and Muslims are meeting each other on a daily basis in almost every corner of the world. The awareness that Christians and Muslims have of each other's faith has also grown extensively. One aspect common to Christianity and Islam is the fact that believers actively invite other people to become adherents to their faith. This inviting attitude has its basis in their respective Scriptures:

> Matthew 11:28: "Come to me, all you who are weary and burdened, and I will give you rest."

> Surah 16:125: "Invite [all] to the way of thy Lord with wisdom and beautiful preaching; and argue with them in ways that are best and most gracious."

Many Christians and Muslims are dissatisfied and disillusioned with their own faith for various reasons, and are looking for an alternative faith to satisfy their felt needs and search for a new life. For a variety of reasons, it has become more common for people to change their allegiance from Christianity to Islam and from Islam to Christianity.

I have personally witnessed this change of allegiance with many people, both in Africa and Europe. For instance, in 2000 there was a public event in Zürich where Muslims presented their faith in an informal and attractive way. The relevance of Islam for people in Europe was explained, literature was sold, and oriental food was given free of charge. There were Swiss people who had already converted to Islam and many who found Islam very attractive but had not yet made a decision to embrace it formally. Most of these people told me that they grew up in a Christian environment and professed to have been Christians before.

On the other hand, I met a businessman from an Islamic state who had been a Muslim all his life but recently converted to Christianity. He secretly obtained and read a Bible in his own language. As he traveled in Europe, visited churches, and spoke to Christians, it became clear that becoming a Christian was right for him. For reasons of persecution, it was not possible for him to return to his home country as a Christian. He was prepared to pay the cost of his conversion: to leave his family and business behind and start a completely new life in Europe. This business-man pointed out that he knows of many more people in his home country who are disillusioned with Islam.

Many more incidents today prove the contemporary relevance of examining the fact of conversion between Christianity and Islam. A number of new publications also underline the importance of this theme, such as Jean-Marie Gaudeul's *Called from Islam to Christ*[2] and J. Al-Sain's *Ich Kämpfte für Allah: Eine Frau auf der Such nach der Wahrheit* ("I Fought for God: A Woman in Search of Truth").[3]

How do the Christian and Islamic communities respond to this change of religion in both directions? In my experience, both in church practice and in Christian missiology, conversion is usually understood as being only towards Christianity and with only one valid, strictly religious motive.[4] I contend that such a view is missiologically inadequate in the context of Christian-Muslim relations. It should be acknowledged that conversion moves both ways and is based on a combination of motives. For this we need a holistic missiological understanding of conversion to help promote understanding and respect between faith communities.

Psychology of Conversion in a Religious and Culturally Pluralistic Society

Worldwide, religious pluralism is an undeniable fact and poses a new challenge to the Christian church. Kauuova observes that "where the non-Christian religions had been seen as objects of mission and evangelism they are now 'partners' in this whole activity. They are 'shareholders' in the public arena."[5] It is therefore necessary that a new Christian theology of religions needs to emerge. Kritzinger emphasizes the same notion when he says:

> We must begin to view other religions also as *missionary* movements. The fact that Christian theologies of religions developed initially in Christian missionary circles often had the result that other faiths were viewed as "target groups" only. . . . What we now need to do in Christian missiology is to analyse the mission of other religions . . . to be able to understand how and why they are growing.[6]

This implies that the churches need an adequate missiological understanding of conversion. In relation to Islam, it will help churches to have more understanding of and respect for Muslims. It will also increase understanding of Christians who convert to Islam and of the reasons why Islam is growing. The importance of acquiring this understanding is highlighted by Kritzinger:

> A Christian theology of religions that does not tackle these questions head on will quickly become irrelevant to the unfolding new society. Nicolson (1991:81) rightly says that if religious groups are unable to accept religious pluralism, they will be "irrelevant to the establishment of a democracy."[7]

Often Christians fear that, by accepting other religions as equal and entering into interfaith dialogue, they have to give up their missionary zeal and that they will no longer be "true Christians." I disagree with this sentiment and would like to emphasize what Kritzinger said in this respect:

> This does not mean that the content of faith (the *fides quae* in scholastic terminology) is to be regarded as irrelevant in interfaith dialogue. . . . Dialogue is an encounter of *commitments*, which are firmly (but not arrogantly) held by all the participants. This is therefore not a call to adopt a posture of theological relativism or to create a new "world religion," but to say farewell to arrogance in relation to people of other faiths.[8]

For Bosch, both dialogue and mission can be understood only with the meeting of hearts rather than of minds. He proposes an honest seeking after dialogue.[9] This whole issue brings a Christian into a dilemma. How do we maintain the tension between being both missionary and dialogical? Bosch observes that "we are dealing here with a mystery" and that Christians need to accept this tension.

Christians need therefore to see conversion as not just a one-way but a two-way movement. Kritzinger goes a step further when he says:

> A theology of apostasy should be an integral part of a Christian theology of religions. This is in keeping with the change from a one-way to a two-way theology of religions. . . . [A] Christian theology of religions will understand Christianity not only as a missionary faith but also as a faith being addressed and challenged by other living religions.[10]

Conversion happens between Christianity and Islam in both directions, but also happens in various ways within the fold of Christianity. In an attempt to clarify the various possible types of conversion, Figure 8.1 illustrates the types of conversion, with special reference to Christianity and Islam.

Whereas each of these types of conversion is interesting and significant to study, the special focus of this article is on the conversion movements P1 and P9 ("tradition transition").

FIGURE 8.1 TYPES OF CONVERSION

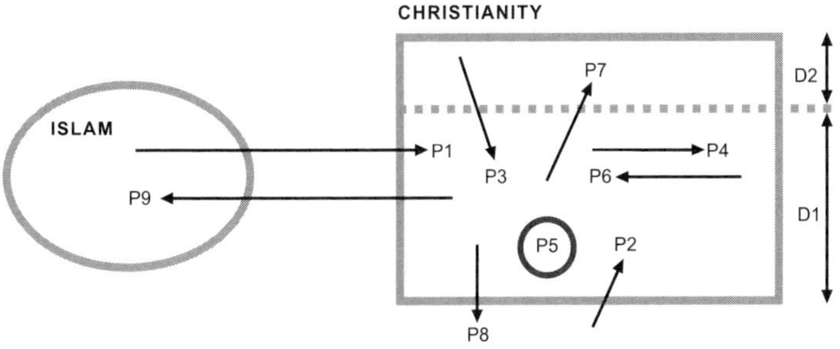

KEY:

P1 = A person converting from Islam to Christianity (how churches most commonly understand conversion). Rambo[11] calls this "tradition transition."

P2 = A person converting from a nonreligious background to Christianity. Rambo calls this "affiliation." Such converts can also be called "first-generation Christians."[12]

P3 = A person converting from one denomination to another (D2 to D1) within Christianity. Rambo calls this "institutional transition."[13] It is also called "denominational switching."

P4 = A person converting within the same denomination (D1) of Christianity to a deeper spirituality. Rambo calls this "intensification."

P5 = A person with no actual conversion experience. Often called a "nominal Christian," who was "born and bred" in the Christian tradition.

P6 = A person converting within Christianity and the same denomination, having a negative spiritual growth. P6 is a potential convert away from the Christian faith and in opposite movement to P4. This movement is often labeled "backsliding."

P7 = A person converting from denomination D1 to D2 within Christianity (P7 is in the opposite direction of P3): according to Rambo termed as "institutional transition."

P8 = A person converting from Christianity into a nonreligious environment. This type of conversion is called "apostasy" or "defection" by Rambo.

P9 = A person converting from Christianity to Islam. In Rambo's terminology, this is also "tradition transition" (see P1).

An Analytical Grid: Five Conversion Motives

Questions about human motivation have long been raised in missionary circles. Social scientists have brought forward different recommendations on how to classify conversion motives. Rambo, for example, refers to the suggestions of Lofland and Skonovd[14] to distinguish six categories of conversion motives:

1. Intellectual: A person seeks knowledge about religious or spiritual issues.

2. Mystical: A sudden and traumatic burst of insight, as in the case of Saul of Tarsus.

3. Experimental: Active exploration of religious options.

4. Affectional: Interpersonal bonds as an important factor in the conversion process.

5. Revivalist: Individuals are emotionally aroused and new behaviors and beliefs are promoted by the pressures exerted (by using crowd conformity).

6. Coercive: Different levels of pressure exerted on the person to participate, conform, and confess.[15]

Such a categorization is useful as a model for basic consideration. It needs, however, to be adapted to each particular situation.

In the context of my research I have identified five operational conversion motives. This analytical grid of five motives was constructed out of my readings in the missiology and psychology of conversion.[16]

Religious

This motive is sometimes called the "intellectual" motive for conversion. It is the motive that has been traditionally called the "true" motive for conversion.[17] The understanding of the religious/intellectual motive is that a person actively seeks knowledge about religious or spiritual issues via literature, television, lectures, and other media. In my study it means that a person actively acquires knowledge of the Christian or Islamic faith.

Some converts interviewed were seeking religious knowledge about Christianity or Islam because there was a problem or "crisis" with their experience of their original faith. The main reason given was that of not being able to understand the teachings or rituals. This aspect can be described as the "push" dimension of conversion. Since such persons could no longer understand and agree with the teachings of their faith, they felt "pushed" to leave it and explore an alternative religion. Since the new religion was experienced as "better" and "more understandable," it "pulled" the person to accept it. Therefore, in this religious motive one can often identify both a push and a pull dimension.

Mystical

Rambo and Robbins also discuss this motive.[18] According to Rambo, a mystical conversion experience "is generally a sudden and traumatic burst of insight, induced by vision, voices, or other paranormal experiences." A "paranormal" experience is usually described as an experience that cannot be easily explained scientifically or rationally.[19] The prototypical conversion in respect to mystical experience in the Bible is commonly attributed to Saul of Tarsus on his way to Damascus (Acts 9). In religious terminology it has the understanding of direct intervention by the spiritual divine power. In the conversion narratives described by William James, the mystical factor plays a central role.[20] J. H. Kroeger is convinced that in such conversions it is the Holy Spirit who "is at work in ways that pass human understanding."[21]

The term "supernatural" is also sometimes used in this context. Cowie describes this term as something that "cannot be explained by natural or physical laws" but rather has its original cause in the "world of spirits."[22] If people speak about supernatural experiences they usually refer to a significant dream, a vision, or an impression. It is an extraordinary happening or event that is usually sudden and unexpected. The level of emotional arousal is extremely high—sometimes involving theophanic ecstasies, awe, love, or even fear. Raschke discusses the term "revelation" in this context and gives the definition as "an enlightening or astonishing disclosure."[23] A revelation is therefore an extraordinary disclosure that a person receives. This extraordinary insight enables a person to make a step in a direction that would otherwise not have been easily taken—such as a change in religion.

McKinney, in her case study among the *Bajju*, pointed to the important role of dreams and visions in conversion.[24] Dreams and visions can serve either to initiate conversion or to confirm it, or both.

Some psychologists have attempted to explain visions as "paranormal" experiences: "Persinger has speculated that individuals within the 'normal,' ostensibly nonseizure, population who have experienced significant mystical or paranormal religious states might in fact have had what he describes as 'microseizure', i.e., slight abnormal electrical discharges of the limbic, emotional brain sufficient to sustain a mystical experience."[25]

In their section on "Epilepsy, mystical experience, and conversion," Warren Brown and C. Caetano differentiate between two neurocognitive models of religious conversion: (a) conversion seen as the result of abnormal experiences that have their origin in a malfunctioning brain; and (b) conversion seen as an extension of normal mental activity, differing from other mental activity only in its content and perceived significance.[26]

In a footnote they mention a third possibility, which would be that "conversion is an entirely supernatural event, occurring entirely outside of neurocognitive systems." In my study, I did not search for the origin of the mystical experiences reported by the interviewees. I refrained from trying to determine whether a mystical experience comes from within or outside the neurocognitive system. What should be clear, though, is that I do not regard these experiences as the result of a "malfunctioning brain." It was not my aim to critically assess whether such an experience had in fact taken place. If a respondent reports such an event, I accept it as a reality for that person.

Affectional

Lofland and Stark originally identified this conversion motive.[27] It stresses interpersonal bonds as the decisive factor in the conversion process. A person experiences affection as being loved, nurtured, and affirmed by another person or group. Van Butselaar calls this the "personal motive" and describes it as the "outgrowth of interpersonal relationships."[28] Interpersonal bonds are widely viewed as providing "fundamental support for recruitment."[29] In my interviews, this conversion motive appeared primarily in the form of affection for a person admired for his/her religious activities. Such a person was either a friend or a relative, from the same or the opposite sex.

Described thus far, the affectional motive can be interpreted as a positive "pull" factor, drawing the convert to accept the new religion. However, the affectional motive can also function as a negative "push" factor. Negative affectional factors are often traumatic events such as the death of a family member or a divorce, which constitutes a crisis in the life of a particular person and may push him/her into a conversion process. A convert may therefore enter into conversion due to an affective "push" or "pull" experience.

Sociopolitical

Rambo does not mention this motive. Van Butselaar calls this the "social motive."[30] It relates to the functioning of the individual within his or her sociopolitical group. In this category a person is motivated for sociopolitical reasons to change his/her religious allegiance. This motive featured strongly in my interviews, since many converts mentioned the sociopolitical situation as a reason for embracing another religion. The political climate in South Africa during the apartheid era "pushed" many black people to look for another religion, since for them the ruling government was experienced as "White Christian oppressors."

Kritzinger regards the slogan "Christianity is the religion of the Whites" as representing a "mood of Black consciousness looking for its roots." He is of the opinion that the reality of racism was responsible to "establish a negative image of the Christian faith in the minds of many Black people" and this resulted in a "growing interest in Islam as a religion of Africa." African people in South Africa began to see Jesus as the author of racism and not as the one who died to break down the dividing wall between peoples. Muslims have taken advantage of this situation and have promoted Islam as the "religion based on equal rights and justice."[31] Today there are many black Muslims in South Africa, almost all of them coming from a Christian background.

Material

Rambo does not mention this motive but Van Butselaar includes it.[32] It is particularly important for my research since various converts mentioned it. There are many poor people who find themselves in such a desperate situation that they will change their religious allegiance if it can somehow improve their lot. Maslow calls this the "physiological need," which is one of the basic human needs.[33] This motive has sometimes been criticized as an "impure" conversion motive.

Included in this conversion motive is the desire for benefits such as food, clothes, gifts, housing, etc. I also viewed an offer of employment or a scholarship for studies as a material motivation for conversion. Poverty constitutes a crisis that sometimes "pushes" a person into a conversion process leading to a change of religion.

Analysis of the Conversion Motives

In my research I interviewed twenty converts, ten who converted from Christianity to Islam and ten from Islam to Christianity. The narratives reveal that between two and four of the motives I have identified played a role in each conversion process.

From the interviews it appeared that when more than one motive was operative the conversion process usually started with one motive but then moved on to the others, sometimes leaving the initial motive behind, especially when the material motive initiated the process. In other cases the original motive persisted as a key factor throughout the process. Various other combinations or constellations of conversion motives were found.[34]

Religious

My research findings reveal that eighteen out of twenty respondents experienced this motive as vital in their conversion process. The converts acquired knowledge of the new faith and compared it with the old. If the new faith appeared superior to them, that became a motivation to accept it. The main issue mentioned by converts to Christianity was the love displayed in the Bible through Jesus as well as the warmth among Christians. The converts also found "hope and assurance" which they hadn't experienced before. In these cases, Islam was perceived as a religion with meaningless ritualistic practices and utterances in Arabic that most people in South Africa did not understand. By contrast, converts expressed their joy at having a "living relationship" with Jesus and guidance from the Holy Spirit.

On the other hand, a number of converts accepted Islam because they said Christianity was not practical and was against common human reason. They experienced the Christian faith as replete with irrational doctrines such as the Trinity and Christ's incarnation. In contrast, they found Islam to be accommodating to the findings of modern science, which therefore appeared as the only viable option for an enlightened man or woman.

Mystical

It is significant that six out of ten converts to Christianity said that a supernatural experience contributed greatly to their decision to convert, whereas none of the ten converts to Islam mentioned this motive. All six of these converts emphasized that this supernatural encounter happened towards the end of their conversion process and that it was the "final straw" which convinced them to make a commitment to Christianity. The converts appeared to be convinced that God had spoken to them in a direct way.

Affectional

Of twenty converts, eighteen mentioned this as a motivational factor in their conversion. It can be assumed that the reason why people convert (in both directions) is often not that they are intellectually convinced about the new religion but because a "friend has shown them the way."[35] Frequently marriage results in accepting one's spouse's religion. In the Muslim community, the non-Muslim spouse is usually expected to convert to Islam.

Sociopolitical

Five out of ten converts from Christianity to Islam indicated that the sociopolitical situation in South Africa was a reason for them to convert to Islam.[36] This fact confirms Rambo's hypotheses: "Indigenous cultures that are in crisis will have more potential converts than stable societies."[37] Conversion thus becomes an act of revolt against the religion and society in which the converts were born and brought up. It is a break from their past, with all its painful memories.

Material

This motive appears in five conversion narratives. If people see that their basic needs can be fulfilled they are often prepared to change their religion. People with serious physiological needs often display a high availability for conversion. People likely to fall in this category are the unemployed, young people who would like to study but have no money, refugees, and recent immigrants. Many poor people in South Africa have recently become Muslims in order to get food or a job.

Other emerging aspects:

- Converts often have a strong desire to witness to their newly found faith.

- Many converts have to endure opposition and persecution. It is significant that five Muslim converts to Christianity faced persecution compared to only one Christian convert to Islam.

- The ritual of commitment is seen as a final break with the past and as a public confession of embracing the new faith.

Conclusion

My empirical findings suggest that the conversion process is usually driven by a variety of motives. A human being should be viewed holistically as a person with different needs, all of which play a role in the movement to conversion. It is therefore questionable to distinguish between "pure" and "impure" conversion motives. A sound theological anthropology views a human being not only in spiritual terms but as a whole human being, who is situated in a specific economic, cultural, religious, and political context. One cannot expect a decision as fundamental as conversion to a new religious community to be made solely on the basis of the truth claims of the new religion.

As Conn observes, "The conversion door swings both ways."[38] I believe the Bible supports a view of conversion that includes a two-way movement. There is no controversy to declare a person a "convert" in Christian terminology if this person turns towards Christianity. But can a person also be declared a "convert" if she/he turns *away* from Christianity? It appears that the Bible uses the term "apostate" in such cases. I propose that it would be to the benefit of missiology to adopt a more holistic view of conversion and include both ways of conversion in its definition.

Apostasy in the Old Testament is described in terms of "turning away" or disobedience to God in a particular situation (e.g., Exodus 32:8). The Bible teaches that it began with the transgression of Adam and Eve in paradise. God dealt with sins of apostasy in radical ways (see, for instance, Genesis 3; Exodus 21:17; 32:10, 35). In the New Testament, apostasy appears to be a continual danger to the church, and there are repeated warnings against it (cf. 2 Thessalonians 2:3; 1 Timothy 4:1–3; 2 Peter 3:16–17).

Jesus seems to have taken a different attitude toward apostates, since he did not support the use of the death penalty as was often the case in the Old Testament. One such account is recorded in John 6:60–71, where many disciples deserted Jesus since they could not understand his teaching. In terms of the categories used above, one could describe this as a "religious" conversion motive, dominated by a negative or "push" factor. The reaction of Jesus was that he was not afraid of losing disciples. He gave them the space to make up their minds, so they were in fact free to leave. Jesus revealed the same attitude when he met the "rich young ruler", where it is pointed out that Jesus loved him (Mark 10:21).

As Christians we are challenged to emulate this attitude of Jesus: to show genuine love to those who are in the process of turning from the faith we belong to—not wanting them to leave, but refraining from all coercion to make them stay. Our understanding of conversion to our religious community—and consequently the nature of our self-understanding as Christians—is directly related to our understanding of conversion away from it.

Implications for Contextual Church Praxis

The theology of conversion proposed in this paper emphasizes two dimensions that have often been neglected: the wholeness of the human person and the two-way direction of conversion. This has two consequences: all conversion motives discussed above need to be accepted as playing a valid part in any specific conversion process; and missiology should give as much attention to those who leave as to those who join.

This understanding of conversion has a number of practical implications. First, it encourages a faith community to take adequate measures to care for new converts who join the community, acknowledging that there is a whole variety of motives "pushing" or "pulling" the person to make such a move. Secondly, a faith community should take special care of people who wish to convert to another faith.

In order to guide converts more meaningfully, a few practical steps are recommended to a Christian faith community:

- Within each faith community there should be a small specialized group consisting of members trained to welcome new converts from another faith.[39]

- This group should show genuine interest and care for converts and lead them into a deep study of their new faith and its religious practices.

- In due course, the convert should be introduced through this small group to the larger faith community.

- If the convert is a single person, he/she should be "adopted" into a family of the new faith community.

- By applying these guidelines, the faith community will take care of the spiritual and social needs of new converts in their group in an organic way.

In addition, this small group should also be trained to counsel and care for people who are contemplating converting away from Christianity to another religion, such as Islam, in the same loving attitude. First, this would mean trying to encourage them to review their Christian faith before converting. Should a person still want to convert to another faith, the group should be sensitive to that desire and even assist him/her in investigating it thoroughly.[40] Finally, when the person converts to another faith, the church should let him or her go in peace and Christian love.

CHAPTER 9

NORTH AFRICAN WOMEN AND CONVERSION: SPECIFICS OF FEMALE FAITH AND EXPERIENCE

EVELYNE REISACHER

When North African women from an Islamic background decide to follow the teachings of Jesus, they face issues felt to be specific to them as females. I sought to understand how women view their conversion in comparison to that of men in the same sociocultural context.

From the narratives of fifteen North African women interviewed, several common themes emerged which represent what the majority of these women experienced or felt. These findings resonated with my own observations in the context of my living with the North African Christian community for two decades in France.

Methodology

In order to ascertain what was unique to female conversion I interviewed fifteen North African women who have become Christians either in France, Morocco, Algeria, or Tunisia. Interviews lasted no longer than thirty minutes to an hour, in order to discern the two or three issues mentioned first.

I knew all these women well, having interacted with them over many years, but this was the first time I discussed the specificities of female conversion with them. Interviews were conducted either face-to-face or over the phone.

The questions asked were as follows:

1.   According to you, what are the differences between your conversion and the conversion of males in your culture?

2.   If your own brother instead of you had converted, what would have been different?

3.   Describe experiences from your conversion that typically relate to the fact you are a woman.

4.   If you would mentor a Christian worker, what are the things you would tell him or her are specific to women's conversions?

5.   What are the concerns of Muslim women which would prevent them from investigating Christianity?

The various issues North African women identified are hereafter listed in random order not indicative of importance. Future research is needed to rank them.

I was also curious to find out the reaction of North African men to the comments of the women I interviewed, but my schedule did not allow for interviewing more than two men. I include their comments so that the reader may see their perspective on what women said about them.

The limited number of interviews does not allow for generalizations but rather outlines a number of issues for further investigation. Since it only deals with North African women, no conclusions can be drawn for women from other regions of the world.

Fear of Rejection

Women mentioned their fear of being rejected by family and relatives after conversion. Malika, for example, was forced by her family to stay home for several weeks, and consequently lost her job. Her parents wanted to give her the opportunity to change her mind and return to Islam. They told her that it was terrible to reject God and that awful things would happen to her as a result. They were afraid that, because she was now a Christian who had left Islam, she would go to hell after her death. Family members of those who convert feel it is their duty to bring them back into the Muslim community in order to save them from hell.

Aicha was asked by her family to choose between them and her new faith in Jesus. She was estranged from her family for several years but has since reconnected with them. It was not easy for her to deal with this physical separation after conversion, since she was not raised to be disconnected from family and did not find any group or community which provided the same kind of social and communal support. She slept in the streets for several days after leaving home, and wandered from place to place without being able to bond with anyone. Her family was worried about her and was sad, but used rejection as a means to make her become aware of the punishment she would endure from God as a consequence of renouncing the teachings of Islam.

Kheira and Zoubida, who were not rejected, fear that something bad may still happen to them—for example, that their family will send them to North Africa or marry them to a Muslim. Fatima asked me, "Did you shun conversion because you were afraid of what would happen afterwards? No? I did and wondered what my parents would say: Would they forbid me to go to meetings, would they marry me to a Muslim? I was terribly afraid that they would not allow me to convert, because girls do not have the same freedom as boys."

Djamila told me, "I fled. I left home without saying anything. I could not receive a phone call, could not go to church, therefore I preferred to leave. Today I forgive my parents. They had suffered during the war with France and during immigration. This explains why they reacted like that and resisted when I converted." Djamila now regrets the decision she made at her conversion to leave home and be away from family.

As several women mentioned, the family fears that the sin of embracing the Christian beliefs for someone coming from Islam will not be forgiven. One woman quoted Sura al-Nisa (4) 48: "Allah forgiveth not that partners should be set up with him; but he forgiveth anything else, to whom he pleaseth; to set up partners with Allah is to devise a sin most heinous indeed."[1] Another woman quoted Sura Tawba (9) 2: "Allah will cover with shame those who reject Him."[2] She felt that her decision caused her family to feel this shame.

Women perceived rejection from family as more difficult to cope with for them than for men. Conversion painfully disconnected these women from the ones they love most, and is a hard experience for parents who fear their child will be eternally lost.

Greater Resiliency

The majority of interviewees stated they are more resilient than men. Since it is more difficult for women to convert, they need more strength to persevere in their new faith. Zohra said, "If a woman wants to keep on in Christianity, she has to be tough, she has to go against the current. . . . I noticed that in the Christian fellowship I attend the majority of women who carry on are not afraid to fight for their new beliefs." Fadila agreed: "There are lots of pressures for women, but we don't easily give up."

Zakia said with a firm voice: "Women, when they choose to follow Jesus, will follow him to the end!" Zoubida added: "Men do not always follow their commitments. They have more freedom in their choices than women and do not face as much pressure at the moment of their conversion. Some men return to Islam after their conversion because it did not cost them much to become Christians." Zakia added: "Once women have jumped so many hurdles before conversion, they do not want to return to Islam. They stay on the path they have chosen and follow Jesus Christ." She continued: "Women have a mother's heart. They are more sensitive and more committed to the Lord's affairs than men. They are more sensitive to the Lord. "

Why did these women think they were more resilient than men in regard to conversion? I only interviewed women who have been Christians for several years. Those who have given up Christianity along the way might have answered differently.

Of the two North African men I interviewed, the first one agreed that women are more inclined to investigate Christianity, but after conversion need greater resiliency as they face greater social and family pressures. Hamid at first disagreed, saying that both sexes face the same degree of difficulties, but eventually agreed when Yasmina said that because women experience more resistance from relatives, extended family, and society, they become more resilient after overcoming that and continue in their faith.

Is resiliency after conversion a particularly female characteristic? I met North African men and women who showed great strength in the midst of tremendous difficulties. However, nine out of fifteen women, when asked about the specificity of female conversion, spoke of greater resilience. Why they feel so, and what the practical implications for ministry to both men and women are, is worth further investigation.

How Jesus Views Women

Women were attracted to Jesus because they were touched by the way he dealt with women in the Gospels. Several were drawn to Jesus Christ because he considered them equal with men, although they did not define this equality.

Several women shared that in Jesus they found their real identity as a woman. They considered this as a major difference with male conversion. Yasmina said, "The first thing that touched me is that Jesus accepted me as a woman. This transformed me. The fact that Jesus accepted me was the greatest gift. He loved me as I am, as a woman. This made it easier to accept my status as a woman."

Zakia said that it was easier to accept who she was: "Jesus gave me the chance to express myself and to be who I want to be. There is a big difference with before. Now I am free to think, to live as a believer, as a Christian!" The women say Jesus sees them as important and respects them.

Ali, one of the male informants, added: "Women are submissive, with fewer privileges than men in the area of education and work. But," he added, "these women feel more freedom when they read the biblical passage which says that in Christ there is neither male nor female, but all are one in him."

Women did not refer to theology to explain differences between male and female conversion, except when they talked about Jesus who touched their lives in a very unique way compared to men.

Female Social Status

Women find it more difficult than men to define their place in society after conversion and what their attitudes should be as female Christians living in a Muslim context. Ali explained: "Women are often seen as the representatives of Muslim religion. It is therefore much more difficult for them to convert to Christianity. Women also embody family; they bear children; they symbolize the private sphere, whereas men symbolize the public sphere. It is much more difficult for women to become a Christian. Religion is both culture and family. When they convert, they go against family and culture."

Fatima said, "Socially, the situation is different between men and women. Since before conversion the woman is already defined differently in terms of roles and obligations, the problem for her is to define how conversion affects these roles and obligations. I do not believe that we can say it is easier or not easier to convert. But it is what comes after conversion that will be experienced differently between men and women." One informant said that Muslim family and societal structure gives women less opportunities to make independent choices.

Interviewees were afraid their conversion would affect their status in the society. Zohra said, "Everything girls do brings more shame to the family." Malika commented on her own conversion: "I was afraid it was going to destroy something but I did not know to what extent it was going to be destructive."

Ali agreed that women were afraid to convert, because they were afraid of what others would say. Hamid underlined that men are less afraid of what other people will say about their conversion than women. He insisted: "Women want to make sure that everyone is happy about their decision, and if they see that people in the family are going to react, they will be afraid to take the decision. They want everyone to agree with what they do."

The informants I interviewed come from a more traditional context, where the roles of men and women are well-defined. The status of women is not monolithic in the Muslim world, and references to submission and male-female relations must be understood in light of the context where these women live. Other women may have said that submission is not an issue.

The Male Guardian

The majority of informants told me it was harder for females to convert if they had to submit to a husband or father who did not agree with their choice. In some Muslim regions, women need a *wali*, or male guardian, to be responsible for them as they perform certain tasks such as traveling or being out in public. According to certain Islamic schools of law, guardians have their say when a woman wants to marry and will make a number of decisions on her behalf.[3] The guardian is usually her father or an uncle, brother, or a man close to the woman's family. There are places in the Muslim world where the role of the *wali* is considered obsolete. Elsewhere it is not. In the case of our interviewees, the majority expect that for a decision like conversion, which has numerous family and social implications, they need to be concerned about the reaction of their guardian.

The women I interviewed did not ask the advice of a guardian before conversion. However, they said it was hard to go against the approval of older members of the family. Several mentioned concern about the reaction of their father and brother. Yasmina said, "My brothers were flexible. I thank the Lord for that. My brothers were not tough. . . . They were flexible because religion was not their priority. If they had been deeply religious, it would have been another story."

While women were worried about the reaction of their guardian, they also felt something was missing when he did not bless their choice. They did not like the idea of making such a decision as conversion alone and missed the approval and support of their family. All women I met pray regularly for their family and long for parents and other members of their family to become Christians so that they can feel their support.

The North African women interviewed shared about visions or dreams they received prior to their conversion which almost played the role of an invisible *wali*. Fadila, Baya, Warda, Yasmina, and Malika received a supernatural confirmation from God in the form of a dream or a vision which helped them to make the decision to become followers of Jesus. Farida had a dream in which she said Jesus told her to follow him; Fadila said an angel appeared to her who told her that she was making the right decision in accepting Jesus. Baya waited long before she dared to accept Jesus in her life, and finally made the decision after seeing a bright light and hearing a voice next to her telling her to follow Jesus.

Marriage Ties

Two of the women were single, three were divorced, and the rest were married. According to Fawzia, married women have more restrictions. It is harder for them to become Christians than single women because of the community. Zakia, recalling her own experience, added that it is very hard to be married to a Muslim man after conversion because the wife has to submit to her husband. According to Hamid, single women carry fewer responsibilities within their family, especially if they are young and still live under the authority of their parents. Life is less complicated for them. However, if the woman's husband is Christian, it is better than not being married. Zohra shared the same view and said that it is important for women not to stay alone and that converts must be helped in finding a husband.

Further comments on marriage focused on childrearing. Farida underlined that when a woman converts her husband fears that she will not raise their children as good Muslims. Kheira, whose husband divorced her because she had converted, said that she will allow her children to decide on their own: "You need to give them the freedom to be what they want to be. They should not be mistreated. Conversion should be an option for them and they should be free to decide what they want to believe."

Zoubida explained that North African women are expected to pass on to their children Muslim values, and if they become Christians this may not happen. According to her, boys do not have this same responsibility and consequently are less accountable. She continued, "If boys do not go to the mosque for a while, people will say: 'It does not matter, perhaps they will go later.' But married women are expected to raise their children according to Islam and cannot afford to have periods of 'spiritual laziness.'"

Kheira shared this regarding the problem of raising children as Christians in a Muslim family: "My sister has two boys and she is a believer. It is harder for her than for me. I have girls and my parents do not react as strongly. Her boys are now fasting during Ramadan!" "What makes it harder for female converts is the responsibility mothers have to raise daughters as Muslims," said Fatima.

My Mother

Mothers held an important place in women's statements. Yasmina said: "I was so afraid of what my mother would say; no one else mattered, except my mother! I was of course happy when I became a Christian. I was overwhelmed with joy, but I also suffered because I thought of what it would do to my mother. In a way, she was glad about the positive change in me, but at the same time she was totally against my decision. I was afraid of the consequences and how my mother would cope with it."

Malika explained: "My mother thought I had done something wrong or I had been manipulated. I was worried and felt extremely sad because she did not understand me. This made me sad." Djamila was hesitant before conversion because she did not want to face her mother. She decided she would never tell her. She came to meetings for many years without being able to make a decision, always preoccupied by the perceived reaction of her mother. Once, during a meeting, she suddenly broke out in tears and accepted Jesus, but has still not told her mother.

The respect due to parents bears more strongly on girls' reflections before conversion. Zoubida said, "The problem lies with my family. How am I going to deal with them? In our culture, there is great respect for parents. As women, we have not as many opportunities to make changes than men. Men do not ask themselves the same questions. Before conversion, they are freer, and this is also true after conversion." Yasmina underlined that men are less worried about their mother's reaction: "They also think of the mother, but not in the same way. They show less sensitivity in this area."

Zohra said, "As a girl I hid my conversion. The priority is the mother, first the mother." One informant highlighted that same concept by quoting a hadith: "A man enquired: 'O Apostle of Allah. Who is the most proper person for my good association?' He replied: 'Your mother.' Then he asked: 'Who is next?' 'Your mother,' he replied. Then he asked: 'Who is next?' 'Your mother,' he replied. He enquired, 'Who is next?' 'Your father,' he replied."[4]

Emotions

The issue of emotions came up in four interviews. Women contended that they are more in touch with their emotions and therefore find it easier to embrace Christianity. They emphasized the importance of sensitivity, and said that if men would get in touch with their emotions they would be more open to receive Jesus.

Yasmina said: "I personally believe men are harder to convince than women. In my family, for example, boys have a hard time to accept Jesus. They think too much, they speak words with their mind, but they do not want to discover the Word of God and understand it." She added, "My brothers do not want to investigate Christianity seriously. God touches the heart of those who search his Word. My brothers think too much with their head and do not want to discover who Jesus is with their heart."

Ali stated that women were more emotional than men and therefore more inclined to convert to Christianity. He added: "Men think and reason too much; they want to play tough, and, because they do not want to listen with their emotions, they do not want to accept the message of the gospel. They do not want to be touched by the message of love, whereas women are more open."

The Public Sphere

In many cases, women felt more restricted in their whereabouts than men—a factor which influenced their conversion.

Farida mentioned that the issue of access to public space is crucial in conversion. Many women will not have access to places men have access to. When women go out, everyone in the household wants to know where they go, whereas men can easily leave the house (for example, to meet other believers) without giving an explanation. Young girls would usually go out with their sisters, mothers, or other people from the household. Therefore leaving the house, especially on Sunday morning, to attend church meetings looked awkward.

Yasmina insisted: "Girls cannot go out as easily as men. That's a hindrance to conversion." She explained that to be able to grow spiritually she decided to move out of her parents' home because, being single, she was not supposed to do things alone. But her moving out created new difficulties easily avoided by staying home.

Soraya said that boys have more freedom than girls: "Girls cannot move as freely. When my husband became a Christian, everything was easy for him. He was accepted. For a girl, it is shameful to leave the house. . . . Furthermore, conversion is the worst thing for her. A girl is completely rejected. I was afraid to lose my family. That is why I did not leave the house; I was afraid to be rejected."

Fawzia said, "In our culture, it is more complicated for girls to convert. They must stay at home, and on the top of that, if they convert it is even worse." Zohra said that boys have more freedom in everyday life: "My brother was not threatened when he became a believer; I was threatened to be taken back to my parents' home country. My brother followed me to work every day after my conversion and picked me up when he found out I was a Christian; my mother said, 'You are not my daughter anymore.'"

Women have fewer possibilities to develop relationships with Christians, said Malika, for whom the only place she was able to interact with Christians was at school. The rest of the time, her mother would make sure that she would be with Muslim friends. The sons of her family had more opportunities to meet Christians than the daughters.

Conclusion

Through my study I have identified nine issues North African women say are specific to their female status:

- fear of rejection
- greater resiliency
- how Jesus views women
- female social status
- the male guardian
- marriage ties
- my mother
- emotions
- the public sphere

These issues were not listed according to order of importance. How women rank these issues would require further research.

A number of conclusions can be drawn. Women perceive more gender differences in the social area than in the theological area. It is in the realm of social interactions that there are major divisions in regard to conversion. I draw here a parallel with how Muslims divide religious activities. They use the word *'ibadat* to describe worship of God, and the word *mu'amalat* to define believers' social interactions. In this study women expressed little gender-specific difference in the way they worship God in Christianity, but a number of differences in terms of social relations. Women are preoccupied by their relationships. They are not so much concerned by new relationships but rather by how to deal with the ones they had before conversion and especially those with the members of their family.

The only time women refer to worship is to talk about Jesus and the importance he has for them, compared to how he touches men's lives. They are able to connect with Jesus. I have known these women personally for many years. Their conversion is genuine and their relationship with Jesus is meaningful. They have all made a clear statement about their desire to follow Jesus. They seem to have fewer difficulties in relating to God than in relating with their community.

The relationships that matter most to these women are close relatives—an issue specific to them as females. They show a genuine interest for relatives and concern about how conversion affects their relationship. Islam says that the family is the core of Muslim society. North African women realize that their decision, by affecting this core unit, will also affect the society.

Women are also preoccupied by anthropological questions. They want to understand who they are and why they accepted Christianity. They try to explain their behaviors by making comparisons with men. Men are less emotional but at the same time less resilient. Men have another status and role in the society. Informants also express the difficulty of defining their roles as Christian women living in a society that does not necessarily embrace their values. They are in search of their identity as Christians. They reflect and ask questions on how they can follow Jesus within their own society, which seems more difficult for them than for men.

North African women feel deeply hurt by how their affectional bonds changed because of their conversion. They express both the desire to be close to their family and the pain of feeling rejected. They understand that it is not easy for their family to cope with their decision. Many would do things differently if they could.

During this research, something puzzled me. I know these women well, and the joy that they have to follow Jesus. I have observed their zeal, their commitment, and their deep bond with God over the years; yet I found that these women expressed more difficulties, concern, and heavy-heartedness than joy. Perhaps they knew me well enough to feel confident to share deep concerns spontaneously. To someone less close to them, they might have revealed another mood. Or maybe the issues they mentioned are still unresolved and painful.

Most of the women came from a traditional cultural and sociological background. Their views do not reflect the views of all Muslim women. Some younger women may say that they are too old-fashioned. Others may say that they are too influenced by current trends of reform. It is important to remember that this research only deals with interviews of fifteen women. However, as I have met with hundreds of women in the Arab world and in other parts of the Muslim world, I have observed similarities with what these fifteen North African women expressed. Of course, these observations have not been systematically analyzed and each context would require further research, taking into account all the factors that influence how conversion affects the life of women versus men.

CHAPTER 10

EXPERIENCING JESUS:
REFLECTIONS OF SOUTH ASIAN WOMEN

MARY MCVICKER

Muslim women in the Indian subcontinent experience[1] Jesus as real and true in their lives as a part of their process in coming to faith. In 1966, a wealthy woman from a well-educated, respected family in the village of Wah, Pakistan, began to encounter peculiar things she could not explain.

> Normally I never dream, but this night I did. The dream was so lifelike, the events in it so real, that I found it difficult the next morning to believe they were only fantasy. Here is what I saw.
>
> I found myself having supper with a man I knew to be Jesus. He had come to visit me in my home and stayed for two days. He sat across the table from me and in peace and joy we ate dinner together. Suddenly, the dream changed. Now I was on a mountaintop with another man. He was clothed in a robe and shod with sandals. How was it that I mysteriously knew his name, too? John the Baptist. What a strange name. I found myself telling this John the Baptist about my recent visit with Jesus. "The Lord came and was my guest for two days," I said. "But now he is gone. Where is he? I must find him! Perhaps you, John the Baptist, will lead me to him?"

This dream led Begum Bilquis to a Christian family in search of answers. Muslims know about Jesus, but who is John the Baptist?

Finding the wife at home, Begum Bilquis relayed her dream. "Strangely, I had difficulty controlling my voice as I related the experience. Even as I told her, I felt the same excitement I felt on that mountaintop."[2]

For Muslim women, coming to faith is a combination of Jesus actively touching their lives and the reality of what truth means for practical living and future security (physical, spiritual, and social). In Maharashtra, India, Taranum was desperate for children after years of marriage. Every attempt, remedy, and doctor failed, emptying the family of all its resources. Miss Joshi taught about Jesus who listens when she prays. To the dismay of her mother-in-law, Taranum decided to ask Jesus. "If Jesus answers prayer, then let him give me a child," she thought. Within a couple of months Taranum was pregnant. Soon a healthy baby was born. She knew Jesus listened to her cry! Her family did not like it, but she wanted to follow the one who blessed her with not just one but now three active children.

For most Muslim women in South Asia, having children is everything. The stigma of being barren is removed from her and the family; the daily barrage from family and neighbors reminding her that she has failed her most important role as a woman in the community changes to advice on how to take care of the children. She gains security for her family and self to be cared for in the future by her children, and most of all she fulfills her duty to Allah to be a faithful mother who teaches her children the path to God.

The President of India, A. P. J. Abdul Kalam, depicts the intimate interaction that characterized his relationship and experience with his mother:

My Mother
    Sea waves, golden sand, pilgrims' faith,
    Rameswaram Mosque Street, all merge into one,
    My Mother!

You come to me like heaven's caring arms.

I remember the war days when life was challenge and toil—

Miles to walk, hours before sunrise,

Walking to take lessons from the saintly teacher near the temple.

Again miles to the Arab teaching school,

Climb sandy hills to Railway Station Road,

Collect, distribute newspapers to temple city citizens,

Few hours after sunrise, going to school.

Evening, business time before study at night.

All this pain of a young boy,

My Mother you transformed into pious strength

With kneeling and bowing five times

For the Grace of the Almighty only, My Mother.

Your strong piety is your children's strength,

You always shared your best with whoever needed the most,

You always gave, and gave with faith in Him.

I still remember the day when I was ten,

Sleeping on your lap to the envy of my elder brothers and sisters

It was full moon night, my world only you knew

Mother! My Mother!

When at midnight I woke with tears falling on my knee

You knew the pain of your child, My Mother.

Your caring hands, tenderly removing the pain

Your love, your care, your faith gave me strength

To face the world without fear and with His strength.

We will meet again on the great Judgement Day, My Mother![3]

In another urban setting in India, Mumtaz made friends with Mary, a social worker. They shared their problems with each other, prayed together, and visited each other's homes. For two years Mumtaz watched how Mary and her husband interacted with one another. Mumtaz told

Mary, "Coming to your home is like going to a mosque . . . we find so much peace at your home."

How much more are humans dependent in their interconnection with the Divine for transformation? *Experiencing* Jesus is the primary ingredient for Muslim women coming to faith in South Asia. Does not God choose to reveal himself in meaningful and relevant ways to women?[4]

Processing Information

Most evangelical approaches to Muslims prioritize the message, and rightly so, with a commitment to communicate the truth of the gospel. This approach normally relies on traditional communication theory: the sender encodes the message, puts it through a channel, and the receiver decodes the message.[5] Following this model, the message revolves around the processing of information through the content, delivery, and reception of the message.

Outreach strategies among Muslims which include women incorporate excellent cross-cultural and receptor-oriented approaches. Resourceful tools, including chronological Bible storying[6] and inductive Bible studies,[7] provide methods to guide South Asian Muslim women to faith and growth in Christ. While the use of stories and relevant themes seek to understand the receptor, often the approach or telling of the story remains in the cognitive realm.[8]

Does the Message Impact Women?

In two areas where Muslims have been coming to faith in South Asia in significant numbers, women are not readily joining men in becoming followers of Jesus Christ. Often the gospel is heard by men and moves through their relationships with one another rather than across gender lines within kinship, though there are exceptions.

The perception of women in the Indian subcontinent is reflected through Manu's view that "a woman must be her father's shadow in childhood, her husband's in her youth, her son's in old age."[9] Mahatma Gandhi worked tirelessly to overcome this oppressive worldview of women and the superstitions attached to it. He believed in woman: her value, her education, and her ability to shape the nation. While the South Asian and particularly Muslim woman centers on her family and home, she "usually compromises on issues with her husband and is willing to subordinate her interests for the welfare of the home and married life"; yet her influence is not to be overlooked. "When it comes to matters of principle, she becomes the guiding force that inspires the husband. This is the basic strength of the Indian woman."[10] In this basic strength, Muslim women across South Asia can be a primary key to move their family and community to faith.

The challenge is to *connect* with Muslim women. South Asian Muslim women communicate and learn by doing. Women long to have their felt needs met. Rather than processing information or convincing through logic, Muslim women are experience-oriented, often searching for love and spiritual power.[11] A cognitive approach alone does not bring change in the women's lives. They need to connect through experience on a relational level—with humans and the Divine.

Multisensory Communication

In order to understand why the message often fails to reach women in South Asia, we must understand the communication and learning styles of Muslim women. Most are oral communicators "who learn from experience and association—not from logic. They organize content by association with events. They learn by interaction with others. Oral communicators can produce beautiful epic poems and ballads. Oral communicators need to hear something several times in order to memorize it."[12]

Rather than a transfer of messages, British anthropologist Ruth Finnegan conceptualizes communication as humans interconnecting through multiple modes in dynamic, active processes.[13] As humans actively interconnect with one another using multiple spheres, including the five senses, body movements and gestures, space, time, emotions, and artifacts in dynamic ways, this process is called multisensory communication.

For Muslim women in South Asia these active processes enable, trigger, and confirm an understanding of the message.[14] Begum Bilquis had a second dream three days later which aroused so many questions in her spirit that she was prompted to visit the Mitchells, a Christian family.

I was in the bedchamber when a maid announced that a perfume salesman was waiting to see me. I arose from my divan elated, for at this time there was a shortage of imported perfumes in Pakistan. I greatly feared running low on my favorite luxury. And so in my dream I happily asked my maid to show the perfume salesman in.

He was dressed in the manner of perfume salesmen in my mother's day when these merchants traveled from house to house selling their wares. He wore a black frock coat and carried his stock in a valise. Opening the valise, he took out a golden jar. Removing the cap, he handed it to me. As I looked at it I caught my breath; the perfume glimmered like liquid crystal. I was about to touch my finger to it when he held up his hand.

"No," he said. Taking the golden jar, he walked over and placed it on my bedside table. "This will spread throughout the world," he said.

As I awakened in the morning, the dream was still vivid in my mind. The sun was streaming through the window, and I could still smell that beautiful perfume; its delightful fragrance filled the room. I raised up and looked at my bedside table, half expecting to see the golden jar there. Instead, where the jar had been, now rested the Bible![15]

Begum Bilquis recalled, while driving home from the Mitchells', "I experienced for the second time that same fragrant Presence I had sensed in my garden earlier that day!" As Jesus touched her through her senses, something was happening in her spirit. Upon arriving home, she read a little from the gospel of John. "If John the Baptist was a sign from God, a sign pointing toward Jesus, was this same man pointing *me* toward Jesus, too?" She put the thought out of her mind until she received a note the next day from Mrs. Mitchell to read 2 Corinthians 2:14 and continually reread the passage.

The knowledge of Jesus spreads like a lovely perfume! In my dream, the salesman had put the golden dish of scent on my bedside table and said that the perfume "would spread throughout the world." The next morning I had found my Bible in the same spot where the perfume had been laid! It was all too clear.[16]

Women Experiencing Jesus

"Allah is simply not close, not real, not vital, nor practical to a woman's life. He is an abstract force to be obeyed, not loved. Intimacy with Allah is not a part of a Muslim woman's thinking."[17] Yet this is where God is breaking in and what South Asian Muslim women are discovering· experience with Jesus!

For the past three years, Mumtaz struggled immensely in her new faith. Her husband physically abused and constantly troubled her. She thought maybe God forgot her—and her Christian friend Mary, too, since she was "out of station" for so long. She sat down hopelessly and told God her need. At that moment there was a knock on the door. It was Mary. (Mary had just returned to the city with several unexpected emergencies, but that day she was deeply impressed to go and visit Mumtaz; she could not shake the feeling that she must go.) That day Mumtaz discovered that God hears her in her most desperate moment.

Physical Manifestation

Muslim women seek help for their pain and suffering: "a sick child, infertility problems, thwarted marriage negotiations, a misbehaving or lazy child, an abusive marriage, a failing business, general trouble in the household."[18]

Often from a place of desperation—physical, economic, or emotional—Muslim women move toward faith through a physical manifestation of Jesus.[19] In Nepal, Shabnam listened to the young man as he told the story of the one who came for *him*. The story captured Shabnam and her daughter, who was particularly impacted, but she was determined to remain on the straight path she knew through Islam. Soon after her daughter began to follow *Hazrat Isa al-Masih* (Holy Jesus the Messiah), Shabnam suffered from severe stomach pain. When her daughter prayed for healing in the name of *Hazrat Isa al-Masih*, instantly the pain disappeared. Shabnam knew he touched her body: she was free of the all-encompassing pain. Through healing, provision, or other miracles, Jesus touched the core aspect of her life and family, and it affirmed her understanding of who he is.

Experiential Knowledge

As educated Muslim women in South Asia debate aspects of the gospel, knowledge alone does not suffice.[20] Yet when women have access to God's Word, combined with supernatural revelation like visions or feeling the presence of Jesus, seeing an act of God confirms biblical truth, and this *experiential knowledge* guides them to faith.

Like Begum Bilquis, a refined Shi'ite woman named Farida encountered Jesus in her mind and through a revelation of the Spirit. Farida had discussed Islam and Christianity with many pastors and leaders but was exasperated by their ignorance. Dr. Lincoln (a married woman) and she, however, would talk into the night about beliefs and doctrine. Dr. Lincoln and Farida prayed and fasted together. The doctor modeled what it meant to follow Jesus. Though all of these factors contributed to Farida's coming to faith, the key was a supernatural encounter. In a vision, Farida saw a picture of a priest coming (whom she believed Dr. Lincoln represented). This visual connection with the Divine was so real that it confirmed the authority of Christ. God confirmed his Word to Farida; the visual picture gave a sense of security. The study of the Word was made practical as she experienced it through her senses and emotions.

Behavioral Experience

Muslim women who interconnect with followers of Jesus and experience how they act toward others taste *behavioral experience* that impacts their journey of coming to faith. In expressions of respect and care for others, living a good example before God and before people, listening and availability, praying together, and practical help, Christian women modeling faith results in a change in personal character and understanding of God's character.

Mumtaz learns to walk by faith through watching Mary and her family. Mumtaz tells Mary, "I see the way you manage your children. My husband even says, 'Go to Mary and learn to be like her.'" She ponders, "If I go, my children will be like yours."

A similar response came from Taranum's community. She remembers Christians on occasion walking through the lanes and passing out handbills. "They wanted to tell us about Jesus, but Miss Joshi *shows* us the love of Jesus."

Watching the character of Jesus Christ through film has proven equally effective. In a slum community in the east, women are drawn to the kindness of Christ and his ways in the *Jesus* film. While the men displayed limited outward interest, they tell the women, "Let's see that film again." They remember the miracles of Jesus.

While physical and cognitive experiences of Jesus tend to differ according to social, economic, or educational backgrounds of the women, behavioral experience is a significant aspect for most Muslim women growing in relationship with God.

Social Dynamics

The social dynamics revealed in her experience of community shape the Muslim woman's life. And multisensory communication creates her sense of belonging. Fostering belonging, identity, and a sense of security provides invitations to faith. Fortunately for Begum Bilquis, her faith was strengthened through an affirmed sense of belonging as she came to faith.

> Her basic questions were laid to rest through regularly soaking in the Scriptures and regularly worshiping with God's people on Sundays. . . . She wept for joy when we sang, "But I know whom I have believed and am persuaded that He is able to keep that which I've committed unto him, against that day"—especially the verse which goes, "I know not how the Spirit moves, convincing men of sin, revealing Jesus through the Word, creating faith in Him." Begum Bilquis was either in our home, or I in hers, just about every day for three years. I would not call

myself her discipler—we were sisters in Christ, learning from him together.[21]

Relationship

In India, Shahida Lateef notes three aspects of the Muslim woman's context affecting her social position: "being Indian, being Muslim, and being a woman."[22] This spirit of rejection associated with these roles—not uncommon to South Asian Muslim women—is one of the reasons that women respond to multisensory communication including touch, visual portrayal, sense of hot and cold, a song or story they feel and remember, or manifestations of power. Their thirst is quenched as they experience Jesus through horizontal and vertical relationships.

In the city of Dhaka, one woman witnesses the power of relationship:

> My main work is to listen to them. This gets their heart more than any other thing. The women are poor and no one gives them the time of day. They are illiterate so it is easiest to teach them to pray first so that they can build a living relationship with the Father. Most of the work is done by themselves once a few have been trained. [Daisy] is very mature and just loves them to the Father. The growth or change is evident in their awakening of a conscience and subsequent radical change of character. The most important area of concentration is to make sure that the discipler lives out a holy life which has power and lives as a good example before God and before the people. Love is the key.

Relationship is developed through time and experience; and, in its midst, multisensory communication creates fellowship.

Experience in Growth and Nurture

Experiencing Jesus is a living, participant faith for Muslim women in South Asia who follow him. Jesus must become real to all their senses, to every part of their being. As one older woman of faith says, "Muslim background believers live on rituals not a scientific faith." The assurance of God's promise for salvation through Jesus Christ is not merely a theological understanding.

Theology and words are important, but for Muslim women coming to faith, participation and experience are essential.[23] Anything that is real or has value is expressed through doing.

Muslim women in South Asia live a faith of praxis. Islam encompasses all of life. If a woman is to follow Jesus, she not only needs ways to experience him but tools to know how to live her faith. For a Muslim woman coming to faith in South Asia it is a practical, life-applicable, dynamic experience with Jesus.[24]

CHAPTER 11

BARRIERS BECOME BRIDGES: AFRICAN ACCOUNTS OF STAGES OF COMING TO FAITH

CHRISTEL ERIC

A Muslim seeker encounters at least five barriers when considering allegiance to the Messiah: religious, social, economic, psychological, and that of spiritual bondage. All these barriers reveal underlying fears:

- Fear of the unknown, of upsetting family and community

- Fear of being ostracized by family, husband, and close friends

- Fear of losing children, home, and all other security

- Fear of losing financial support (school fees, education, food)

- Fear of persecution and suffering, curses and the evil eye, and even the wrath of God

In my twenty-three years of ministry in Africa I have learned that establishing contacts, building friendships, instilling mutual trust, getting involved in people's lives, and having an open door and heart can help people overcome barriers. God can transform apparently grim facts and hindrances into bridges and steppingstones for sharing the gospel.

Doubts and disappointments about their own religion, longing for a pure life or a true relationship with God, challenges of Christian lifestyles, or puzzlements of their own findings in the Qur'an are often crucial and necessary struggles before a person is able to accept Christ and walk in him. The following examples, most of them people I know, show how God works through family problems; financial difficulties; sudden unemployment; displacement through war or other political uproar; despair of life; longing for forgiveness and acceptance; longing for a good marriage, a faithful husband, and obedient children; the experience of answered prayers; dreams and visions; and the love and exemplary life of Christians.

Building Friendships for the Sake of the Gospel

Shenas was a successful businesswoman with two lovely children, a nice home, nice cars, and many friends, yet deep inside she felt lonely and misunderstood. Neither materialism nor alcohol could suppress deep sadness and depression. With her marriage in shambles, she was tortured with suicidal thoughts. Feverishly she tried to get more involved in religion, going to the mosque to pray and meditate in the light of Aga Khan. In her search for answers she turned to books on psychology, philosophy, and New Age—to no avail.

A Christian friend kept inviting her out for lunch, but she would decline. One day her Christian friend appeared at her doorstep, stating boldly: "I will not allow you or Satan to destroy your life completely! Let's go and talk." Shenas was so surprised that she followed her and agreed that her friend could pray with her.

While she listened to her friend's passionate prayer, her burden lifted and love and peace filled her heart. She began to laugh and cry at the same time; everything seemed to have changed. She went home a new person. As she arrived her husband was leaving the house. Enveloped in the evening sun he looked so handsome and different to her that she greeted him with a big smile. Seeing this sudden friendliness, he wondered if this was a new trick.

Shenas went to her room to read Scripture. She did not have a Bible, so she opened the Qur'an. Her eyes fell on Surah Maryam, where Mary had a child without an earthly father. She came to the words about Jesus, "Peace will be on me the day I die and peace will be on me the day I will be raised again." She saw that, contrary to what she had believed as a Muslim, Jesus had been raised again. Who was this Jesus and what had he done? Was he really "the way, the truth, and the life"? Shenas was a devoted Muslim. What would her community say if she would follow Jesus? An enormous **social barrier** arose.

She kept going to the mosque to pray. While praying to Jesus, she heard a voice: "Why do you come here? I am not here!" (That stopped her visits to the mosque very quickly!) She realized she needed to learn what God expected of her as a Christian. Through more reading she gained understanding of her new life in Christ.

The change in her was so drastic that her husband told her one day, "Whatever it is that changed you, I want it too!" Soon her two children followed the example of their parents—a miracle we seldom experience: a whole family following Christ together.

Mark her stages:

1. Shenas was unhappy and experienced deep sadness and emptiness.

2. Allah seemed distant and unresponsive to her prayers. Increased religious fervor only increased disillusionment.

3. Her Christian friend showed sincere concern, although not belonging to the same family, clan, or tribe.

4. She acknowledged that the relief and change she experienced after the Christian prayed came from God.

5. The Qur'an's picture of Jesus startled her. He was dead and alive again. Had the Muslims fooled her? She started to doubt her own religion.

6.   She got a Bible, read Christian books, and understood that Christ died for her sin.

7.   After she heard Jesus' audible voice, she realized that she couldn't combine her old and new life; a choice must be made.

8.   She accepted Jesus into her life, experienced forgiveness and cleansing from her sin, and claimed the promise of eternal life.

9.   Her struggles and change in life became a viable witness to family members. She led her husband and children to Christ.

Shenas has since been faithful to reach out to her own community with great zeal.

Main Reasons for Her Conversion

- Hopelessness in her own life

- Disillusionment about Allah

- Boldness of her Christian friend, and her effective prayer

A Young Hafiz Is Challenged about His Religion

Yasseen enjoyed growing up in a well-respected, upper-class devoted Muslim clan. A rite of passage from childhood to manhood demanded that boys at the age of ten undergo special Islamic training in a specific madarasa boarding school. For two years they would learn about Islam and would be taught the Qur'an so that each would become a young Hafiz (one who knows the Qur'an by heart). At age twelve, Yasseen was already the celebrity and pride of the extended family. What higher status could one achieve than being a young proud Hafiz?

Suddenly his family was shaken: His uncle, a high ranking officer in the Sudanese army, became a Christian while sent by the government to check on a Christian conference. They immediately took away his wife and children, his job, and ultimately his freedom. He was imprisoned for over three years. Yasseen could not understand how all this pressure would not bring his uncle back to Islam. On the contrary, it made him only more determined to follow his newfound faith.

Yasseen loved his uncle and tried to convince him from the Qur'an of his error. In the process he "stumbled" over the prophet Jesus. Why did the Qur'an speak so much about *Nabi Isa* (Prophet Jesus)? He wanted to have a Bible for himself, so he went to his imam. The imam was upset about his questions and said he did not want to see a Bible or study one, because it is corrupted.

Yasseen wanted to know when the Bible was corrupted—before Muhammad or after Muhammad. His imam brushed him off by saying "Before Muhammad." Yasseen then asked the imam: "Why did Muhammad refer to the Torah to find out what punishment is written there for people who were caught in adultery? If Muhammad knew that the Bible was corrupted, why would he want advice from it?" Immediately the imam corrected himself, saying that the corruption must have taken place after Muhammad.

Yasseen asked him more precise questions: "Who changed the Bible? Where is the original now to compare it?" If it was only changed after Muhammad, then it had been in existence for 600–700 years already; there should be an original somewhere. Yasseen was disappointed and, disillusioned, stopped going to the mosque. He was eighteen years old.

His uncle's son got sick with cerebral malaria. When his uncle took him to hospital, all the doctors were on strike. Friends of his uncle appeared and offered to pray for the young boy. Yasseen was mad: this boy needed a doctor, not prayers from Christians. The friends persisted, so he left the room for them to pray. When he returned, the boy was sitting in bed, well and happy and wanting to go home. Yasseen did not believe the change and forced him to stay overnight till the doctors would examine him the next morning. He was puzzled about the obvious miracle that had taken place.

One of the Christians approached him. Yasseen was so intrigued by his smile that he allowed him to sit down and talk to him. This elderly man started sharing with him about the Creator, Adam and Eve, and how they spoiled a perfect relationship by rebelling against God. Suddenly the man asked him: "How many times did Adam and Eve sin?" It was the first time Yasseen realized that *one* sin was already enough to separate a person from God. "What about me? Is there any hope for me?" His sin sprang at him while the Christian shared chronologically through the Bible, from Genesis to Revelation, throughout the night—explaining not only the holiness of God, but also his love and mercy in sending Jesus Christ as Savior.

When the friend arrived at Revelation 3:20, Yasseen knew that he had to make a decision. Salvation seemed too easy. If one would have asked him to fast for two months instead of one or to pray ten times a day instead of five, this would have been more acceptable than to accept freely what Christ had done for him. All his life he had learned that he had to *do* something for his religion. The **religious barrier** seemed too high.

The second overwhelming difficulty was what had happened to his uncle. He had started so successfully in life and now was robbed of everything, even his freedom. Yasseen did not want to be a social outcast. Here the **social barrier** hit him. He had a special place as the only son in the family. Why should he give all this up?

But God's Spirit took hold of him when the Christian read Isaiah 43:1 to him: "The Lord who created you says: Do not be afraid, for I have ransomed you. I have called you by name; you are mine." When his partner

inserted his own name, *Yasseen*, into the verses, his resistance melted, and he surrendered his life to the Lord.

He soon finished high school, living as a secret believer until he graduated. His mother first noticed that something was different when he constantly defended his uncle while the clan discussions tore him down or accused him. As the pressure grew, he left his parents' home and moved in with Christian friends and looked for work. A few years later, he met a European girl and was married in Europe. Today he is ministering among his own Arabic-speaking people.

Note Yasseen's stages:

1. He was confused about his uncle becoming a Christian and his determination and conviction despite persecution.

2. He became puzzled over his own findings about Jesus in the Qur'an.

3. Disappointed by his religious leaders, he started to have doubts about his own religion and stayed away from the mosque.

4. Amazed by the healing of his cousin, he discovered that Christ answers prayers.

5. He realized that good works do not redeem from sin.

6. He realized that God was not interested in his works, but in himself.

Main Reasons for His Conversion

- Divine "shock therapy" in saving his uncle
- The miracle of healing and answered prayer
- The meaningful sharing of the gospel by friends of his uncle

- Realizing the impossibility of self-redemption in contrast to the finished work of Christ on his behalf

Trapped in the Chains of Ethnicity and Culture

Saina, from North Sudan, was forced into marriage at age fifteen and was given the responsibility to look after her younger siblings. With determination she completed high school and, after her child was weaned, entered university. During her studies, she got divorced and moved to another country. Disappointed by Islam, she kept saying: "If you are born in Islam, you should never be a woman!" But that did not change her conviction that "North Sudanese people must be Muslim, otherwise they cannot survive."

A "Christian" man embraced Islam in order to marry her. The marriage was rocky but their little girl seemed to make up for some of the disappointments. Saina longed for her husband's love and for acceptance by her friends. We had many discussions about the Islamic and Christian faiths. She revealed practices and traditions that portrayed Islam from a very different and frightening side. Whenever I shared the hope of the gospel with her, she would usually conclude: "It sounds so good, but it is not for me! I'm a Sudanese!"

One day her husband threw her out. I took her home with me. For three days, she buried herself in the bedroom and cried. We kept talking; I phoned all my friends to pray. One morning she said: "I'm going home. I can't live like this." Two hours later, a cheerful, beaming Saina returned to say: "I have experienced God. All that you told me is true. I want to become a Christian now!" On the way home she had prayed: "Jesus, if you are real and if you are God, let my husband and me be reconciled this morning!" When she arrived home, she asked for forgiveness for what had happened between them. Her husband turned around and embraced her, admitting that he, too, was guilty.

She remembered how she phoned a friend the evening before her husband threw her out, asking for advice. Her friend had told her to pray seventy times, "Allah u-akhbar (God is great)!" She said, "I prayed it 700 times and it did not help. Now I prayed only once what was on my heart, and Jesus answered. He must be the true God!"

Through the miracle of answered prayer, she received personal proof that Jesus Christ is God. A twofold work occurred: She had enough information from God's Word to start praying to God personally. Although she could not make a commitment on what she had heard, God put his own stamp on it by answering her prayer, so that everything became real and desirable. At this point she could overcome the **social barrier** and accept Christ personally.

Stages in her life:

1. She was disappointed by a society that dictates to women how to live.

2. She denied her disappointments, trying to defend having to remain a Muslim.

3. She was disillusioned by her friends' fighting and backbiting.

4. She envied the lifestyle of Christians and their family life.

5. Looking for answers, she compared the Bible and the Qur'an.

6. Thrown out of her house because of marriage problems, she was able to witness Christians' love towards one another.

7. Longing to experience God, she received answers to her prayer and total forgiveness.

Main Reasons for Her Conversion

- She heard the Word of God in an applicable way.

- Her experience of God's direct answer to prayer made him real and trustworthy.

- Her strong desire for the assurance of complete forgiveness and living with a Christian family intensified her longing for a new life.

A Brother and Sister from Ethiopia

Yusuf fled his home country to find a better future in America. In the refugee camp in a neighboring country he met compassionate Christians from nearby churches. As a proud Muslim, he challenged and debated intensely with them. Why were they so patient and kind to answer all his questions, and even allow him to follow them to their homes?

Yusuf was lonely, displaced, and confused, but he had time to think and discuss. His Christian friends kept coming to the camp and were able to answer his questions. This impressed him greatly. As he pondered the biblical message and compared it with Islam, he realized that nothing in the Qur'an matches the sacrifice Jesus Christ made for humankind. Perhaps God brought him here to learn about him, because at home he would never have been able to do so. He came from a tribe with not even a handful of Christians.

Suddenly his life had another dimension and a different perspective than just going to America to find a better life. When he accepted Christ, he also accepted the challenge to be a messenger of Christ.

His steps towards Christ:

1. He was challenged by the lifestyle and love of Christians.

2. He liked the freedom to study God's Word.

3. He became concerned about his family who had never heard the true message.

4.   He realized that only God could change his misery as a refugee.

Immediately after accepting Christ, Yusuf enrolled in a Bible school. He wanted to bring this message to his own people.

Main Reasons for His Conversion

- He was uprooted and confused.

- He had time to study God's Word while getting to know people who were willing to be questioned and who never lost their patience.

- He realized that God offered a greater purpose in life than the freedom and success America seemed to promise.

His Younger Sister

As soon as Yusuf felt strong enough in his faith, he visited his family. Everyone in the family was angry and ashamed about Yusuf's conversion, and they made him leave as soon as possible. When he returned a second time, his younger sister realized that pressure would not change his mind. She wanted to trap him with the right questions. He listened and answered patiently. She was faced with questions about Jesus she could not answer. Her brother stressed four particular points:

1.   Jesus is the only prophet in Islam and in the Bible born of a virgin without a biological father. His birth was absolutely unique.

2.   Jesus is described as sinless in the Bible and in the Qur'an. Surah 4:171 calls Jesus "holy." Muhammad was told by Allah to ask for the forgiveness of his "mistakes."

3. Although Jesus does not enjoy the same honor and veneration as Muhammad, Muslims believe he is the only prophet who comes back to earth for judgment.

4. Jesus is the only prophet alive today, the only prophet who did not die. Even though the Qur'an denies the crucifixion of Jesus, everyone knows that he is in heaven now.

These points moved her to see that Jesus is truly more than a prophet. Her brother then read Jeremiah 31:3, "The Lord says: 'I have loved you with an everlasting love. With unfailing love I have drawn you to myself.'" This overwhelmed her: God was personally interested in her. In this first talk with her brother, she accepted Christ. After she had overcome the **religious barrier**, she was ready to follow Christ, although only thirteen years old at the time.

Her brother gave her his own Bible and left the next day. She treasured the Bible and read it secretly under the blanket every night till her father found her out. Yet how to pray and to enter into a vibrant relationship with Christ she learned only during persecution, times of starvation, and being cut off from the outside world.

The parents were speechless: it was one thing to have a son turning to Christ far away from home, but that a daughter turned her back on Islam under the very roof of her parents was too much. This shame had to be removed from the family. The best solution was to marry her off to Saudi Arabia. Her brother knew he had to get her out of the home and, as the oldest of the family, could arrange with the family to get guardianship of her. In this way she could leave Ethiopia and continue her schooling in the nearby country where her brother resided.

Main Reasons for Her Conversion

- Her keen mind and inquisitive spirit

- Not going with the flow, but finding her own convictions

- Her astonishment to find logical answers in the Christian faith and to reason about subjects foreign to her in Islamic classes

- The uniqueness of Christ and God's great love expressed in his Word

Later I asked her: "How did you feel when your family dropped you at the airport, knowing that you would never see them again?" She spontaneously said: "First I cried a little, but then I remembered that I can read my Bible now whenever I want to and that no one will hinder me ever again—then I rejoiced!"

A Couple Finds Their Way out of Darkness into the Light of Christ

Fatuma and her husband Musa were both madarasa teachers. Musa was a keen reader and loved to exchange books with his Christian neighbor, each one trying to convince the other about their "right religion." Musa was fascinated by the book *Delivered from the Powers of Darkness*. As he read, he realized there is a greater power than that of witch doctors and imams. He wanted this power. He asked his neighbor, "How can I get the power described in this book?" His neighbor shared about Christ's unmatchable power over evil spirits, nature, sickness, and even death. Although Musa had learned much about the Bible in his training as an imam, he saw now for the first time the truth and teaching of the Bible and accepted Christ.

He kept his decision a secret, because he did not know how his life would continue as a Christian. He had no other profession than being a Muslim teacher. What could he do with his Arabic and Islamic knowledge outside the mosque? Who would he be? Would anyone still respect him, honor him, give him the high place and position he had now as an imam?

The social and psychological barriers hindered him from making a public declaration of his new faith.

Stages he went through:

1. He was open to reading Christian books, even if only to dispute better with Christians.

2. He studied the Qur'an to find out more about Jesus, because he was scared to read the Bible openly.

3. He wrote to a Christian organization for books and Christian literature to understand more of this new faith.

4. He wanted to go to church with his neighbor, but it took weeks of intercession by the Christians before he could put his foot over the entrance of the building.

5. He was in a serious accident. Where would he go if he died? Would God accept him as a secret believer? He realized that God gave him another chance to live.

6. He got an offer from his Islamic mission to go to Iran for further studies. When he shared this with a Christian, he was challenged: "How long do you want to limp on both sides? You need to make a decision which way to follow."

7. He met sporadically with another Christian who had sent him literature. He concluded that he can follow only one master and made a clear decision to follow Christ.

Main Reason for His Conversion

- A desire for more power led him to the one who is all-powerful.

When Fatuma realized that her husband accepted the Bible as true and Jesus as his personal Savior, she was enraged as **economic barriers** hit her. How could they live? Where should they go? She was pregnant with their first baby. The first thought was to leave him, yet her husband had been good to her. How would she survive as a divorced woman? He confessed that he had been a secret believer for a year but could not hold it inside any longer. He was convinced that he found the truth in Christ and did not want to teach wrong theology any longer. When he resigned from the madarasa school he lost his house, his friends, his income. His wife left the Muslim training center at the same time, still a Muslim. Both sets of parents rejected them totally.

A Christian family opened their home to them. While staying there, watching the family, learning more about God's Word, Fatuma felt comfortable and opened her heart to the gospel. Although they could only rent a small room in a slum area to continue life as a couple, she was not worried about economic problems. She started to work as a "house lady" and enjoyed Christian fellowship with her new employer. She trusted God to look after her family.

Her stages to faith:

1. She was angry that her husband had deserted Islam.

2. She had no other complaint about her husband who cared well for her. He was so excited about his newfound faith.

3. She was willing to leave their madarasa with him, while still a Muslim. She experienced persecution from her family, even before she was a Christian.

4. Staying with the Christian family she realized that she had no hope or assurance of salvation, despite being a religious teacher.

5. She learned that she needed to accept Christ on her own accord.

Main Reasons for Her Conversion

- Her husband's changed life and joyful conviction about his new faith

- His willingness to leave everything behind to follow Christ into an unknown future

- Living with a Christian family and being enveloped into their activities, including family devotions

- Studying the Bible regularly, which brought her full assurance that Jesus is the way she wanted to follow

Storytelling Helps Overcome Barriers

Khadija was one of the first ladies to join a Bible study. Every Saturday we would meet in a school for a "Chronological Bible Storytelling class." Khadija had many questions. After getting married she stayed away, and only returned when the Bible study had turned into a sewing project. The leader of the group challenged her about her indifference towards Christ.

Early one morning, Khadija appeared at my doorstep with a question: "Is it true that the Qur'an and the Bible both tell us that Jesus is in heaven right now?" I nodded as she continued, "In our last session we learned that Jesus is busy preparing a place for us in heaven and is coming back to take us with him to God. Muhammad is still in his grave in Medina, where so many people go and visit him every day. Shouldn't I rather follow the living one, who will be our judge one day, than the dead one, who is still in the grave waiting for his own judgment?"

I asked her, "Why did it take you so long to understand this?"

She replied, "I had to be sure that I have a very good reason to believe that Jesus was truly the *only way* to God. Now I can see why Jesus could say, 'I am the way, the truth, and the life!' Jesus knew long before his death how he would die; it was not an accident but God's plan from the beginning, so that, through his death, he would take away our sins and become the way to heaven for us. We know nothing like this about Muhammad. He died naturally and is still in the grave. We still have to say, 'Peace be upon him,' like he has obviously no peace in himself. I want to follow the living one, so that if I die tonight I know I'm going to heaven, because I'm forgiven."

Khadija battled with a **religious, theological barrier** for five years, in spite of attending the storytelling classes on a regular basis. She passed through various stages:

1. She had many questions and challenged every story she heard.

2. She married a Muslim man and stayed away for a time to live as a pure Muslim.

3. She returned disillusioned about life, miserable in her own faith.

4. When questioned about her doubts and fears and need of help, the ice finally broke.

5. Over many years of listening to story after story, her trust in the Word of God grew.

Main Reasons for Her Conversion

*   She had consistent exposure to God's Word and the conduct of Christian friends.

*   Her many years in the storytelling group gave her time for a change of worldview as well as religious view. She could see

the difference between a relationship and a religion, between following the living one and venerating the dead one.

What Might Happen if I Showed the *Jesus* Film in My Home?

Medina missed the lesson one day. On my way home I visited her small but neatly kept home. She was burdened. Her sister had been sick for a long time. People say she is cursed. Medina asked: "Can a curse make you so sick that you die from it?" I replied, "Yes, there are curses with great effect, but not everyone who is sick is cursed. The world suffers from the consequences of a curse, right at the beginning when God created people. That's why we are getting sick and eventually die."

Medina interrupted and related the story to her husband as she heard it some months before. "But did God not promise us that he would send a Savior to free us from this curse? How can I be protected from any curse people might put on me?"

As I repeated the stories of Jesus, she was so attentive. Suddenly her eyes changed from sparkling to doom. I needed to leave. Medina accompanied me to the fence. "I know this is the truth. I want to follow Jesus, and I need him to protect me and my children! But what about my husband? I'm scared."

I knew she spoke the truth. She was dependent on her husband financially. Her life was a constant misery because of her in-laws and her husband's treatment. The only highlight in her life was her involvement in our sewing project, where she earned extra money and learned stories of hope from the Bible. She was blocked and bound by **economic and social barriers**.

A few weeks later, my living room was bustling with the laughter and busy chatting of twenty-five ladies, more than half of them still

Muslims. It was fun to see their joy and excitement, which obviously arose from this close fellowship. As they watched the *Jesus* film, I could hear them laughing, crying, sneezing, and even shouting. After the film, I asked them to write down what it meant to them and bring the notes to the next meeting.

Medina wrote down her thoughts immediately, leaving me a note that she needed to see me soon. She told me how convicted she was by the film, and how much she needed Jesus in her life to help her to cope with problems and difficulties. She asked Jesus to forgive her anger and hatred towards her in-laws and to cleanse her from all unrighteousness.

She went home rejoicing. She was so happy about the little New Testament in Swahili and Arabic that I gave her. She showed it to her husband; when he saw the Arabic script, he said: "This is a good book; you can go on reading it!" She enjoyed this support only for a time, and became a wonderful instrument to lead other ladies of the sewing project to Christ before her husband ended her life with a paraffin (kerosene) stove. Was the price too high?

Stages to her conversion:

1. Life was miserable; she had a terrible, violent husband and cruel in-laws.

2. She was looking for help to cope with her social and economic needs.

3. She needed greater protection than any human being could give her.

4   She listened to the stories for more than a year.

5. She had felt an echo in her heart that Jesus is the help and answer she needed.

6.   She fell into a vacuum, fearing the consequences; the price just seemed too high to pay.

7.   She watched the *Jesus* film; Christ's display of love and power convinced her that she wanted to follow him, no matter what the cost.

Main Reasons for Her Conversion

- Her constant fear of her husband and his family drove her to find help and protection in Jesus.

- In the Bible stories she found many examples she could identify with and drew new hope for her own life.

Loving More than Convincing

I have worked with a storytelling group for over eight years. It is a very effective approach for reaching whole communities—to give unreached, illiterate, or semiliterate people a chance to learn about God, human nature, sin, law, and reconciliation with God. This does not exclude the use of secular stories, metaphors, or themes about the domination of men, cleanliness, self-worth of a Muslim woman, marriage, or raising children. For the more educated woman, the *Al-Kitab Bible Correspondence Course* is another fantastic tool to help them understand the trustworthiness of the Bible and God's wonderful plan of salvation.

Still, my main focus in reaching out to Muslim women and youth is not so much how I can *convince* the person, but how I can truly *love* her.

CHAPTER 12

FACTORS LEADING TO CONVERSION AMONG CENTRAL ASIAN MUSLIMS

HASAN ABDULAHUGLI

In 1991 change came to Central Asia with the independence of the new sovereign republics of the former Soviet Union. Home to many millions of Muslims and many holy Islamic religious sites, my country has increasingly been captivated by a return to a moderate resurgence in Muslim religious practice and a rewriting of Central Asian Islamic historical identity.

Our president has attempted to maintain a stable socialist trajectory away from agricultural dependency and toward an increasingly production-based market economy. At the same time, he has tried to navigate the country through a preservation of moderate Islamic expression, maintaining unique Central Asian cultural distinctives while keeping in check potentially subversive elements of radical, militaristic minority organizations still active within the region.

It is against this background of transitional economic hardship and social displacement that our country has seen a new interest in spirituality. More than a decade after the fall of communism and state-sponsored atheism, the vast majority of nominal Muslims here are seeking God with renewed zeal. Many are turning to a revitalized commitment to stricter Islamic practice. Others have sought a restoration of the more ancient, traditional spiritualism. However—especially among youth and the rural poor moving into larger cities—life is difficult and Central Asian Muslims are increasingly open to the gospel.

My goal is not to present an overall evaluation of the increasingly strong but small movement of Muslims to Christ in Central Asia. Rather, as a former Muslim now planting churches among his people, I seek to discuss firsthand experiential factors contributing to conversion growth among members of the growing church in one region of my country. By assessing these factors, we can draw conclusions for future church planting work in the region.

A Dream

In the fall of 1996, just a few short years after I came to faith in Christ, I was working almost twenty-four-hour shifts as an engineer. It was hard work. Often I was not able to see my family for days at a time. I shared my faith with my coworkers, but usually they mistreated me, calling me a *kofir* (infidel) or worse. I struggled, because deep inside my heart I could feel God's call on my life to serve him completely. Yet I worried what would happen to my family.

Then one night I had dream. I saw field workers cutting stalks of ripened wheat. The plants had already grown beyond harvest time. God said to me, "Go join them."

But I was afraid. I knew there was great danger for me and my family if joined the harvesters. I protested, "But what about my children, Lord?" The Lord directed my eyes to the top of the very highest peak of one of the mountains that surrounded our city. At the top was a cradle, in which lay my only son at the time, peacefully awake. I was terrified: one slip of his cradle and my son would fall off the mountain to his death. Suddenly God gave his command and the cradle quickly flipped upside down, then completely turned back to its original position again. I yelled out, thinking my son was dead. But I looked and saw that he was happy and peaceful, as if nothing had happened at all. The Lord said, "Do you see? I took care of your son. I can take of your family. Now go into my fields."

Church Planting in Central Asia

I share this dream through which God called me as a church planter, not to say that dreams are the normal way God speaks to us, but to show that from the very beginning it was God (not me) that was at work.

My wife came to faith two months after I did in 1994. As I witnessed, my brothers, mother, nephews and nieces, and then some of my neighbors came to Christ. After my family was converted, we began to share the gospel with others we knew from our ethnic group. In 1996 God organized a small church in my home. By 1999 we had grown out of our home and asked permission to meet on Saturdays at a local Russian Baptist church. But in 2000, after our baptisms became more and more public, the local mosque near our home began to persecute many of our new believers. They threatened to stone me because rumors were spread that women were swimming naked during our baptisms. We decided to divide the church into house churches rather than meet as a large group.

By 2001 we began to see the value of the church being led not by one pastor but by a group of elders sharing responsibility, giving advice to one another, teaching and praying together. John Piper's short paper on *Biblical Eldership* helped us greatly; I translated it into our language. In the summer of 2001, God through us appointed our first two elders and in 2002, another two elders. We began to see the church grow spiritually as each elder took responsibility to teach and preach and lead their own new disciples to Christ.

Today our church membership unofficially is about 100 members across four regions. Since the church is still continuing to grow both in new conversions and maturity, and since two more new elder candidates have emerged, my wife and I are planning to begin a fresh church planting effort in another regional capital one hour's drive southeast of our city.

Historical Background

My country became independent from the former Soviet Union in 1991. In the last twelve years, even though we respect our governmental officials and pray for them, our country has suffered greatly. Factories have shut down. The majority of our people cannot find work. Land which was fruitful in the Soviet era is now very tired. It seems that God is preparing our people's hearts by all these hardships.

Since atheism is no longer forced upon us, new interest in God has awakened among my people. Many react to the difficulties by learning how to be better Muslims: praying, fasting during Ramadan, going to the mosque on Fridays, and reading the Qu'ran and the hadith. Some are turning to the "ancient ways," visiting fortunetellers, sacrificing animals at the graves of Muslim "holy men," and learning secret chants and curses, along with many other practices that had been forgotten during the Soviet years. But the majority seem to have lost all hope, trusting no one—not the government, educational institutions, television, not even the mullahs, teachers of Islam. It seems God is preparing my people for the only true hope: Jesus Christ in the gospel.

The Church Situation

The size of the church among my people is difficult to know accurately because of government controls on believers and information. There is not one single registered church among us. Some fellowships share registration privileges under Russian or Korean denominational registrations. Many meet in home churches. From my own personal contacts, we estimate that a few thousand believers gather in unofficial meeting locations, with perhaps a total of six thousand followers of Christ in my country today.

Findings of My Survey

The data presented here is information I have collected myself, surveying close to 100 Christians in the south-central region of my country—people of all ages, almost equally from both genders, across all denominational and nonaffiliated church backgrounds, from registered and nonregistered churches. The results are not official or scientific, but based completely on personal interviews. Here are my observations.

Most Believers Come from the Middle or Lower Classes

Of those surveyed, 65–70% lived in villages or had moved from villages to a large city. A full 85% had either little or no educational background; 60% had no profession and the majority were unemployed. Christians appear to come from the same classes of people that early Christian believers were from:

> For consider your calling, brothers: not many of you were wise according to worldly standards, not many were powerful, not many were of noble birth. But God chose what is foolish in the world to shame the wise; God chose what is weak in the world to shame the strong; God chose what is low and despised in the world, even things that are not, to bring to nothing things that are, so that no human being might boast in the presence of God. (1 Corinthians 1:26–29 ESV)

Most Believers Are Not from the Older Generation

A full 80% were between the ages of 18–40. Many of these had tasted life in the Soviet Union and were disappointed with life after independence. Also, 70% did not know the Qur'an or the hadith well at

161

all, while more than 75% had never practiced the five so-called "Pillars of Islam."

Why was there so little Islamic influence among believers? In my country, most Muslims do not become serious about their Islamic faith until after retirement age, which for men is 60 and for women is 55. Almost none of the believers in this survey had reached the age where serious dedication to Muslim practice usually begins, making them open to the gospel.

Most Believers Had Experienced Opposition to Their Faith

Of those surveyed, 77% said they had been persecuted. More than half had bad relationships with the people in their neighborhoods because of their faith.

Two Main Influences: A Christian Social Contact or a Supernatural Event

A full 53% of believers said that it was the changed life of a friend or spouse that brought them to faith. After that, 41% said that an answered prayer, a miracle, or a healing convinced them to come to Christ.

Conclusions

From the survey and my eight years of experience in church planting, I have drawn several conclusions.

Rural Poverty and Relocation Is a Leading Factor in Conversion

The most open people to the gospel have been those who have tasted hard economic conditions in traditional villages and then have moved to the city, away from the social pressures of family, neighbors, and the mosque and into the freedom and love of Christian communities located in urban areas.

The Economic and Political Situation in Central Asia Is Turning People to Christ

Of course, many are turning to Islam, but people are tired of life, especially in the villages. Yet, when disappointed and hopeless, they see love between the Christian brothers and sisters, and they are interested to hear about Christ.

Miracles and Dreams Seem to Help People Come to Christ When There Are No Relationships with Christians

Many converts are first drawn to Christ through supernatural experiences. After that, preaching, evangelism, and Christian example among relatives and friends seem to continue the process. We are always looking for God to heal and do miracles. Yet after unbelievers see the changed lives of people they know and trust in their social networks, and then hear the gospel, they seem to believe more quickly.

Persecution Is Normal

When someone comes to faith in Christ, they are immediately persecuted. It takes time for each believer to pass through persecution, yet afterward they are stronger. Persecution should not stop us from preaching, church planting, or teaching. Instead, we should be bold and tell people even more about the gospel.

Other Religious Practices Like Traditional Religions and Islam Cannot Compete against True Christianity

Muslim leaders and those who practice traditional religion require strict obedience to many rules and laws. Yet my people have seen the bad example of these same strict religious leaders, many who were installed in their positions during the Soviet era. These leaders take bribes, swear, drink, and lead immoral lives. We are tired of the empty promises of these religious leaders. But when the gospel is preached, telling of the love and mercy of God and the love among brothers and sisters, and when they see a godly example in the lives of believers, Christianity wins in the hearts of the people.

Time Is Short

People are coming to Christ, but many more are becoming stronger in the Muslim faith. We long to proclaim the wonderful name of Jesus Christ to every last unreached member of my people. We also want to extend his love to others through fellowship, discipleship, and outreach.

Appendix: Survey Data

General Information

Age of believers survey: Over 40, 20%; 18–40, 80%

Location: Urban, 35%; Rural, 65%

Gender: Male, 60%; Female, 40%

Education: High (postsecondary), 15%; Middle (secondary school graduates), 50%; Uneducated, 35%

Profession: Some profession or trade, 40%; No profession or trade, 60%

Employment: Working, 35%; Not working, 65%

Family and Community Situation

Some other member in family is a believer: 96%

Economic situation before coming to faith: Good, 10%; Average, 30%; Poor, 60%

As a believer, how is your relationship with people in your neighborhood? Good, 20%; Fair, 13%; Poor, 67%

Islam and Other Religious Practices

How first did you hear the gospel? From friend, 40%; Preaching, 17%; Holy Book (Bible), 12%; From relative, 10%

Did you know the Qur'an and hadith well before coming to faith? Yes, 30%; No, 70%

Was there someone in your family who was a strong religious Muslim? Yes, 65%; No, 35%

Was there somebody in your family who did fortunetelling, sorcery, or other ancient religious practices? Yes, 68%; No, 32%

Did you ever follow the Five Pillars of the Islamic faith before you came to faith? Yes, 25%; No, 75%

Previous Knowledge of Christian Faith

Did you know the New Testament, Torah, or Psalms before coming to faith? Yes, 18%; No, 82%

Other Possible Influences

Did somebody offer money for you to come to faith? No, 100%

Did you see a dream from God before you converted? Yes, 15%; No, 85%

What kind of things affected your coming to faith? Changed life of a friend, 22%; Attracted to different life of believers, 18%; Answered prayer, 16%; Changed life of a husband or wife, 15%; Miracle, 14%; Healing, 11%; Curiosity, 4%

After Coming to Faith

Have you been persecuted? Yes, 77%; No, 23%

Have you been baptized? Yes, 52%; No, 48%

Do you think Muhammad is a prophet? Yes, 4%; No, 96%

CHAPTER 13

"COMING TO FAITH" IN PAKISTAN

EDWARD EVANS

"The tears of my mother were harder to bear than the beatings from my father," commented one Muslim background believer. Having been involved for many years with Pakistanis from this background, in 1998 I undertook a research study on the phenomenon of conversion in Pakistan.

Setting the Scene

Pakistan is a young nation with an old history. Only in 1947 was it carved with difficulty out of ancient India. Emerging as the world's first ideological nation-state, Pakistan has claimed Islam as its *raison d'être* from the start. Its Muslim population of some 150 million is already the second largest in the world and is on course to overtake Indonesia's in the next ten years. Situated at the crossroads between Asia and the Middle East, Pakistan has a geopolitical significance which keeps it often in the world news.

Culturally, too, it combines elements from Arab and South Asian societies. For many centuries the region now comprising Pakistan remained predominantly Hindu but with a gradually growing Muslim population. These two communities coexisted mostly in peace until the twentieth century. Meanwhile, starting in the 1870s and for the next 50 years, sizeable numbers of outcaste Hindu clans turned to Christianity in the Punjab. They had come from the lowest rungs of the social ladder and are still perceived as such, despite some upward progress in subsequent decades due to education. Today approximately 2.3% of Pakistan's population is measured as Christian, with 1.5% Hindu and 96% Muslim.[1]

In addition to these converts from Hinduism, some well-educated Muslim converts, though few in number, became significant leaders in the church. However, they represent only a yearly trickle of known cases, in contrast to apparently greater numbers moving from Christianity to Islam. There is also an unknown number of Muslims who secretly believe in Christ but who are not in a position to make their faith public.

Aims of the Study

My first aim was to investigate the phenomenon of conversion from Islam in Pakistan. What patterns may be discerned in the gender, age, and family background of those who have converted? What happened to their faith after conversion? What (if any) Christian influence did they have on their families? It was outside my scope to research into what factors had led these individuals to change their faith.

My second aim was to find out in what ways and to what extent Pakistani converts to Christianity are punished by their families and communities as a result of their decision.

My third aim was to explore religious, historical, and sociological factors which influence the attitudes of Pakistani Muslims towards apostates, and hence to reach tentative conclusions on why some converts are punished more severely than others.

Sources

I gathered conversion accounts from 70 Muslims who had converted to Christianity in Pakistan. These accounts came from several sources:

Academic Studies. To my knowledge, the only prior academic study on conversion in Pakistan was conducted by Finnish missionary Seppo Syrjänen in the 1970s.[2] Of his 36 interviewees, 23 were relevant to my study.

Biographies of Converts. I had 11 written accounts about or by Pakistani converts (some of whom overlapped with Syrjänen's interviewees).[3]

Firsthand Acquaintance. Seventeen individuals were known to me personally. They had told me their stories, and I knew something of their circumstances through my own observation.

Oral Information. Information on 26 additional converts was given to me by those who knew them personally.

For their own safety, these individuals are identified by pseudonyms, unless their stories have already been published using their real names.

All individuals were Pakistani citizens who converted to Christianity in Pakistan between 1947 and 1998, and whose decision became known to their Muslim families. They were all "primary" converts, in the sense of being the first Christian in their family. I excluded from my study the following categories:

- "Secondary" converts, including women who later followed their husband's or father's primary conversion
- Pakistani converts who kept their faith entirely secret
- Muslims of Pakistani origin who converted to Christianity in the West
- Non-Pakistani Muslims converting in Pakistan

I sought to make the sample as representative as possible, by including converts from most time periods and ethnic groups.

Methodology

I sought information on each convert's gender, ethnicity, and family background, the story and circumstances of their conversion, and particularly the reaction of their Muslim relatives and neighbors. I categorized the severity of this reaction, ranging from "murder" (the most serious category) to "neutral reaction" (the least serious category). I also tried to find out the eventual outcome several years later, in terms of the converts' faith and their relationship with their families.

Finally, I assessed the range of actual treatment experienced by my sample group against theoretical Islamic teaching on apostasy and also in the light of religious, historical, and social factors in Pakistan. Although not based on a systematic questionnaire survey, this sample of 70 primary converts is, so far as I know, the largest yet collected in Pakistan. The research may be extended by others in future. I will now examine the related findings.

The Phenomenon of Conversion in Pakistan

Gender, age, and the relationship of converts to family or a larger group who also convert are significant factors in describing and understanding conversion.

Individual or Group Conversion

At no time anywhere in Pakistan have large-group conversions from Islam to Christianity taken place. Individual conversion is the almost invariable route, as evidenced by each one of the 70 cases recorded in this study.

However, my research had deliberately focused only on "primary" converts, who were the first in their families to take this step. It should be remembered that in many of these cases other family members later received Christ as a result of their influence. These "secondary" conversions may be considered as group conversion, albeit usually on a small scale.

Typical Age at Conversion

Syrjänen found that 64% of his interviewees had converted to Christianity between the ages of 16 and 25. My comparable figure of 59% confirms his findings. In Pakistan, as in most cultures, this is an age at which people search for identity and question their roots. Older people are typically more set in their ways, more concerned about dishonor, less idealistic, and less open to change than younger ones.

Gender

Of my sample of 70 primary converts, only 7 (10%) were women. Generally, it is harder for Pakistani women than for men to be the first in their families to step out from Islam. It is harder for them psychologically to "think outside the box" of what they have been told to believe from birth, harder physically to move out of the home to meet Christians or find out about Christianity, and much harder to *declare any change of faith* to their relatives who will view this act as bringing great dishonor upon them. Pakistani women are punished much more severely than men over issues of family honor.

By contrast, considerable numbers of women were able to convert to Christianity after their father or husband had done so first: at least 20 such women, under the influence of the 63 male "primary" converts in my sample. In no case in my sample was a wife able to convert first and later bring her husband to faith in Christ.

Eventual Outcomes

Of 49 cases where I had information, the eventual relationship of the convert to his or her family was as follows:

Eventual relationship with family	Number of cases	%
Some family members became Christian	11	23
Convert was fully reconciled to family but they remained Muslim	8	16
Family maintained a "truce" with neither hostility nor full acceptance	16	33
Family remained antagonistic towards the convert	4	8
Convert reverted to Islam or at least outwardly conformed to Islam	10	20

In only 8% of the known cases did the convert remain in a long-term antagonistic relationship with the family. In all the rest contact was restored, even if only at the level of a "truce." This confirms Syrjänen's conclusion that "only in some cases the separation of a convert from his family was a single blow, absolute and final."[4]

In my sample, the proportion of converts influencing their families for Christ (23%) approximately equaled the number returning to Islam (20%). Few of those who reverted did so with any enthusiasm; typically, they conformed outwardly (even to the extent of reciting the Islamic creed) while remaining secret but weak Christians at heart. Ahmed said, "With a heavy heart I went to the mosque."[5] Some, however, chose deliberately to return to Islam, including Rafiq, who had in the meantime even become a pastor! The reasons for reversion probably include disillusionment with the Christian community, weariness from opposing their families, the need for a job, and the desire to marry and settle down.

A comparison of age at conversion with the eventual outcome suggests that, while young Pakistani Muslims may enter the fold of Christianity more easily than older ones, they may also leave it more easily:

Age at conversion	Later conformed to Islam	Later led some relatives to Christian faith
Under 25	9 (32% of this category)	5 (18% of this category)
Over 25	1 (5% of this category)	5 (26% of this category)

Older converts, especially those already married before their conversion, were more likely to stick with their decision. Of the 15 already married converts, not one returned to Islam. Moreover, nearly half of them were able eventually to bring their wives or other family members to Christ. Typically, the relatives who converted were his wife or sister, sometimes his mother or younger brother, but very rarely a more senior male family member. Converts' children usually followed their mother's choice, only converting if she did.

Range of Punishment Received by Converts

Categories A–G were developed to classify the range of punishment received by converts from their relatives and neighbors:

Category	Severity of response	Number of cases	% of cases
A	Murder	4	6
B	Life-threatening	8	11
C	Severe	23	33
D	Moderate	24	34
E	Mild	6	9
F	Neutral	5	7
G	Positive	0	0
	TOTAL	70	100

Category A: Death of the Convert

It is striking that only one out of 60 male converts (1.7%) was killed, but three out of seven female converts (42%)! The reasons for this huge discrepancy are discussed below.

Category B: Life-threatening Punishment

In most of these eight cases, according to the converts' own accounts, an actual attempt was made on their lives—nearly always by a male family member (e.g., father or elder brother). In some cases they were beaten so harshly as to threaten their lives.

Category C: Severe Punishment

This category, accounting for a third of all cases, covers a wide range of coercive treatment. Many in this category were single young men. Beatings and physical deprivation were commonly reported, accompanied by threats of even worse punishment if the convert did not recant. Sometimes at this stage he ran away of his own accord; sometimes he was expelled by the family; sometimes he lost his job. Nonviolent coercive measures included cutting the convert out of his inheritance or arranging his marriage with a Muslim relative. If married, his wife and children may have been taken from him, at least for a while.

Category D: Moderate Punishment

This category accounts for another third of the cases. Converts frequently reported intense emotional pressure from their close family members and boycott from the wider circle of relatives. Bilquis Sheikh described the "devastating hurt" which her conversion caused to her aunt, and her own distress when excluded from family gatherings.[6] Converts also faced attempts at reconversion, and occasional court cases. Several lost their jobs.

Category E: Mild Punishment

Six cases (9%) fell into this category. These converts received relatively mild pressure, extending no further than family disapproval.

Category F: Neutral Reaction

Five of the converts (7%) experienced a neutral reaction from their families; all five, significantly, were Sindhis (discussed further below).

Category G: Positive Response

Not one of the 70 converts came into this category.

Overall, more than 90% of the converts in my sample were punished in some way for their apostasy. Only rarely were converts actually killed, but nearly half experienced "life-threatening" or "severe" punishment, typically at the hands of their close male relatives.

Factors Influencing Severity of Punishment for Converts in Pakistan

Islamic Law of Apostasy

"Muslim attitudes are still influenced by the premodern *shari'ah* [Islamic law] that forbade Muslims to convert from Islam," states Mayer.[7] This is certainly the case in Pakistan.

Commentators differ over whether the Qur'an's thirteen references to apostasy require punishment in this life or only in the hereafter.[8] Most hadith are less ambiguous: for example, "He who changes his religion, kill him."[9] The four schools of Sunni law specified severe punishments for apostates. Even though apostasy is technically not a *hadd* offense, it was treated as such by the majority of jurists who agreed that any male apostate who failed to recant within a fixed time period should receive the death sentence.[10]

Hanafi law, which is the most prevalent in Pakistan, considers that "an apostate is an infidel enemy." It requires the dissolution of his marriage and property rights, and even authorizes members of the public to take matters into their own hands by killing a (male) apostate.[11]

Although these stipulations of shari'ah are not recognized in Pakistani law, some jurists and ideologues continue to promote the traditional teaching on apostasy. Thus one Maulana Yousaf, concerning the wife of an apostate, confirmed that "the Shari'ah does not allow her to live with that man."[12] And the hugely influential Abul A'la Mawdudi advocated the death sentence in his book *The Punishment of the Apostate*. He argued that out of "mercy" for the apostate, and to protect society from the "poison" of his continued influence, it is better "to punish him by death and thereby at one and the same time to put an end to his own and society's misery."[13]

This attitude towards converts certainly affects attitudes in Pakistan today. The man who killed Rahila Khanan, his own sister, claimed he had "done his religious duty by killing an apostate from Islam."[14] And although it is rare for the death sentence actually to be carried out against Christian converts, the opinion that apostates ought to be killed has been frequently expressed. Convert Aslam Khan commented, "When a Muslim sees some other Muslim leaving Islam, he wants to cause that Muslim harm as much as he can, and if possible, even kill him."[15]

Many in my survey experienced to some extent the "civil death" accorded them by shari'ah theory. Several converts were cut out of their inheritance. In six cases, their spouse or other relatives threatened to dissolve the marriage (though rarely did this take place in practice).

As might be expected, converts from more religious families were punished more severely:

Religious background	Severity of punishment (more severe ——— less severe)							
	A	B	C	D	E	F	G	TOTALS
Religious	0	5	10	9	1	0	0	25
Moderate	0	0	2	5	1	2	0	10
Easygoing	1*	0	2	2	3	3	0	10

* In this case, the attitude of the family was irrelevant, as it was outsiders who killed the convert.

The Legacy of Colonial Rule

British rule in the area comprising present-day Pakistan began in 1840. Its legacy has influenced contemporary attitudes to converts in three ways.

In the realm of law, the Pakistani government maintained, almost without change, the legal and administrative apparatus left behind by the British. This included the Indian Penal Code of 1860, under which apostasy was not illegal.[16] This still holds true in Pakistan today—as confirmed in the test case of convert Tahir Iqbal. Though a lower court remanded him for apostasy, a higher court ruled this incorrect. So instead he was charged with desecrating the Qur'an, which under Pakistan's blasphemy laws does carry a death sentence.[17]

The English-medium education system introduced values of tolerance which still influence the attitudes of upper-class Pakistanis. One such was M. A. Jinnah, the founder of Pakistan, who stated, "You may belong to any religion or caste or creed—that has nothing to do with the business of the State . . . there is no distinction between one community and another."[18]

Protestant missionaries, though not directly supported by the colonial administration, were allowed freedom for their work. Muslims still today suspect that missionaries win their converts from those who "are very poor and susceptible to temptations of money and facilities in life."[19] In 1992 an Urdu weekly alleged that missionaries were enticing young men in Lahore with pornographic films, girls to marry, and visas to the West![20]

Social Status of Pakistani Christians

My landlord in Pakistan once dismissed a woman he had employed to wash dishes. "Why did you do that?" I asked. "Because I discovered she is a Christian; she will pollute our utensils," came the reply.

In a class-conscious society like Pakistan, the association of Christians with sweepers works as a powerful deterrent to conversion. Esther John was asked by affronted Muslims, "How could you leave Islam to become a low-caste Christian?"[21] Gulshan Esther's relatives refused her a lift because "we don't want to pollute our car."[22] The landowning relatives of a woman convert I knew near Lahore were furious with her for associating with "the Christians who clear away our buffalo dung."

However, even such deep-seated prejudice can be overcome through personal acquaintance. Several of Syrjänen's interviewees were attracted by the lifestyle of Christians, describing them as "superior in human respect," "honest," "brave," and "prayerful."[23] My collected data furnishes further instances of Muslims being positively impressed by individual Christians. Through education, many urbanized Christians have risen somewhat socially over the decades.

Rarely are Pakistani Muslim converts gathered in sufficient numbers to form a viable church of their own. Indeed there are some advantages in joining churches of the dispersed Punjabi Christian community which are found in almost every corner of Pakistan. This at least offers the opportunity to find Christian marriage partners. However, integration into Punjabi churches, especially for non-Punjabi converts, is likely to lead to some loss of their own identity as well as of contact with their Muslim community. Occasionally it is possible for a convert to belong to both communities at once, for instance attending church on Sunday and a convert fellowship group on a weekday, as Zafar Ismail advocates.[24]

Family Dishonor

Numerous anthropological studies reiterate the importance of "family honor" (*izzat*) as one of the most cherished values in Pakistani societies.[25] Indeed the English words *honor* or *prestige* provide barely a glimpse of the richness of the Urdu word *izzat*. Izzat is a shared quality; each member's behavior will contribute to, or detract from, the prestige of the whole extended family. Conversely, one individual's misdemeanors may bring enormous disgrace, or *be-izzati* (the opposite of *izzat*), crashing down on the whole clan, who "feel as if they were injured in the very depth of their personality . . . they will have to accept the lowest place of respect in the society."[26]

This appreciation of izzat in Pakistanis' cultural matrix explains much of the punishment given to converts. In the West a person's choice of religion makes little or no difference to his relatives, but in Pakistan it affects the whole family's reputation. "Auntie, do you realise what this means for other people?" sobbed Bilquis Sheikh's niece.[27]

It is incumbent on senior male family members, as guardians of family honor, to control the behavior of younger ones. This explains why a convert to Christianity is subjected to the same sliding scale of punishment as applies to young Pakistanis for any other disgraceful behavior: arguments, ostracism, threats, beatings, disinheritance, expulsion, and finally murder. The greater the public be-izzati attaching to the offense, then the more severe will be the punishment.

In dealing with the shame of apostasy, Pakistani families typically seek first to contain the news to themselves, warning the convert to recant or at least keep his decision secret. But if news does leak out, then they resort to the opposite tactic of punishing the apostate publicly, thus proving to the community that they are taking appropriate action.

This need to save face motivated the father of Shafiq in handling his son's apostasy. As one of the wealthiest businessmen in Pakistan, and also a Syed (descendant of Muhammad), the damage to his own prestige was devastating. But he could not make his son recant. So he arranged a lavish reception for his highborn friends and, in front of them all, made his son an offer: "Come back to Islam and you will receive my wealth; refuse, and I will cut you off for ever." By going public in this way, he showed his friends that he had dealt correctly with his son's apostasy, and thus to some extent salvaged his own izzat.

Even more than in its sons, a family's izzat is invested supremely in the modest behavior of its females. "The chastity and good name of a woman are the most sensitive points of honour . . . a woman's acts reflect her husband's status and honour," writes Akbar Ahmad concerning the Pathans.[28] This is why some 600 "honor killings" take place in Pakistan every year: mostly of women and nearly all by their close male relatives.

Thus it is no surprise that in my sample the most severe punishment for apostasy is meted out to women. All three murders of unmarried female converts can be explained in terms of revenge for be-izzati. As females, they brought dire shame on their family by refusing their marriage arrangements, running away from home, and (in the case of Esther John) even engaging in Christian evangelism. Hence drastic steps were required to restore honor. This is despite Hanafi law, which requires the death sentence for male apostates only! Clearly, actual practice is governed more by societal values than by Islamic law.

Other Social Factors

Personal independence, ethnicity, and social class were also significant factors which were analyzed in my study.

Degree of Independence. My data shows that the severity of male converts' punishment depended considerably on their degree of independence in the family:

Age and marital status	Severity of punishment (more severe ———— less severe)							
	A	B	C	D	E	F	G	TOTALS
Male aged 20 yrs or less	0	3	11	6	2	1	0	23
Male over 20 yrs, single	1	2	5	8	2	2	0	20
Male over 20 yrs, married (including divorced or widowed)	0	0	5	8	2	2	0	17

It is significant that not one of the married men were subject to murder or life-threatening treatment (categories A and B). These converts could not be pressured as much as single young men living at home, nor did their acts of dishonor affect their parents so directly. Again, single men typically fared better if their father had died or if they had no elder brother. And if economically independent they also tended to face less pressure.

Ethnicity. The severity of punishment appears to relate to ethnicity:

Ethnicity	Severity of punishment (more severe ——— less severe)							
	A	B	C	D	E	F	G	TOTALS
Sindhi	1	0	8	7	2	5	0	23
Punjabi	2	6	7	7	1	0	0	23
Pathan	0	1	1	7	0	0	0	9
Muhajir	1	0	3	2	1	0	0	7
Other	0	1	2	1	1	0	0	5

Most male converts receiving lightest punishment were from the Sindh. This correlates with anthropological studies which seem to indicate Sindhis (apart from the Syeds) are typically less concerned for izzat than Pathans or Punjabis.

Social Class. My survey also suggests that, in going up the social scale, the average treatment of converts grew somewhat more severe.[29] I believe this is because they have more izzat to defend than the lower classes, overriding their otherwise rather modernist, individualistic, and tolerant outlook. An important factor in some lower-class families is that

Socioeconomic class	Severity of punishment (more severe ——— less severe)							
	A	B	C	D	E	F	G	TOTALS
Upper	2	2	4	1	1	1	0	11
Upper middle	0	1	3	3	0	0	0	7
Middle	0	1	4	8	4	1	0	18
Lower middle	0	1	5	8	1	0	0	15
Lower	0	0	4	3	0	3	0	10

whenever a son's contribution to the family income is badly needed, his apostasy is more likely to be tolerated.

Modernity and Urbanization

Generally speaking, the more close-knit a community, the harder it will be for a convert to survive. In the traditional village, everybody knows one another. Religious leaders may easily stir up aggression against converts, especially through public announcements from the mosque. As one secret convert told me, "There are many kinds of media in this country, but the most powerful of all is the loudspeaker medium: the *maulvis* can ruin your life and that of your family. We live in fear of them."

Conversely, in a big city it is easier for converts to live anonymously (with regard to their neighbors) and independently (with regard to their families). In one fairly large town Hamid has been able to keep his shop running all through the years. When people complained to the civil officials about his conversion, the response came, "Does he do his job well? Is he a troublemaker? If not, then what difference does his religion make?"

Rapid urbanization in Pakistan is accompanied by a growing individualism. This will not only give Muslims a greater choice to convert, but will probably also affect the attitudes of their families. The reaction of a Punjabi businessman to his brother's conversion, "It is his own choice," may become more common, especially among the urbanized middle classes.

Avenues for Further Research

The survey led to some interesting conclusions, which I have noted, and also raised the following questions which might fruitfully be followed up in future research.

183

Social Factors Favoring Conversion

Further study could be carried out to investigate which ethnic and socioeconomic groups in Pakistan are more open to conversion than others. Why is it that Pakistan has yet to see a people movement anything like on the scale seen in some other countries? In the absence of large-scale movements to Christianity, what factors might favor at least a limited cascade effect, with primary converts bringing their nuclear and extended families to Christ?

The Traditional Christian Community: Help or Hindrance?

One Pakistani said to me, "The greatest resource for Muslim evangelism is the Pakistani church. And the greatest hindrance for Muslim evangelism is the Pakistani church." The reasons for this paradox are clear to anyone familiar with the Christian community in Pakistan. But it would be instructive to compare this positive-and-negative situation with a country where there is no Christian population. What different dynamics are at work? What conclusions may be drawn concerning the missiological impact in countries which have long-established Christian minorities?

Secret Discipleship Versus Open Witness

Pastorally, a critical balance should be struck between an overbold, insensitive witness which cuts the new believer off from his family and leaves him socially isolated and an overcautious approach which leads to compromise and spiritual stagnation. How is this balance to be discerned and taught? Missiologically, which is the greater danger: For a convert to be cut off from his family and hence lose his witness before they have even had the chance to observe his changed life, or to be so submerged in his old culture that he loses his witness anyway?

Globalization Versus Islamization

The influence of modernity might tend towards increased tolerance for converts in the future. On the other hand, a vigorous counterreaction to Western influence was already gathering pace in the 1990s, and has increased all the more since the American invasions of Afghanistan and Iraq. This has led to lethal attacks on Westerners and Pakistani Christians since 9/11. Some (not all) Pakistani Muslims view Christians as allies of America's "crusade" against Muslims.

In such an atmosphere Pakistani converts to Christianity will be considered as traitors and may be punished as such. Caught in the interplay between the forces of modernity and neotraditionalism, they need somehow to be able to exercise individual choice without ceasing to belong to the *ummah* (the Muslim community). Is it possible to remain loyal to the Muslim community while holding a non-Muslim faith? Can apostasy and treason be separated? As Kenneth Cragg asks, "What . . . can be done to encourage in Islam the truth that becoming a Christian is not ceasing to belong with Muslim need, Muslim thought, and Muslim kin?"[30] This is a crucial question, not just for Pakistan but throughout the Muslim world.

CHAPTER 14

A HANDFUL FROM AN UNREACHED MEGAPEOPLE

P. I. BARNABAS

Southeast Asia is one of the world's most populous regions, with more than 500 million people—half of them Muslim—and includes the world's largest Muslim country. Although only two of the area's nations are officially Muslim kingdoms, throughout Southeast Asia it is very difficult for a person or family to come to faith in Christ.

One of the World's Largest People Groups

One of the largest unreached people groups (UPG)[1] is found in Southeast Asia. Islam is very dominant among them, and its presence dates from the early sixteenth century. However, according to some historians there is evidence that by the fourth decade of the fourteenth century there were some people who had already embraced Islam. Today, according to official statistics almost 100 percent of this people group is Muslim; membership in the UPG is synonymous with being Muslim.

When Islam was introduced, this people group had an indigenous belief which had already adopted aspects of Indic religion (Hindu/Buddhism), and elements of these previous religions still exist in daily life. Thus, they received Islam as a new item of clothing to wear over their former religions. This new clothing was torn in many places to fit the body of this UPG, and through these tears we can see the old cloth—commonly known as folk Islam.

In general, these people seem to be more Islamic than some other groups in Southeast Asia. Islamic artifacts are more obvious, and many use Islamic symbols openly. The women often wear the veil along with other Islamic clothing. Men also wear a kind of robe or hat associated with Islam. Mosques are spreading everywhere, and all varieties of Islamic schools cover the area.

Every year more and more people of this group make the pilgrimage to Mecca—almost twenty thousand in 2004. During the 1990s there was a noticeable movement by this group towards a more Islamic attitude with specific political attempts to implement *shari'a* law for all Muslims and a wider general movement to Islamize every element of life.

The Cost of Christianity among This People Group

In the past, Christianity was recognized as the religion of the European. The European colonization of Southeast Asia began in the Malay Peninsula in 1511. Islam became the counterbalance to European colonialism. During the colonial era, when an indigenous person became a Christian, neighbors would mock him or her with nicknames like "black European," and he or she would become an "outsider." In some cases Christian converts would forfeit familial inheritance rights.

In the mid-1960s, a movement brought many Chinese living among this people group to embrace Christianity. Christians from other people groups also live among them. However, among the indigenous people Christianity remains a *deviant* religion, and Islam remains the *modal* religion: only 0.07 percent of the indigenous people are confessing Christians.

Praise God that, in the midst of all the above, some indigenous people are Christians. The majority may consider these people deviant, but these believers have the courage to be so. Since the mid-1960s, some thousands have embraced a new faith in response to a wide variety of approaches in reaching them for Christ. Some responded to conventional evangelistic approaches while others responded to more contextual approaches, whether *cultural* contextualization or *Islamic* contextualization.

Some new believers have faced stark opposition from relatives or local communities. In some cases this has grown into open persecution where it is almost impossible for a single indigenous person to formally become a Christian. These difficulties often depend on the attitude of the official leaders of the community. Some indigenous Christians have had to move to relatively safe areas, while others have simply backslidden to their previous beliefs.

In the last fifteen years the opposition to the Christian church in this area has, if anything, intensified. Many church buildings have been burned, ruined, or closed and sometimes the congregation has been refused permission to rebuild.[2] It has also become more difficult to get permission to build new churches or other buildings used for Christian ministry.

Lessons from a Handful That Came to Faith

In the midst of the above difficulties it is interesting to discern the motives of those who have become Christians. Even though a tiny minority, they are strong in Christ, and some have stood firm for a very long time. All have faced some difficulties, but most have continued on their faith journey. Surprisingly, there has been an uninterrupted continual flow of them making decisions to join the earlier *musafir* (pilgrims on a spiritual journey).

A discussion on the relative features of contextual approaches and their impact on new believers' attitudes and ideas is beyond the scope of this short article. My focus is solely on the general motives expressed by these people in making decisions to come to a new faith from a Muslim background. To understand these motives, I distributed open question-naires randomly among first-generation Christians of this UPG. So far I have received 118 completed questionnaires.

These 118 respondents represented 53 men and 65 women. Eight were teenagers (14–19 years old), 53 were in the age range 20–40, and 57 were in the age range 41–83. The youngest respondents were two 14-year-old boys who both came to faith three years ago. The oldest respondents were two men (both 83) who came to faith 23 and 27 years ago respectively.

Out of the 118, only 14 came to faith in the last two years (seven in the last year). The oldest of these new believers was 50 years old but was also the youngest in Christ, having returned the questionnaire just two months after making a decision. Four of these 14 are still recognized as Muslim among their relatives and neighbors but regularly attend a Christian gathering. Thirty-one respondents came to faith 20 or more years ago and two of these more than 40 years ago (a 66-year-old man and a 65-year-old woman who are both considered faithful Christian believers). The majority (73) of respondents came to Christian faith between two and 20 years ago.

Out of 118 respondents, 30 claimed to have been faithful Muslims who faithfully performed daily *salat* (prayers), while 40 admitted they never practiced salat; the remainder (48) were somewhere in between these extremes (occasionally practicing but not devout). Twenty-six respondents claimed to have faithfully kept the Ramadan fast while 37 admitted that they never fasted during Ramadan. Again the majority (55) were somewhere in between these extremes (they usually started the fast but did not continue it for the whole period of Ramadan). Only 14 claimed to have once been passionate to visit Mecca. Since daily salat and fasting are the most prominent marks of a devout Muslim, one can conclude that the majority of respondents were not devout Muslims. Sociologically, however, they associated strictly with Islam.

All respondents claimed that some of their immediate families or close relatives are still Muslims. It is interesting that only 50 of them claimed to have faced clear opposition from their family, relatives, or neighbors when it became known they were Christians. The other 68 respondents reported that their families and relatives did not react negatively. It was normal for family, relatives, or friends to be unhappy to learn that they became Christians, but many respondents were not rejected. At the time when the majority of respondents came to faith, there was no strong objection from neighbors; rather, the local Muslim community was open-minded.

All but two of 118 respondents wrote that they are satisfied with their new faith—a good indication that they are happy with a new faith and community, even though many have to face opposition. I have no idea why two of them are not satisfied; perhaps they are still struggling in their new faith.

Motives and Sources

My questionnaire was designed to obtain information regarding the motive that inspired a faith decision as well as the primary influence (people or resource) that started this faith journey. This table shows the reasons or motives why these UPG people decided to follow Christ.

Primary motivation for decision	Percentage of respondents
Assurance of salvation	66
Christian lifestyle witness	11
Blessing	9
Healing	7
Forgiveness	6
Marriage	1

Sixty-six percent came to faith because they were passionate to have eternal life in Christ. They heard about this magnificent Christian belief and contrasted it with their old beliefs. Some still explained this motivation in Islamic terms (such as a desire to experience salvation "here and in heaven"). One added that he received his first information regarding Christian assurance of salvation from a fellow Muslim, right after finishing salat. This was followed by a sign from God. After long contemplation—as well as his eldest son joining a church—he came to faith in Christ. Today his whole family is Christian.

Related to assurance of salvation, 6% wrote that the desire to receive forgiveness was their main motivation. They understood their need for real forgiveness from God and were satisfied to believe in Christ as the way of repentance and forgiveness. Significantly, the second-largest reported motivating factor (11%) was Christian lifestyle witness (the character and loving attitude of Christians). One respondent wrote that he was impressed by the lifestyle of his navy commander who was a Christian, and he wanted to be like him.

A desire for a healing provided motivation for 7% of respondents, while a more physical blessing motivated an additional 9%. Only one person (less than 1%) came to faith because of marriage. This woman was attracted by the greater stability of Christian marriage (i.e., divorce is not permitted). I have heard many Muslims testify regarding the stability of the Christian family.

The Power of Personal Connections: Family, Clergy, Friends

The following table shows the primary influences (people or resources) that encouraged these faith decisions. Respondents reported from whom or where they first heard the Christian gospel message.

Primary influence in hearing the gospel	Percentage of respondents
Family	36
Pastor/evangelist	25
Friend	22
Christian worship gatherings	5
Boss/teacher	3
Dream	3
Tract	2
Bible	2
Self-interest	1
TV	1

It is interesting to note that among this UPG the largest number of people came to faith through a family member (36%): parents, uncles, aunts, grandparents, brothers, sisters, children, or sons-in-law. When a member of a family has come to faith, he or she will naturally share this new experience with other members of the family. This natural family line of witness is a phenomenon reported in the New Testament (John 1:40–42).

Some respondents reported that they heard the gospel for the first time from their own son or daughter. They then shared their new faith with relatives, continuing the family line phenomenon—which is very usual among communal people groups. According to historical data in Southeast Asia, many churches have been started by this family line, for example among the Malay, Javanese, Sundanese, and Chinese.

The second-largest grouping reported that they had first heard the gospel through an evangelist or pastor who talked personally to the respondent (25%). A faithful and diligent personal evangelist or pastor can lead many indigenous people to faith. One respondent wrote that she heard the gospel that opened her mind and brought her to Christ from a pastor of her mother-in-law.

The third-largest grouping first heard the gospel through a friend (22%). Obviously the definition of *friend* is not specific and encompasses many kinds of friendships (workplace, guests, school, neighbor, etc.). Three respondents wrote that they heard the gospel for the first time from their neighbors.

Only two respondents wrote that they heard the gospel for the first time from their boss. One respondent reported that his high school teacher shared the gospel with him 20 years ago. The group reached by employers, bosses, and schoolteachers accounts for three, or almost 3%, of my respondents—the same number as reached through dreams.

Other Means for the Message

Only 3% of respondents began their journey to faith because of a dream. This contrasts with the experience of other Muslim people in some Islamic (especially Middle Eastern or South Asian) countries. Perhaps God uses more ordinary means among this UPG because they are more open to these means. Family, other relatives, friends, pastors, or evangelists are ready to share the gospel of love with this UPG.

Out of 118 respondents, only two first heard the gospel through tracts and only one through television, despite the fact that there are Christian sermons broadcast every Sunday. The Muslim community does not normally watch Christian programming. The grouping "mass media" (tracts and television together) accounts for only three or less than 3% of respondents. While this number is quite low, these media methods can be very important in reaching individuals in a context hostile to the gospel without this individual being known by anyone else (family, community). I myself first knew about the way of salvation through Jesus Christ from a tract.

Six respondents (5%) began their faith journey after hearing Christian praise or experiencing Christian worship gatherings. One of these joined a Christian retreat with her friend and another heard the gospel in chapel when he was in prison. In some areas, Christian worship gatherings experience difficulties from surrounding communities, yet this can be an effective way of reaching people.

Only two respondents began their faith journey through directly reading a Bible. One borrowed her friend's Bible and read it many times at work. The other had a friend who was a vegetable vendor and lent her Bible to her.

Conclusion

My research has amazed me by demonstrating how much God loves this people group. God has rescued many of them through many ways and means and is still working through a great variety of people and methods. Data from a leading institution working among this UPG indicated that in 2003 more than 200 people have come to faith.

An initial review of the data from my questionnaire would suggest that the most important task must focus on equipping the three groups who together brought the gospel to 83% of respondents: family members (36%), Christian ministers (25%), and friends (22%). Secondly, the role of laypersons must not be underestimated in the growth of this UPG church, as 58% of my respondents were reached through laypersons (i.e., family members and friends).

George Hunter III wrote many years ago in *The Contagious Congregation: Frontiers in Evangelism and Church Growth* that "most people who become Christians receive communication and an invitation from a credible Christian who is more often a relative or close friend than a stranger, and whose conversation is often spontaneous rather than pre-planned."[3] When the Billy Graham Evangelistic Association conducted the International Congress on World Evangelization (Lausanne II) in Manila, July 11–20, 1989, most participants admitted that they came to faith through a personal approach by lay Christians.

Especially in ardently Muslim communities, mass evangelism is almost impossible, whereas personal evangelism can occur everywhere in normal situations. Personal evangelism is like a strong wave under the surface: unseen and yet powerful in its influence. Most of my 118 respondents came to faith through personal evangelism. Lay people among this UPG should be better encouraged, motivated, and equipped to share the love of God. In doing so, they will become a fantastic tool in the hand of our mighty God.

SECTION 3
Understanding
Some Movements to Faith

HINDRANCES TO EVANGELISTIC GROWTH AMONG MUSLIM BACKGROUND BELIEVER CHURCHES OF THE "JIJIMBA" PEOPLE OF WEST AFRICA

DAN MCVEY

A church planting effort among the Jijimba[1] people group of West Africa during 1992–2003 resulted in the establishment of more than thirty-five assemblies of believers from a Muslim background. These churches are found within a thirty-mile radius of Dejani, the traditional center of Jijimba culture and chieftaincy in the eastern reaches of the sovereign land of Jojan. After many years of hardened resistance to the gospel message, eastern Jojan is proving more receptive in recent years. However, after the initial establishment of a Christian congregation in the communities, the rate at which subsequent converts are added to the body of disciples is dramatically lower than expected in light of the receptivity level and numbers of converts in the first phase of evangelism. ("First phase" is the initial evangelism and organization of an assembly of believers meeting at least once a week. "Second phase" is defined as the efforts to continue to evangelize after a congregation of believers is established.)

A survey was conducted from April–June, 2003, consisting of information gathered from existing churches, detailed interviews with church leaders, discussions with the evangelistic team spearheading the work, and discussions with traditional leaders and opinion leaders of the tribe. The survey was designed and organized by a team of Jijimba church leaders and evangelists and one expatriate worker. The form and structure of the survey were determined by the felt needs of these local leaders.

Contributing Factors to the Success of First Phase Evangelism

A variety of methods have been used in church planting. The most common and effective has been preliminary contacts in a village with opinion leaders and chiefs, followed by discussions with small groups of villagers who have expressed interest in learning more about Christianity. Out of this develops small study groups, usually of three to six people and rarely reaching twelve or more. The primary agents of evangelism are Jijimba Christians who have been brought to faith in Christ through similar methods. Two evangelists work as full-time church leaders whose primary responsibility is church planting, with six lay workers involved in outreach. The same men are involved in church maturation, with the help of another five to seven local church leaders.

The *Jesus* film and other methods are used in public presentations when allowed by village leaders and where Muslim opposition is not too intense. Making the Bible available to Muslims through public reading, infant naming ceremonies, funerals, private discussions, etc., is a primary means of communicating the message that God's Word does not change, is worthy of respect, and deserves a hearing.[2] Knowledge of the Qur'an itself is very limited, due to general illiteracy and the specific lack of knowledgeable readers of Arabic and Islamic prayers and teachings in the Hausa Ajami script. This creates a hunger for the word of the Lord.[3] Chronological Bible lessons and public showings of films on the lives of the prophets (Abraham, Joseph, Moses, David, etc.) are periodically used with great effectiveness.

Prayer is the primary tool of evangelism. Evangelists and church leaders have scheduled times for fasting and prayer weekly. The Jijimba people continually renew allegiances to ancestral spiritual powers as well as Islamic cosmological strongholds through festivals, rituals, and liturgical devotions. Thus the weapon of prayer is essential. Prayer ministry and empowerment are strategically important in the conflict of spiritual kingdoms in Jojan.[4]

Similar methods have met with extraordinary results when adapted to animistic tribal groups in the same areas of this West African state. When the first phases of evangelism are done among these groups, the ranks of initial converts are soon expanded with additional converts. However, in contrast to this level of receptivity among animistic groups that has seen the same denominational group plant 600-plus churches in close proximity to the Jijimba between 1992–2003, the response of the Muslim Jijimba people has exhibited a different nature.

When we go through the preliminary steps of church planting in a Jijimba community and a congregation of believers is actually established, we normally witness the conversion of a few individuals who have family and relationship links that promise further positive developments regarding evangelistic and ministry opportunities. The overall level of interest in villages we are able to enter with the message is usually quite high in the beginning, for the villages usually either deny us access to the population completely or they exhibit a level of curiosity and openness that gives hope to greater response.

Subsequent interest in the gospel message declines sharply once a group of believers begins praying and worshiping together. In some cases there are no new converts for several years. Are we penetrating only one family or clan group in each village, thus limiting potential converts? Is there a marginalization of believers that promotes this sluggish, or nonexistent, continuation of interest on the part of the villagers? If so, what factors encourage this marginalization, and how can they be overcome—if at all? Are there discernible causes to this characteristic we have found in every community where we have evangelized? Are there definable obstacles to second phase evangelism, and are there measures that can be taken to mitigate the causes of the lower rate of conversion and minimize obstacles?

Survey Results

A postsurvey analysis was done through a series of discussions within the evangelistic team, on a broader scale with church leaders of the area, and with selected traditional and opinion leaders. A total of 35 churches in the Jojan area were included in this survey, comprising 81% of the Muslim background believer (MBB) churches of this particular denomination. These represent 98% of the MBB churches of this fellowship among the Jijimba people, and all are found in small villages, except for one congregation in a district capital. Only two of the churches were established before 1993, with eight (23%) established between 1994–1998, and 25 (71%) established between 1999–2003. In terms of the numbers of believers actively participating in corporate assemblies and prayer (not including children), the numbers are as follows:

5–20 members	21–40 members	41–60 members	60+ members
22 churches (63%)	8 churches (23%)	3 churches (9%)	2 churches (5%)

As to marital status, only one church reports that less than 10% of the members are married. Eight churches have 11–25% of their members married, and 13 churches have 25–50% married. The remaining churches emerged as five having 51–75% of members married, while eight assemblies reported having more than 75% of members married. These figures are important, for they confirm that the gospel has been embraced by mature adults to a significant degree.

Six of the churches (17%) report that all members come from one extended family, or more precisely one clan, which is much larger than the familial links of the extended family.[5] Two members of the same clan may not have any contact or relationship except in times of tribal/clan festivals or funerals of the most senior clan or family elders. What would be termed a "nuclear family" would trace familial relationships back to a common grandfather. The ties and obligations at this level of family are very strong, providing essential structures for marriage, reproduction, economic interdependence, and inheritance. Four churches (11%) reported that members were from two clans, and four had members from at least three clans. The majority (19 churches) reported that members are from four or more clans.

Considering the small size of most assemblies of believers, the presence of three or more clans among them indicates that receptivity is probably not based predominantly upon clan affiliation. If the church became identified with a restricted number of families or clans, one or two for example, we would hear the complaint or accusation that the church is only for a certain segment of society. Rather, the opposite is spoken of the church: that communities have been impacted by reaching into a variety of families and clans. The fact that we often have members of rival extended families or clan groups within the same congregation supports the conclusion that family ties are not the predominating factor in conversions, although the natural flow of relationships within families/clans does serve as a positive factor in conversions.

Part of the survey covered a wide range of topics, to which 121 of the more mature members and opinion leaders among the believers responded (77 men and 44 women; 58% of the men and 50% of the women were over 40 years of age). They related personal experiences of coming to faith in Christ as follows:

- 69% believed in response to a public presentation of the gospel

- 18% were attracted to faith through the influence of Christians' lives

- 8% reported that some influence in childhood predisposed them to Christianity (a Christian school, relative, or friend)

- 3% attributed their conversion to "friendship," meaning their close relationship with an agemate brought them into proximity with the gospel

- 1% credited a radio broadcast

Of those who reported that public preaching or a presentation of the gospel in their village brought them to faith, 88% were converted through initial preaching in their locality. Among these respondents, 23% had some form of contact with a church or Christian believer in their localities before; however, all but two communities reported that there were no functioning churches or active Christian believers in their proximity at the time they came to faith.

Dreams were significant factors in being drawn to Christ for 76%: 49% of these had dreams of themselves praying or singing in a Christian setting with feelings of security and guidance, 25% saw Christ in a dream or were called by Christ to follow him, and the remaining 26% were given warnings or directions to follow Christ.

In terms of what drew them to learn of Christ, the interviewees gave the following responses:

- the power and goodness of Jesus (35%)

- lifestyle of Christians (22%)

- desire for salvation (17%)

- the search for guidance and protection (11%)

- dissatisfaction with Islam (6%)

- acts of kindness done by Christians (5%)

- drawn to Christ from their earliest childhood, whether by familial influence or spiritual inclination (3%)

Regarding persecution suffered since becoming a follower of Christ, 81% gave specific details of rejection by family, threats, attempts on their lives, extreme insults, false accusations, forced divorces, etc., whereas 19% gave no specific details or indicated that they did not wish to speak about their suffering. Among leaders, 54% indicated that their first time to meet a Christian was at the initial preaching in the village; 28% had at least met a Christian before they encountered any presentation of the gospel (usually a national from the southern parts of the country where Christianity is dominant). Others had schooled with Christian classmates or had met relatives or neighbors who were Christians—this response from some who had lived in more urban settings, particularly during the dry season when villagers migrate to the south looking for work.

When asked what influenced them to leave Islam, 38% expressed attraction to a positive aspect of Christianity (the person and power of Jesus, the Christian way of life, healing of an illness due to Christian prayer, kindness done by Christians), whereas 56% expressed something negative about Islam (no truth, peace, happiness, salvation, or love in Islam). For 83%, Christians are seen in a very negative light in their villages with the labels "pagan" and "hypocrite" being the most common epithets. The remaining 17% said that Christians are viewed in a more positive light due to their influences for good. Of these church leaders, 3% still go to the mosque at times for prayers, and 5% go to imams for advice and teaching from time to time.

When asked why they think Muslims reject the message of Christ, other than because of the obvious fear of persecution, 43% said it is based on what Christians believe about Jesus and that they do not pray according to Islamic law. Thirty-five percent also said that this rejection is based on the blindness of Islam and the fact that the Islamic way of life is radically opposed to the Christian manner of life. This question was geared towards understanding what elements of the gospel Muslims find most offensive.

Twenty-eight percent said that the best approach to Muslims is through friendship and living a good life before them, while 29% said that the message of Christ should be presented to the villagers primarily in private settings, for example when working on the farms. Nine percent emphasized the importance of prayer as a strategic component, both in praying for Muslims and praying with them in times of trouble and need. As to what distinguishes the followers of Jesus from Muslims in their villages, the answers were as follows:

- character/way of life (69%)

- truth of God (14%)

- method of prayer (8%)

- name of Christ (2%)

Seven percent indicated that there is little difference in the lifestyles of Muslims and Christians.

Seven Hindrances in Second Phase Evangelism

The issue of the lower than expected rate of conversion in the second phase of evangelism was examined thoroughly. Seven distinct reasons contribute to the difficulties in making additional converts after an assembly of believers has been established. These were deduced from questions relating to makeup of the membership, methods and dates of conversions, reasons for rejection of the gospel by the Muslims, prevalence or absence of evangelistic efforts within local communities, level of maturity among leaders, to what degree the believers hold to an exclusive view of the gospel, public perceptions of the believers and the church, and internal/external attitudes toward the public role of Christians in their local communities. Because statistics must be interpreted by qualified analysts from within the culture when at all possible, particularly when related to attitudes, cognitive responses, and social structures, great care was given to prayerfully study the results in a context of seeking spiritual insight and practical assessment of the situations of the churches.

God's Calling

The foundational spiritual factor of God's calling is the first and primary consideration. The Lord's declaration to the apostle Paul, "I have many people in this city" (Acts 18:10), serves as a principle directive that he alone is "the Lord of the harvest" (Luke 10:2), controlling response to the gospel through his eternal grace and will. The examples of Acts 16:6–7 and Acts 16:14 confirm that the Lord Christ is the one who prepares the ground for evangelism and opens the hearts of hearers. Our Lord revealed that no one may come to him unless called by the Father (John 6:44–45); therefore, any discussion about the readiness or reluctance of people to respond to the message of salvation in Christ must be prefaced by this acknowledgement of the sovereignty of God. It is not evangelists or believers who have power to strategize people into the kingdom; it is God who calls and to him all glory is given.

This principle is seen in the manner in which communities were entered with the gospel. In the early years, basic research and preliminary surveys led to programmed outreach into the first seven churches established. However, the subsequent 28 churches all came into being through individuals or small groups from the communities asking believers to explain the gospel message to them. Even among the first seven churches, most were established through contacts that emerged from casual discussions or acquaintances of evangelists in the area who were working among other ethnic groups, which in turn led to serious consideration of organizing an evangelistic effort among the Jijimba people. Through the conversion of several influential individuals, the work took on a life of its own as guided by the Holy Spirit into a vibrant fellowship of believers, withstanding persecution and growing from grace to grace.

Limited Population

Another reason for this slowness of secondary conversions is the limited population—the field for harvest in each community was limited in terms of prospective hearers. The average population of a community, with the exception of one large district center, is 25 compounds, each having on average 15–20 residents for a total population of 400–500, half of these being children under the age of 15. When a group of 20–30 adults out of a total population of 200 has already heard the gospel, the low population limits the number of possible future contacts and is impacted by both the positive and negative aspects of familial links within the communities. Communication capabilities are enhanced and curiosity levels are higher with one clan; however, the possibility of the gospel being identified with one clan, which may be in a state of perpetual tension with other clans, results in prejudicial barriers.

A Pause for Observation

Christianity is so new in these villages that the actual establishment of a body of believers leads to a pause for observation by the rest of the population. This is recognizable from the gap in time between the initial making of converts and the subsequent opening up to further evangelistic efforts (second phase evangelism). Noting that 81% of believers were converted immediately following initial evangelistic efforts in their villages in contrast to a definite drop in the rate of second phase conversions, church leaders and evangelists consulted not only with Christians, but also with non-Christian traditional rulers, family heads, and opinion leaders, seeking to understand this from the standpoint of unbelievers.

Once a group of believers is actually identified as followers of Jesus Christ, the majority of inhabitants in the village enters a phase of observation—a wait and see mode. Imams, whether native to the village or coming from a nearby area, begin preaching opposition and warnings concerning the presence of the Christians. Very often curses are cast on the believers, along with the ever-present threats, insults, and rejection. The general population waits to see the outcome. Will the Christians survive? Are they serious in this faith? Are they receiving gifts that lure them into Christianity? How will they function as members of the clan and community? These as-yet-unknowns discourage anyone from interest in learning about Christ.

Persecution

The fourth hindrance to second phase evangelism is persecution. Islamic invectives against the faith of Christians and the persistent, methodical harassment of believers are effective deterrents to subsequent conversions. Many in these communities, some very prominent citizens, confess that they recognize the truthfulness and uniqueness of the faith of Christ; however, fear for their lives and positions, as well as disgrace for their family, create seemingly insurmountable obstacles for their serious consideration of the gospel call. Wives are taken away from believers, children are forced away from parents, and properties are confiscated. Some are beaten while others have their lives threatened. Almost all are rejected and alienated from their families; all are attacked spiritually through curses.

Restricted Access

A fifth factor is the restricted access granted to believers and evangelists to engage members of the community in meaningful religious dialogue. Doors that open briefly for first phase evangelism quickly close when the gospel is accepted by a definite group of indigenous villagers. It is one thing for the people to listen to the presentation of the gospel out of curiosity or low levels of spiritual interest, but it is quite another matter when family members, agemates, and neighbors actually believe in Jesus Christ as Savior and reject the finality of Islamic claims of prophethood and salvation.

Due to the communal nature of village life among the Jijimba people, it is usually not possible to approach people with the gospel in a very private or one-on-one manner. Small groups or even gatherings of the entire population of the community are the best ways to present the message so as to minimize suspicion and allow for the widest appeal. Although this allows group pressures to be brought to bear, initial general presentations of the message provide opportunity for the work of the Spirit of God in the hearts of people. Though direct methods of evangelism may not be possible, indirect methods abound, such as naming ceremonies for children, marriage rites, funerals, and communal labor. Christians are able to follow traditional patterns for these rituals and customs while putting their faith into words through prayers, biblical readings, songs, and exhortations that fit the occasion and also proclaim and explain their faith.[6]

Inadequate Time and Effort

The final two barriers to conversion are simply that in some cases not enough effort is put into reaching the community, due to scheduling factors on the part of evangelists and timidity on the part of local believers; and secondly, not enough time has elapsed in some cases for second phase evangelism to have taken place. The process of gathering and analyzing survey information has enlightened church leadership about the value of such studies, enabling them to plan and implement similar research. It has also challenged them through the revelation of weaknesses and recognition of opportunities within and among the churches.

Some of the identified causes for a slower than expected rate of conversions in second phase evangelism are obviously beyond the capabilities of church leaders and evangelists to address: the principle of God's calling, the limited population, and the passing of adequate time for more converts. Persecution will automatically cause fear and hesitancy on the part of potential converts and cannot be answered except through patience and faithful endurance. What church leaders and evangelists realized was that the period of observation that sets in among villagers needs to be fully taken advantage of with increased evangelistic efforts where possible and, most importantly, through the infusion of Christian faith into traditions.

Thus, the issues of lack of direct effort to evangelize, the restrictions on opportunities to reach the populace, and the hesitant mindset of observation can be cumulatively approached through reinvigorated faith and contextualized rites. Of 121 church leaders interviewed, 74 were converted by initial preaching and evangelistic efforts in their localities, and 36 gave specific information about their conversions as being in a secondary phase of evangelism. Of these, ten were converted through some form of public presentation of the gospel, 22 were attracted through the influence of Christians' lives and faith to learn more of Christ, and four stated that it was a friendship that brought them to listen to the message. This demonstrates how the observation period can be used for positive impact. All 36 were won through some form of observation and positive influence exerted by Christians after the initial phase of evangelism.

Needed: A Transforming Worldview

The single greatest obstacle to church growth among the Jijimba has been communicating the concept that one can be a follower of Jesus while maintaining identity as a Jijimba. The history of Jojan is wrapped in the battle dress of conquerors who swept through the savannahs, establishing dynasties and subduing both related and nonrelated tribal groups, especially in the period just before European colonial dominance was imposed in the late nineteenth century. At the height of the Jijimba empire, Islam permeated society from the royal families downward under the influence of Hausa traders and imams. Alliances with the people of the southern forest zone ensured the economic and military position of the Jijimbas, contributing to a tribal identity that associates Islam with all the greatness, security, and fecundity of this very proud people. Therefore, to penetrate this social structure with the message of Christ is a great challenge, for the prejudices of Islam against Christianity, and its monolithic infrastructures against external penetration, are strengthened by the ethnic definition of identity.

The infusion of Christian faith and life into the rituals of naming ceremonies, funerals, weddings, communal labor, and festivals such as harvest and those dedicated to expressions of loyalty to chiefs has gone far in opening the doors for proclamation. Although church leaders realized that their efforts at contextualization need to be enhanced and intensified, their previous attention to this principle has been rewarded by a level of tolerance and acceptance in many Jijimba communities and recognition by traditional rulers. One will often hear statements by Muslims regarding this church that indicate a level of respect not given to churches before. The most common expression is that this church can only be accused of not praying five times a day.

So highly regarded are the evangelists after years of persecution and rejection that, during a recent violent intratribal conflict, it was the Christian evangelists and church leaders who were turned to as peacemakers, even though Christians are found in both of the warring clans. Their integrity, courage, and peacefulness were regarded by tribal elders and chiefs to be characteristics that qualified them to be the most reliable advisors and intermediaries. At one large gathering of chiefs and elders, after a speech by one of the evangelists, a senior chief observed, "If we had all been followers of *Isa al-Masih*, this tragedy would not have happened."

The timing of the survey and the church leaders' role as peacemakers in this conflict have converged at the right time to challenge them to move to new levels of confidence in the Spirit of God and expect the opening of many doors. The survey showed church leaders and evangelists that they are seeing a breakthrough into the hardened resistance that has existed for decades. Furthermore, they have more fully understood the dynamics of their own society and culture regarding spiritual change.

It has been demonstrated quite openly that one can be a follower of Jesus and not lose Jijimba culture or identity. As the observations of the Christians continue, these believers are determined to portray a clear image of Jesus Christ within the Jijimba culture and establish lines of dialogue with community leaders and interested individuals who may be brought to saving faith.

CHAPTER 16

AN INSIDER MOVEMENT
AMONG FULBE MUSLIMS

LOWELL DE JONG

We have been working among the Fulbe[1] for twenty years, but it sometimes feels as if we have only made a small beginning. There is increased openness among the Fulbe, but barriers remain and there continues to be resistance. Some Fulbe are just beginning to follow Christ, but the church seems a more distant reality; among the believers there is much volatility as some experience paradigm shifts while others fall by the wayside. Should we consider ourselves movement developers rather than church developers? Whose business is it to develop the church? As we analyze the movement of the Spirit among the Fulbe in our area we will explore answers to these and other questions, but we will first see what can be learned from the Muslim infiltration of Fulbe culture and society.

The Development of Fulbe Islam

Christianity is just beginning to make inroads among the Fulbe. Islam was at a similar juncture among the Fulbe about 400 years ago. Islam did not move into sub-Saharan Africa through military conquest, and there were few if any Muslim missionaries per se; but rather, as a result of ancient trans-Saharan commercial activities, a steady stream of Arab and Bedouin traders and fortune seekers passed through and sometimes settled in West Africa. Through their influence the royal lineages of the Gana, Mali, and Songhay kingdoms, which controlled large areas of West Africa from about AD 800 onwards, became Muslim. By the late 1500s Islam was beginning to spread among peasant Africans as well as the nomadic Fulbe. By the mid-1700s the Fulbe were sufficiently Islamized to spawn a series of Muslim kingdoms which controlled increasingly large swaths of the Sahel until the arrival of the French in the late 1800s. These kingdoms expanded in the name of Islam, and *jihad* was a common battle cry as the Fulbe completed the task of the Islamization of the Sahel. By the mid-1800s the Fulbe themselves were virtually 100 percent Muslim and had contextualized Islam into Fulbe culture and society.[2]

Thus, Christian mission among the Fulbe is not encountering a people who are superficially Muslim but still animists at heart, Muslims doing the salat prayers and keeping the *Ramadan* fast while dabbling in the ceremonies of Fulbe traditional religion on the side (often called folk Islam). Rather, Fulbe traditional religion is no longer practiced and Islam has been integrated into Fulbe culture to form a mature, stable entity: what we might call Fulbe Islam. In fact, Fulbe Islam has now developed (stagnated) to the point where it in turn has become legalistic and even spiritually moribund, possibly much like Judaism in the time of Jesus.

In the end Islam only moderately altered Fulbe society, primarily through bringing a new eschatology: it introduced heaven and hell and the idea that there would be an end to time when there would be a judgment day. This replaced belief in a cyclical time continuum where the living were simply translated to the place of the ancestors. This fundamental reorientation required changes in some rites of passage plus a new daily spiritual regime, but it changed little in the family, in cattle raising, and in worldview; indeed, it enhanced Fulbe animistic science.[3] At the same time, it slowly and patiently transformed what needed to be transformed to bring the Fulbe into the fold of Islam.

What Can Christian Mission Learn from Muslim Mission?

Christians should take note of several principles that can be seen in the successful spread of Islam among the Fulbe.

Islam Was Patient

It took hundreds of years to penetrate Africa. In contrast, Christian missionaries tend to be impatient. In African Muslim contexts, where missionaries have more freedom than in many other Muslim contexts, hurry-up missionaries can do a tremendous amount of damage with heavy-handed mass evangelism techniques and other methods designed to plant a church "by the first furlough." They can appear to have impressive results in the early phases, thus putting pressure on missionaries around them, but their success is often superficial and short-lived because their methods antagonize the larger community.

Further, pressure is often brought to bear on new believers to organize a church before they are ready, and many problems ensue. Rather, following Muslim example, should not missionaries give new believers "the reins" by permitting them to remain as an informal Bible study and prayer group, for years if necessary—giving them time to contextualize and develop a church at their own pace and time for natural, culturally acceptable leaders to emerge? Generally, this should reduce the level of persecution, but more importantly would give the new movement time to stabilize and separate the wheat from the chaff, which could result in stronger churches in the end. This was certainly the experience of Islam as it percolated into Fulbe culture.

Islam Used an Insider Approach

It was not Arab warriors or marabouts, or even Arab Muslim merchants, who converted the majority of Africans to Islam and confronted

African cultures with change, but it was their relatively small number of African converts who undertook this process. By the eighteenth and nineteenth centuries it was the Fulbe themselves who were instrumental in bringing Islam to many peoples of West Africa. The Fulbe are perfectly capable of repeating this process with Christianity some 200 years later.

Islam Was Selectively Contextualized

Islam capitalized on its theological compatibility with Fulbe traditional religion (similar worldviews, salvation by works, animistic science) and required no more change than absolutely necessary. The result is a very African Islam. However, just as Christian missionaries at times look askance at some of the practices of their daughter churches, so classical Muslims look askance at West African Islam. From their perspective, it has not applied enough *sharia* law to be considered good Islam: the women are unveiled, clothing is not Muhammadan, marriage rites are not Muslim, religious education is inadequate, and animistic science is rife. Careful observation will show that West African Muslims have incorporated the essentials of quranic Islam while discarding Arabic cultural baggage. Again, the Fulbe are perfectly capable of repeating this process with Christianity if we give them the freedom and the responsibility.

Islam, Like Fulbe Traditional Religion, Can Travel Light

Islam is a religion built on law, with libraries filled with thousands of books on Islamic law, and in its fullest form can be heavy, pedantic, and inflexible. Yet it has a knack for stripping away all superstructure and becoming the simplest of creeds and expressions of faith. It does not need buildings; it has little intermosque structure and a streamlined mosque polity. A cleared spot or a portable mat become a temporary mosque where a few Muslims, even a lone nonclerical Muslim, can perform the essentials of Islam.

218

This dovetailed perfectly with the needs of the nomadic Fulbe, as it has with many nomadic groups around the world. In contrast, Christianity sometimes seems incapable of traveling light. It is a religion based on Spirit and grace, but in much of the world it has developed a ponderous superstructure containing endless layers of bureaucracy, and seminaries, and requirements, and programs. Christian missionaries, in spite of good intentions, carry far too much baggage and burden new converts with much extraneous material and structure that exaggerate incompatibility and hinder contextualization as well as communication and portability.[4]

In summary, Islam developed among the Fulbe over the period of a couple of centuries. Islam may have been initially brought to the Fulbe by Muslim Arab and Bedouin traders, but Islam was contextualized into Fulbe culture and the mosque was planted by the first Fulbe converts themselves. The result is a very Fulbe, but essentially Muslim, Islam.

Our Story

Four hundred years later, can we repeat the Muslim story? Could Christianity be implanted in Fulbe culture more rapidly and even more effectively than Islam? Could it penetrate Fulbe Muslim culture even more deeply than Islam? I believe that it can, assuming we work in the name of Jesus and in the power of the Spirit.

In 1984 my family and I moved from Liberia, a quasi-Christian country where nearly everyone would claim to be a Christian, to our present posting, where nearly everyone would claim to be a Muslim. In early 1986 we moved into a small Fulbe village in the Sahel, an outback-like zone on the southern fringes of the Sahara Desert, to work among this proud, seminomadic, cattle-herding Muslim people.

We developed a strategy of Christian presence—that is, a strategy of living among the Fulbe as much like the Fulbe as we could manage, in order to develop friendships and contacts whereby the gospel could be shared. In our context this meant living as a family in grass huts, sitting and sleeping on mats on the ground, wearing robes, eating millet, buying cattle, making a millet field, learning to weave mats, our four children growing up with their children, and so forth. It also meant sitting for hours and hours in conversation with Fulbe while drinking ceremonial Arabic tea. Periodically we would make the nine-hour drive to the capital city, where we maintained a more Western-style house, in order to regain our balance and attend to the more deskbound aspects of our work. This strategy meant a considerable amount of travel, but also permitted us to pursue a long-term, low-barriers approach in the village, where the Fulbe and our relationships with them were our only agenda.

We had several reasons for pursuing this approach. First, we felt that in identifying with the culture and lifestyle of the Fulbe we would be communicating to them that Jesus loved not only them but their culture as well. Becoming Christians would not entail abandoning their culture but rather fulfilling their culture through the transforming power of the gospel. This seemed very important for the Fulbe, who are exceptionally proud of their culture and language.

Second, most Fulbe have never met a Christian and know little about Christianity except for what they learn from their marabouts. They needed to meet Christians, even if imperfect, in order to see them pray, observe their faith in action, and experience the compassion of Christ. Misperceptions needed to be dealt with on a personal level and barriers broken down before the gospel could be communicated.

Third, in much of sub-Saharan Africa, missionaries have the legal freedom to witness to the gospel in almost any manner, even in Muslim contexts. We had observed some missions and their daughter churches using the same evangelism techniques among Muslims that they had used among animists, and these were not producing the desired results. In fact, there were reports of the occasional hostile reaction which were usually couched in terms of suffering for the gospel. We felt new approaches were needed.

Fourth, our primal vision was to see the gospel well up from deep inside Fulbe culture, deeply embedded inside Fulbe hearts both theologically and philosophically. We had only vague ideas of how this could happen, but we suspected that the means of communication would need to be thoroughly Fulbe and that the leadership of any future church would need to be in Fulbe hands from the day there was more than one believer. We would simply establish a Christian presence, serve as evangelists and catalysts, and then step out of the way.

We moved to our little village in the Sahel early in 1986, naively thinking that ten to twelve years should be sufficient to realize our vision. The first years were filled with adjustments to living in this difficult environment. Language had to be learned, culture and customs had to be acquired, children had to be homeschooled and later sent to boarding school. In those early years (the first five to six years) it sometimes felt as if we were accomplishing little, but during that time we were developing friendships with the people, we were observing them and they were observing us, trust was developing and credibility was being established, and I was slowly bringing to life my identity as a marabout of the *Linjiila* (New Testament).[5]

Towards the end of this period we began some development projects which continue to this day. We also began to talk increasingly about religion and even on occasion share some of the gospel. Eventually there was a small stream of younger men, but also the imam of our village and other marabouts, who to one extent or another came to read the Linjiila and to talk about Islam, Christianity, and Jesus. In 1996, after ten years in the village, I requested, and the village agreed, for me to give public presentations on the Linjiila and on Jesus. Four of these sessions were held with encouraging attendance. But after the fourth session the senior marabout, with whom I had spent much time in discussion and Scripture

reading, as well as with his father before him, forbid any further attendance at the sessions, so we had to abandon what was appearing to be a
promising development.

We were discouraged since, after more than ten years of work in the
area, there were still no believers. Shortly after this, one woman, "Sira,"
became a follower of Jesus. In 2000, "Alfa," who had been studying both
with the marabouts and myself for over seven years, finally submitted to
Christ. Since that time, both Sira and Alfa have borne fruit and there are
others who are interested. There are now seven believers, as well as a
number of seekers, in our area; and there are about the same numbers in
one of our colleague's area.

An Emerging Movement?

These encouraging results have come during the past five years. It
appears to us that we may be facing the birth of a movement, since:

- The believers have placed all their hope in life and in death
  on Jesus Christ—he is their only protector/intercessor—but
  nearly all of the believers continue worshiping within the context of the mosque. They are doing their prayers and keeping
  the fast, in Jesus' name.

- The believers are witnessing to their faith in Jesus using appropriate, indigenous means.

- A mentoring model of discipling is emerging where older,
  more studied believers are taking the lead and are considered
  to be a sort of marabout. This is the default setting for leadership development here unless we introduce something new.

- A high level of indigenization and contextualization is occurring.

- There is a high degree of volatility. Many are wrestling with
  basic theological issues. Paradigms are slowly shifting as they

experiment with new ideas. One senses that the movement could continue moving forward or it could suffer setbacks at any time.

•   There is as yet no sign of the development of a church and no one has requested baptism.

These factors taken together point to a high level of indigenous ownership which would be a vital characteristic of any movement. It also shows that in these initial stages the believers are taking Jesus into their context (embedding) rather than meeting him outside in the church or some other venue (extraction). Nearly all of the believers remain insider followers of Jesus and to those around them they appear to be Muslims, but Muslims who are showing a dangerous amount of interest in Jesus and the Linjiila. Nevertheless, they are left in relative peace as long as they do not create a disturbance and practice the Pillars of Islam, thus remaining Muslims in the eyes of the people. The longer this can continue, the longer the believers will have opportunity for growth, both in numbers and in faith, permitting the movement to gather strength.

Our situation at this point leads us to wonder whether more attention needs to be given to an often ignored phase of the missionary endeavor: the movement phase. Could not the missionary task be divided up as follows?

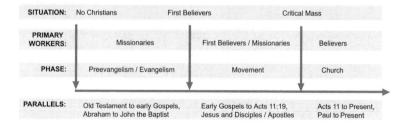

FIGURE 16.1 THREE PHASES IN THE MISSIONARY ENDEAVOR

The Evangelism Phase

The missionaries are the dominant force, characterized by their preevangelism and evangelism activities. In the sweep of redemption history, this would parallel the time from Abraham through the prophets on to John the Baptist, when God prepared the Jews (and the world) for Jesus. In the Bible this would correspond to the Old Testament through the first few chapters of the Gospels.

The Movement Phase

This would begin with the first believers, who would increasingly become the dominant force. The missionaries would retool and begin to recede into the background, taking on a discipling role. In the sweep of redemption history, this would parallel the time of Jesus as he prepared the disciples to go into all the world, and continues on into the early years of the apostolic age. In the Bible it would cover the Gospels and up to about Acts 11:19, when the church at Antioch emerges.

In redemption history this is a wild and volatile phase. There are signs and wonders, miracles, and many conversions, but also persecution, heresies, and backsliding. The disciples are sent out to preach in the surrounding towns and Jesus sees Satan falling from heaven, but later Peter denies him three times. Stephen undergoes a glorious martyrdom, but Ananias and Sapphira experience God's punishment. The power and work of the Holy Spirit is evident at every turn, but this also attracts charlatans such as Simon the sorcerer. Can we expect the movement among the Muslim Fulbe to be any different?

The Church Phase

Our experience and observations lead us to question whether it is the missionary's business to develop the church. Rather, it would seem that indigenous churches ideally emerge from indigenous movements and are best developed by indigenous believers themselves as they study the

Bible under the guidance of the Holy Spirit. The missionary should be completely in the background by this phase. In the sweep of redemption history this would parallel the church age, roughly covering the time of Paul's missionary journeys and onwards. In the Bible this would correspond to Acts 11 and forward.

Cross-cultural missionaries often take Paul and the apostles to be church developer models, but we forget that they were "home missionaries". The apostles and also Paul worked within their own cultures or those with which they were very familiar. They knew the languages, what to say, and how to act; they were evangelist and pastor all in one. I would suggest that the dynamics of cross-cultural ministry are very different from what Paul and the apostles faced and will require a longer and more complex movement phase before churches emerge.

How Do We Respond?

If we are indeed facing a movement, how do we respond? As noted above, in two different areas we have about seven believers. We could organize them into two churches. We have seen many missionaries try to do this in Muslim contexts in West Africa, but the results are almost always disappointing. The church, no matter the external form, struggles and either dies or stagnates due to several problems:

- A church is too high profile and invites opposition.

- New believers are young in the faith and not ready for church. Most are struggling with basic life and faith issues: How do I integrate Jesus into my context? Hasty church development prematurely pushes these issues into the background and brings church organization issues into the foreground.

- To further complicate matters, the first believers are often socially incompatible: some may be from the social fringes of the society; some may have come with the wrong motives and bring dissension into the group; some may have cared little for Islam (and religion) in the first place.

- Faced with a predominance of these kinds of believers, the missionary feels he has to take the lead in the development of the church—which then takes on a strong Western flavor, causing the new believers to lose ownership.

In our situation, we need to give time for a movement to develop, to go through a series of shakeouts, for worldviews to shift, for faith to mature, for the believers themselves to have time to contextualize and indigenize their faith and practice, to experiment and make mistakes, and for leaders to emerge naturally. However, we realize that movements are unpredictable and uncontrollable. It would seem logical that the greater the level of contextualization and indigenization of the movement, the less the missionary has knowledge of and control over the movement. The question is whether we will have the courage to ride out the storm or should we draw the believers into what we may feel is the safer haven of an organized church.

It is important in our situation that we ride out the storm, because if we are indeed riding the crest of a movement among the Fulbe there should be some intriguing changes occurring beneath the surface. With a significant amount of evangelism activities taking place, there should be more happening than just the odd individual here and there becoming a believer, even though this may be all that we can observe on the surface. Rather, as the number of these believers increases, there is a very real possibility that a critical mass of the population is beginning to move up the scale towards Christ. We feel that is what is happening among the Fulbe.

At this point the movement is at a very delicate stage. We feel that if we were to take these first converts and force them to create a church, in addition to the problems already noted above, the critical mass will not yet be ready for this development. It would simply alert them to where they are headed; many will not approve and therefore will bail out. The movement will stagnate and remain underground. In the case where the church would be highly contextualized this may actually speed up the movement, but it is unlikely that we could be so successful.

For the time being, we feel our role is to patiently and faithfully delve into the Scriptures and pray with the believers. The movement should be permitted to run its course, even though this could conceivably

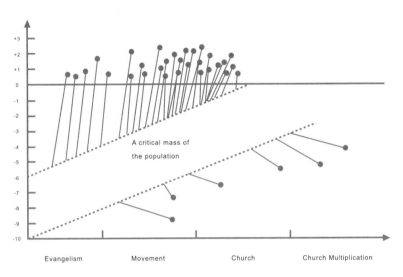

FIGURE 16.2 THE GROWTH OF A MOVEMENT

Key:

- The vertical axis represents a modified Engel/Sogaard scale, zero indicates the point of conversion.

- The horizontal axis is a timeline showing phases in the missionary endeavor.

- The dot terminated lines denote those who are becoming believers ahead of the critical mass which is moving more slowly towards Christ or those who are bailing out of the movement.

cover more than one generation of missionaries. During that time the movement could progress forward or slip backwards, but one has the impression that more than a few of the believers have theologically gone beyond the point of no return. They know and believe who Jesus is; and as this truth takes deeper and deeper root, nothing in Islam will ever look quite the same again.

But what is it that sparks movements? I would propose that one key factor is the embedment of the gospel into the culture. The problem is that no matter how well-intentioned the missionary, no matter how well-educated in the culture, a person from a very different culture will never be able to adequately accomplish this task. I walk with our new believers as they wrestle with the gospel, apply it to their lives, and communicate it to their peers. They are taking me down paths little visited in my mind and walk with Christ. I can do little more than walk with them, observe them, and keep their feet anchored in the Bible. They must take the lead and set the agenda. I am confident that they, filled with the Spirit, will in time plant the gospel deeply in Fulbe culture, more effectively and more profoundly than Islam was implanted some 400 years ago. And out of this movement of the Spirit, the church will emerge.[6]

CHAPTER 17

EMBEDMENT OF THE GOSPEL INTO THE
FULBE MUSLIM CONTEXT

LOWELL DE JONG

If embedment of the gospel is a key factor in setting off movements, how does one make this happen? First of all one must be profoundly dependent on the Spirit, but our responsibility does not stop there. Missionaries must embed themselves physically and socially in the culture, establish Christian presence. This can then be followed by the more complex, long-term process of embedding the message. For us this is just beginning to take on a more meaningful shape as new believers become involved.

"Alfa" has been particularly instrumental in this process. For seven years, as he was studying with various marabouts, Alfa also wrestled with the truths of Christianity. He devoured everything I could give him to read in Fulfulde, and over the years our theologies would interact and influence one another. On the one hand he was powerfully drawn by the Spirit to the truth about Jesus, but on the other hand he was afraid of its implications. What about his father, the chief of the village and a dedicated Muslim? He knew how he would react, but each time we met he was moving closer and closer to submitting to Christ. In August of 2000 we had yet another discussion on the nature of Jesus. This time the fact that Jesus was the Word of God become flesh, and that God's Word is coeternal with his being, finally made an impact. He said for seven days he hardly slept or ate and then he submitted to Christ.

Factors in His Conversion

There was no single seminal moment followed by an emotional conversion. It was more of a creeping-up-the-Engel-scale type of conversion. Nor was there one single factor or event that led to his conversion, but a complex of factors, personal and external, which the Spirit used to lead Alfa along. One key factor was close contact with Christians over a long period of time. He related in a recent testimony that, beyond reading and Bible study, our acts of compassion (projects, assistance to the poor, patience in the face of harassment, etc.) unsettled his and many Fulbe's perceptions of Christians. How was it that these "pagans" who did not know Allah correctly could act like such good Muslims? Why was God's favor on them, predestining for them righteous acts, when they were not Muslims? Both word and deed had impact. But the most significant factor was his seizing the gospel and embedding it into his context.

Embedment of the Gospel Rather than Extraction of the Seeker

I would assume that few missionaries would want the believers that result from their ministry to be physically extracted from their families and cultures. However, we learned that the assumptions we make in regard to what constitutes true Christian behavior will often make this inevitable. Let me explain.

Alfa did not like to contemplate the implications of being extracted from his culture, religion, and village, which he assumed would be necessary if he were to become a Christian. I have since realized that we missionaries unintentionally communicate this in many subtle ways. Alfa would say things like, "If I become a believer my father will chase me from the village." In the early years he would ask me, "If I become a Christian, will I have to leave the mosque?" I would respond, "No, not immediately; but eventually you will want to leave the mosque because you will want to share the saving gospel of Jesus Christ with your family and friends." I narrowly defined the phrase "leave the mosque" as leaving the religion of Islam, at which point he would become an open Christian and witness to his faith. But in Alfa's mind this was code for not only leaving the religion but also everything that was life for him, which would then render further witness impossible. At the time I did not entirely catch on. I did not think I was preaching extraction to him since I wanted him to remain a believer in his culture, but neither did I open the window of possibilities very wide. I now realize that my position slowed his movement towards Christ.

Since then, our thinking has shifted. A couple of years ago Alfa began to transform his Muslim prayers into prayers to Jesus, while I began to understand that he and other believers could remain in the mosque and follow Christ. Subsequently, from that position Alfa gives powerful witness to the true nature of Christ. Our and his stated ultimate goal is that when there is a critical mass of like-minded believers, they will come out of the mosque and develop "a truly Fulbe and truly Christian church."

Theological extraction, as opposed to physical extraction, is more complex because personal issues are interwoven with the theological issues. I found myself time and again instinctively retreating to the security of tried and true formulations of the gospel, but these were not being understood by Alfa nor anyone else. The Fulbe have a high view of Jesus, and I tried to push this even higher by discussing the authority of Jesus. This attracted some attention, and with those who were interested I would proceed to the gospel of the cross as victory over sin, evil, Satan, and death. This seemed to communicate to some degree, but it moved no one, including Alfa. There was something missing in this chain of logic; the gospel of the cross was not communicating. Observing the process that Alfa went through provided an answer: the nature of Christ. From the beginning he had circled around this issue, believing this was the central point, whereas I, being a well-brought-up Pauline Christian, felt the cross was the central point and persistently and faithfully pushed every inquiry in that direction. For me, the nature of Jesus and the Trinity, although very important, was a bone of contention between Christians and Muslims, and discussions of such issues needed to be delayed to a later point or we risked descending into counterproductive polemics.

Alfa did not become a believer until he came to a degree of understanding on this very issue, but he continued to wrestle with it. He returned to Islamic theology and reflected more deeply on the nature of Jesus in the Muslim tradition. His thought processes went as follows:

- He started with the presupposition that God is one and eternal.

- He then raised the question as to whether God's Word can be divorced from God: Is it not coeternal with God in his being?

- He then took up the quranic presentation of the nature of Jesus. In the Qur'an, Alfa understands Jesus to be the Breath of God, having been blown into Mary (21:91), he is the Word of God (3:45), and he is the Spirit of God (4:171)—inseparable elements of a single whole. Word is spoken by Breath and Spirit is the unseen Breath of God.

- He then moved to "therefore": Jesus, being the Word/Breath/ Spirit of God become flesh, is inseparable from God, coeternal with God, and thus none other than God.

- His second "therefore" is this: God cannot lie, and since Jesus is the eternal Word of God become flesh, he too cannot lie; therefore, since Jesus said that he was the Savior and that he accomplished this through his work on the cross and in the resurrection, then it must be so.

That is how Alfa presents the gospel. More recently he has been working off the title which Islam gives to Jesus: the *Ruuhulayi*. All Fulbe are aware of this title and translate it as "breath of God" or even "soul of God," but seem unaware of its potential meaning. Alfa, beginning with Jesus as the Ruuhulayi and using the line of argument described above, is effectively upsetting traditional Fulbe understandings of Jesus. I have heard him discuss this issue with marabouts and laypersons alike, beginning at different points and using different styles but always effectively demonstrating that Jesus is uncreated and coeternal with God.

Implications about Embedment of the Gospel

In order to understand my version of the gospel, a person of Fulbe background would have to be educated in my worldview and belief system. I am firmly convinced that the gospel can be embedded into any worldview and belief system. With Alfa and others now taking the lead we are coming closer and closer to effectively embedding the good news of Jesus Christ into the Muslim Fulbe context.

Implications about the Attitude of the Missionary

In my earlier years I respected Islam before the people, and would use verses from the Qur'an to support my point of view, but in my heart I thought of Islam as Enemy Number One. My basic heart attitude was at odds with the stated goal of my ministry: to embed Jesus into the Muslim Fulbe worldview and belief system. However, in order to embed Jesus into a worldview and belief system, one must be willing to enter therein, walk along with that worldview and belief system as far as is biblically possible, and bring Jesus as the answer to the issues within it. I am not proposing that missionaries become neo-Muslims. Rather, in restudying Islam with a renewed attitude during the past two years, I am realizing that Christianity and qur'anic Islam can indeed walk a long way together. Islam can be viewed as a resource which can be employed in the cause of Christ.

Implications about the Rewards

As Alfa and I walk down this road together we are each experiencing liberation. Alfa was a frustrated believer; now he sees the way forward for him to remain inside his village, culture, and worldview. Jesus has met him there. He is now a powerful witness of Jesus to all around him. I was a frustrated missionary, at times overwhelmed by the fortress that was Islam, but now it feels as if a gap has been blown in the wall, and we can walk right through with the gospel. This has changed my approach to witness, leading to many fruitful collaborative discussions as we explore the true meaning of Christ.

Frameworks of Religion

There is much in every worldview and belief system that can be affirmed; on the other hand, this can also be hostile territory for the gospel. There will have to be transformations, but some of these may not come until later. So where do Fulbe believers begin?

a) Jesus is the ultimate prophet, protector, provider, savior, elder brother. He is the eternal Word of God, the Breath of God, the Ruuhulayi, the king of a new group/kingdom/*umma* of which they are now a part. In Fulbe culture one is always seeking to be allied with a protector or a mediator, not only in preparation for the afterlife but also for life on earth. Once a person of Fulbe background understands who Jesus is and believes in him, Jesus replaces all other pretenders and rises to the top of the stack.

b) Jesus would be the best source of *barke* from Allah both now and in the afterlife. (*Barke* refers to the blessing, the supernatural power, that is available from God for people—the same as *barakah* in Arabic. This is greatly sought after by the Fulbe.) In time they understand that he is the only source of barke. As there is spiritual growth, they should begin to focus more on worship and gratitude, on what they could give back to Christ, on suffering for the gospel, on service, and less on receiving barke.

c) The marabouts of the *Linjiila* (New Testament), whether mission-ary or Fulbe, would be considered to be closer to Jesus and would be seen as potential mediators of barke.

d) There is much emphasis on prayer as the means of acquiring barke.

e) For Fulbe there are two major foci in religion: barke and *sariya* (law). One keeps sariya so one can receive barke. In Africa, every fetish, every spirit or power, every religious manifestation, has its law. Keep the law and you will be blessed; break the law and the fetish may devour you. When Fulbe submit to Christ, they immediately look for the law of Jesus. Communicating Christian concepts of law and grace will require much repetition.

f) Literacy is valued because the *binndi* ("books") contain the *sirri*: the secrets of power. They also seek those who have studied the binndi, since that is where the most powerful sirri can be found. Now that we have translated much of the Linjiila into Fulfulde and the binndi are increasingly available to the average person, literacy is a growing value. The Linjiila is a powerful tool; in time new believers look less and less for sirri and increasingly turn to the Linjiila for encouragement and understanding. They finally begin to accept that there are no sirri in the way of Jesus—all is light.

This is where the Fulbe believers start. They have put their trust in Jesus as their only hope in life and in death: Is this not sufficient for salvation? These new believers could be characterized as similar to those mentioned in John 11:45, "Therefore many of the Jews who had come to visit Mary, and had seen what Jesus did [raised Lazarus from the dead], put their faith in him."[1] These Jews could have no understanding of the cross and resurrection of Jesus, but they saw what he did, they heard what he said, and they concluded that he was indeed no ordinary prophet, and they "put their faith in him."

For the apostles, the urgent need of the day was to demonstrate to the Jews that Jesus was indeed the Messiah and so they focused on who Jesus was. They preached his miracles and the resurrection as proof of his identity; it was only later that a full appreciation for the cross developed. Similarly, the urgent need among the Fulbe is to demonstrate that Jesus was much more than just another prophet of whom Muhammad is the seal. Full appreciation of the cross and its meaning will come later.

My observation is that Fulbe believers retain the same framework of belief that they had in Islam but simply change the names. This is inevitable since this is where they have come from, or rather this is what they have brought Jesus into. As we had hoped, Jesus is being embedded into their worldview and belief system, but the job of discipleship will be to help the believers to develop a new framework. Those coming out of African traditional religions have a similar framework but different names, and consequently as believers have a different focus. Their background is filled with vaguely defined spiritual beings and powers; they more naturally identify with the Holy Spirit than with Jesus. Islam has moved people to focus on Allah and his prophet. Thus when Muslims become believers they more naturally identify with Jesus.

Postscript

When a believer makes comments that come out of his Fulbe Muslim worldview and belief system, this does not mean that he is not a believer. Rather, in the early years these issues must be seen in the context of the believers' struggles as they live between two worldviews. As these issues arise, they need to be taken lovingly to the Bible.

In this same vein, I have had to wrestle with how much I am willing to give new believers freedom to be themselves spiritually—not only in regard to indigenization of the church and worship, but also in regard to their personal expression of faith. To what degree do I expect the new believers to sound like us, to feel like us, to express their faith in the same pious tones as our evangelical-speak? Will not their expression of personal faith be similar to a Fulbe Muslim's expression of personal faith? I have observed a tendency in others and in myself that, when the believers do not sound like us, to then be skeptical of their faith. This can lead us to put subtle, unconscious pressure on them to sound and feel like us. I must keep reminding myself from whence the believers came: there is a battle going on for their hearts and minds as they wrestle with fundamental, life-changing, worldview issues. We must give them freedom to be themselves and accept the Spirit's work in them.

CHAPTER 18

MUSLIM VILLAGERS COMING TO FAITH IN CHRIST: A CASE STUDY AND MODEL OF GROUP DYNAMICS

JOHN KIM

"You have been a refuge for the poor, a refuge for the needy in his distress, a shelter from the storm and a shade from the heat. For the breath of the ruthless is like a storm driving against a wall and like the heat of the desert." (Isaiah 25:4–5)

"Anotoc" is a remote village in a mountainous area of Southeast Asia. The "Bangunda" people of the village, mainly illiterate, have a strong ethnic identity and are proud of their Muslim identity. Recent tensions with native islanders led to the scattering of many Bangunda as refugees on other islands, while a few settled in Anotoc, previously a peaceful village.

During this period a team of national Christians, ethnic neighbors to the Bangunda and mentored by expatriates, had begun ministry in the area. They examined some areas in terms of David Garrison's description of "universal elements" among church planting movements (CPMs).[1] They concluded that Anotoc already had most of the elements for a CPM and could be regarded as the most feasible area for such a movement to develop.

Two months after the study, I was meditating on Isaiah 25:4 when the telephone rang. An urgent voice cried, "There was a strong windstorm which destroyed many houses in Anotoc. Some of the villagers were killed." Surveying the devastated houses, the team and I agreed that Isaiah 25:4, describing God as a shelter from a storm and refuge for the poor, applied to the scene we witnessed. The poor villagers needed God to be their shelter and refuge.

We began by working with Bangunda villagers to repair sixteen houses. The national members of our team naturally shared the gospel by introducing *Allah* as the "shelter and refuge."

After two months, the team invited an "insider" Bangunda evangelist, a C–5 follower of Jesus.[2] Welcomed by the villagers, he preached in the Bangunda language from the Torah through the Injil (New Testament) for about four hours. The villagers were greatly moved and all twenty-five present raised their hands, indicating their decision to accept *Isa Almasih* (Jesus Christ) as their Savior.

Sometime after this, baptism became a hot issue among workers in the network. We decided to let the Muslim background believers (MBBs) take the initiative in this decision.

Meanwhile, a lady in the converts group had been persecuted by her husband. About a year after the group conversion, he had a terrible traffic accident in which some passengers were killed and his own left leg was broken in three places. At first he was taken to a witchdoctor, who proved unable to help. The national team members were called to help him and prayed regularly for the man in the name of Isa Almasih for over a month. The villagers were astonished to observe his rapid recovery. When this influential man decided to give himself to Isa Almasih, a collective turning to the Lord occurred. The team members were very encouraged and continued to interact with the MBBs.

Nine months after this second collective decision, the MBBs decided to be baptized. With the help of national team members and prayer support from other workers in the network, twenty-five Bangunda were baptized, while a second group prepared for a later baptism.

The movement continues to grow. Over one hundred relatives of the believers attended a celebration after the baptism at which an appropriate evangelistic film was shown. Later, two *ustad* (Islamic religious teachers) asked for an *Alkitab* (Bible) and expressed their desire to learn about Isa Almasih in more detail. A new Bangunda believer called a group of neighbors to join him and the national team in prayer, in the name of Isa Almasih, for a sick woman. When she was healed, the neighbors, the woman, and her family all came to faith.

Bangunda leadership is developing. They have planned to produce cassette tapes for the fellowships of Bible verses in Arabic as well as the Bangunda language, along with traditional music. Potential key leaders are expected to grow through this encounter with the Word of God. At the gatherings, national team members teach how to hold culturally appropriate worship services and how to lead groups of MBBs by sharing the Word of God prepared in the cassettes.

A Cluster Model for Understanding Church Planting Movement Group Dynamics

David Garrison defines a church planting movement as "a rapid and multiplicative (exponential) increase of indigenous churches planting churches within a given people group or population segment."[3] Drawing on my background in physics as well as the study of social group dynamics, in this section I will develop a model which helps us better understand the group dynamics essential in CPMs. Based on the model, some suggestions will be given to foster CPMs in Muslim contexts, recognizing the unique role of the Holy Spirit in any such movement.

A Given People Group or Population Segment

A people group or population segment is a set of people clusters in which each cluster has a relatively strong affinity and homogeneity differentiating it from others. In rural contexts, this can be seen in clans in the form of the extended family system. In urban Muslim contexts, the clusters often exist as socioreligious affinity groups centered on mosques or Islamic boarding schools.

Each cluster may consist of a number of family units as well as people working in a similar job field. Families in a cluster or people in the similar job field can be connected to each other by sharing social, religious, political, educational, or professional backgrounds. Sometimes one family unit can function as a cluster itself in a small people group.

Constrained Condition Binding the Clusters as a Whole People Group or a Population Segment

A cluster can be regarded as the unit to which we may apply the homogeneous unit principle (that people prefer to become Christians without crossing barriers of language, ethnicity, or class).[4] A cluster's collective behavior produces the latent possibility of a "people movement."[5] As one cluster moves through collective change this affects other clusters, which in turn may be incorporated into the movement.

The kind of situation that binds a cluster with others can be described as a set of clusters in a context, in which the constraints produce a bounded system (see Figure 18.1). The constraints—historical, social, political, religious, economic—result in internal biases which help maintain stability. In a context under constrained conditions the clusters are correlated and bound in all realms of life.

The constrained condition can be both negative and positive for the entire movement. A negative aspect is exhibited when a cluster is about to move, as internal biases oppose the direction of the cluster's reorientation.

This is intrinsic to the system, maintaining the traditional stability of the group. However, because clusters are networked, movement can result in a sequential disturbance to—and change among—other clusters.

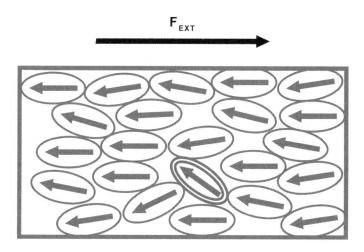

FIGURE 18.1 A PICTORIAL DESCRIPTION OF CLUSTER MODEL

Overall Features of the Entire Movement of Clusters in a People Group

Figure 18.1 is a pictorial description of a people group consisting of clusters under a constrained condition. Each ellipse describes a cluster in a bounded condition, all heading in more or less the same direction but opposed by an outside force (F_{EXT}). Each cluster will be influenced and disturbed to a certain degree by the external force which is, in our application of the model, the gospel impact of mission efforts.

The cluster most likely to be turned by the external force, the most *feasible* cluster to change, is that with the highest degree of freedom and least in line with other clusters, represented by the double-lined ellipse in Figure 18.1. With the consistent application of force, the cluster will go through a reorientation process as a *collective behavior* of elements within the cluster. Along with this reorientation process, other clusters can be motivated to move and thus this movement can spread to the entire system.

This reorientation process is observed both in human social systems and material systems.[6] Over time, a people group undergoes change as more and more clusters reorient, something McGavran described as a chain reaction.[7]

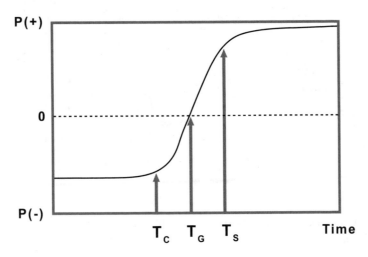

FIGURE 18.2 TIME DEPENDENT BEHAVIOR OF ENTIRE SYSTEM UNDERGOING REORIENTATION PROCESS, SHOWING STRETCHED EXPONENTIAL.

As depicted in Figure 18.2, the movement goes through a period of initial growth (only a few clusters), starting at a threshold of critical time T_C followed by rapid growth and eventually saturation, as denoted by T_S.[8] The horizontal axis of the graph represents time, while the vertical axis represents the number of clusters which have taken the new orientation. What Garrison has described as the exponential increase taking place in a church planting movement is described by the period of rapid growth, T_G in Figure 18.2.

Implications of the Cluster Model

This model gives us a visual understanding of a people group as a set of clusters possessing homogeneity under common constraints in the context, characterized by historical, social, political, religious, and economic backgrounds.

Each cluster is a unit of collective conversion, such as those who together came to faith in Christ in Anotoc village. Collective conversion takes place in a context where a group of people respond to the gospel impact in a cooperative way when the constrained condition is loosened. Since conversion is a reorientation process and the cluster is linked with other neighboring clusters through constraints, it can initiate successive reorientations resulting in a movement.

In Figure 18.1, the orientation of each cluster relative to the direction of gospel impact symbolizes openness to the gospel. When the gospel impacts a cluster having a higher degree of freedom against the constraints, the cluster can be an initiator, resulting in a successive reorientation process. A church planting movement takes place in a period displaying, in a term from physics, *stretched exponential behavior*, characterized by three distinguishable time regions: very slow growth (time T before a critical point T_C), CPM period (the time of growth T_G between a critical time T_C and a saturation point T_S), and the stagnation period (after T_S). In this sense, a CPM is a part of an entire people movement to Christ.

This model helps us extend our understanding of the conversion process from a personal view to a people group approach. Eventually our understanding should extend to the whole growth pattern of the kingdom of God. The kingdom of God is developing in a way far beyond our imagination, as Jesus suggested in the parables of the mustard seed and yeast (Matthew 13:31, 33). It started in the small Garden of Eden with two people, but will be completed as the great Holy City where countless multitudes will praise the Lord (Revelation 7:9). The growth of the kingdom of God in time is an accumulation of the people movements among people groups in space and time. They are indeed the accumulation of all the CPM-like events in each people group.

Group Dynamics and the Family as the Most Feasible Cluster Unit

The family or household is repeatedly emphasized in the Bible as the unit for salvation and a channel of God's blessings. Paul and Silas' encounter with the Philippian jailer (Acts 16) is a clear example of collective conversion of a family unit. In our model, the family may often be the most *feasible* cluster to initiate larger change, further illustrated (Acts 10) in Peter's encounter with Cornelius' household. Of course as the driving force the Holy Spirit plays a special role as motivator, initiator, activator, and controller, resulting in the group dynamics leading to conversion.

In these contexts in which group dynamics were at work, the gospel message was *proclaimed* rather than presented as persuasion or dialogue. Dialogue, aiming for mutual understanding, and persuasion are common ways of communicating in Western culture. However, in Asian cultures communication is often made in the form of preaching or proclamation in a context where group dynamics are at work in a hierarchical social system, including the family.

The family is the smallest unit of a social/blood/kinship affinity group, which I have called a cluster—a unit which by itself can have social influence. The social aspect is shared through interpersonal relationships among family members, but at the same time it can be propagated to neighboring family units. Dean S. Gilliland recognizes both the time factor and the personal and social aspects.[9] Wolfgang Simson recognizes the family approach as a practical model of church planting. His approach "seeks to start a new house-church with a whole, newly converted family, which is then linked with other families into multiplying house churches."[10]

The Holy Spirit and Group Dynamics in Philippi and Corinth through the Lens of the Cluster Model

It is the triune God who initiates church planting movements. Understanding how he works in the light of the cluster model is briefly drawn from two examples from the book of Acts.

In Acts 16 we read of the urgent call of the Holy Spirit upon Paul to go to Macedonia, resulting in Paul's visit to Philippi. In terms of constrained conditions, Philippi, however, seems to be highly opposed to gospel impact. For prayer, Paul goes not to a synagogue, but outside the city—where he meets Lydia, a worshiper of God, an exceptional woman less bound by the constraints of the city. The spiritual and social constraints opposing the gospel are shaken by the midnight earthquake. In this unstable, traumatic setting the jailer and his family are freed from constraints, believe the gospel, and are baptized.

Lydia and her household formed the most *feasible* cluster responsive to the gospel. Meanwhile, not only the slave girl's owners but the crowd were strongly opposed; however, this constrained condition was shaken, allowing collective reorientation. We note also the Holy Spirit's work in leading Paul to the city and to Lydia's family as well as in the earthquake. The dynamic work of the Holy Spirit is an intrinsic property of the spread of the gospel.

In Corinth, the constrained context was disturbed somehow by newcomers from Rome, Jews including Priscilla and Aquila, who were forced to leave Rome by the emperor Claudius (Acts 18:2). This was an intentional preparation by God, as he says to Paul in a vision, "I have many people in this city" (Acts 18:10).

Paul, Priscilla, and Aquila were severely opposed by Jews, and left the synagogue immediately. But the situation totally changed when they arrived next door, at a place looking almost the same as the first in terms of the kind of people (or cluster). They met in the home of Titius Justus, a Gentile "worshiper of God," and soon saw the conversion of Crispus, the synagogue ruler. Not only the synagogue ruler, but also "his entire household" and "many of the Corinthians" came to the Lord and were baptized.

Paul appears to be more passionate in the synagogue, but the positive response is in the second place of teaching. The two clusters look the same in terms of socioreligious atmosphere (Acts 18:7), but the opposite result occurs. Even clusters with the same affinity can have different orientations relative to the direction of the gospel impact. Crispus' household played the role of the cluster described by the double-lined ellipse in Figure 18.1. Their collective conversion initiated the successive reorientation of other clusters—a conversion movement (Acts 18:8).

The Holy Spirit prepared the context and encouraged Paul to continue preaching, "For I am with you, and no one is going to attack and harm you, because I have many people in this city" (Acts 18:10). This story helps us to see that, even though different social clusters appear the same, they may have different orientations to the gospel's impact. Thus, we need to be sensitive to the Holy Spirit in an ambiguous situation to know his clear direction.

Anotoc Village

Let us now return to the story of Anotoc village, interpreting the story through the lens of the cluster model.

The national team members, Christians from a neighboring ethnic group, were looking for a situation with potential for a church planting movement according to the factors described by David Garrison.[11] Anotoc village seemed like a feasible cluster since it had more of those elements than other villages. The team turned away from an "extraction" approach, realizing the importance of keeping the new believers in their context. Through their CPM study, they developed a sense of urgency in evangelization and sensitivity to the Holy Spirit.

The national team members were waiting for a decisive moment while continuing their activities in the village. The moment arrived with a strong windstorm sweeping through the village, a dramatic event which occurred just as I meditated on the description of God as the refuge for the poor from a storm in Isaiah 25.

The Muslim Bangunda villagers are interconnected by kinship, a cluster sharing a common contextual situation under a religious and family-oriented constraint. This constrained condition binding the village members was loosened dramatically by the windstorm. The reconstruction project led to an opening for an insider to freely and contextually proclaim the gospel in this unstable situation, leading an entire cluster of twenty-five people to a collective decision to turn in saving faith to Christ.

Experiencing a collective reorientation, they could remain within their own context. Tensions did arise, however, with some local religious leaders who perceived the MBBs to be somehow "Christianized." In reality, the national team members were cautiously practicing a contextualized approach. One religious leader, a distant relative of one of the new believers, took a position defending the new MBBs from the other religious leaders. He left the leaders' association and established his own mosque in Anotoc, which some of the MBBs still attend for communal rituals.

Baptism eventually became a critical issue which team members left to the decision of the MBBs. During this period, about a year after the first decision, a second collective decision was made as a result of the healing of a critically ill woman and the husband of one of the new believers. Once again a cluster went through a collective reorientation.

The MBBs made a group decision for baptism. The baptism and subsequent celebration were attended by many Bangunda, who were given a chance to watch a contextualized film conveying the message of redemption in Isa Almasih. All these activities were intentionally carried out with principles of group dynamics in mind. A further healing resulted in a group conversion of a cluster which had been influenced by those who had already turned to Christ.

We understand that MBBs should go through a transformation in their social relationships as well as in their personal lives. As long as they receive his Spirit in their lives through Isa Almasih, they will experience continuous life change. As I write, this latest group is preparing for baptism and some leadership discipling is taking place.

Can We Facilitate a Church Planting Movement in Muslim Contexts?

Based on my model and our experience, I would suggest that the following principles may help foster a church planting movement in settings similar to Anotoc.

The unreached people group focus needs to be a cluster focus. We should be aware of the existence of smaller, homogeneous affinity groups—clusters—that can experience group dynamics toward change under certain socioreligious constraints. When a cluster undergoes movement in a constrained condition, the reorientation movement can propagate to the other neighboring clusters.

We need to determine the type of constraints binding clusters. The type of constraint defines the nature of affinity in a cluster. Collective conversion will be more likely in a situation in which constrained conditions are loosened or destroyed. Various constraints are formed in a group's long history of its social, political, ethnic, and economic backgrounds. The first role of a strategy coordinator working in a CPM-driven ministry lies in finding out the constraints binding clusters. We should be sensitive to the work of the Holy Spirit, as many constraints are spiritual.

We need to discern the most feasible cluster (usually a family unit) rather than to approach many clusters broadly. A family, the strongest blood affinity group, can play a role as this feasible cluster.

We need to focus on gatherings or communal activities rather than on individualistic interaction. Building private relationships seems to be a starting point to have a chance to share the gospel. However, individual conversion rarely produces momentum strong enough to break through the constrained condition of a cluster. Many individual converts have to be extracted from the living context and even from their families, whereas a group of people experiencing collective conversion can convey momentum to others around them and keep within the context even through persecution.

The more gatherings of believers are created, the more collective conversion opportunities are given. Muslim societies are deeply engaged in communal activities. Thus, it is not strange at all when social or family-centered communal activities are promoted. When people are gathered, group dynamics are ready to work in an atmosphere prepared by the Holy Spirit.

We need to be aware of the socioreligious hierarchy commonly found in most Asian contexts. A mosque or an Islamic boarding school is often the center of socioreligious activities. In Anotoc, the Islamic leader seemed to utilize the collective conversions as an opportunity to bring the group under his authority. In this hierarchical social system we need to develop a genuine relationship with religious leaders.

We need to maintain a sense of urgency in evangelization. Power encounters often occur when a cluster experiences a dynamic situation. We must proclaim the victory of Jesus. Further, in a socioreligious system under a hierarchical condition, the gospel is often proclaimed or preached rather than explained or persuaded. We must have urgency while we recognize the work of the Holy Spirit, at the same time grasping the group dynamics of context. The Muslim context is indeed a pioneering field, in which the Holy Spirit must be in control.

We need to encourage and monitor the initiating cluster so that the movement can be propagated to neighboring clusters. Existing constraints can be obstacles in initiating a collective movement. Yet, once the first collective movement takes place, it can spontaneously influence neighboring clusters because of networking within the constraints. In Anotoc, the first MBB group kept in contact with national team members, who encouraged them to maintain the momentum which in turn helped lead to successive collective conversions.

Understanding the group dynamics of collective conversion may help resolve the issue of the C4–C5 debate. Since Phil Parshall raised the issue of syncretism in the "C–5" congregation,[12] the topic of contextualization has remained a hot issue.[13] Those who are in the debate tend to see the situation too analytically from an individualistic view in a static position. Having a holistic view of the dynamic Muslim context, we understand conversion and contextualization as a time-dependent process. When group dynamics are at work, decision making can be done in an MBB group within the context—for example, the group decision in Anotoc to undergo baptism. Group decisions are much more effective and powerful than individual ones. The remaining issues will be resolved through biblical contextualization, depending on time and group dynamics.

Finally, we need to be aware of the overall time-dependence of the development of the kingdom of God. Conversion itself is a time-dependent reorientation process, changing direction toward Jesus and away from this world. It critically depends on the contextual situation. Our vision is not the static goal of planting a church, but of seeing a dynamic movement. We live in a dynamically changing world, but tend to seek stable situations. This tendency must be avoided. When we remember the overall time-dependent behavior of the development of the kingdom of God, we can maintain a sense of urgency in evangelization and understand what we see now as a part of eternity. The process may develop very slowly in the beginning, as described by Figure 2. However, remembering the entire pattern of the kingdom development, we await the critical time when rapid growth will come.

CHAPTER 19

A MOVE OF GOD IN A MUSLIM LAND

RICHARD TUCKER

"Daristan" is a democratic Muslim country that has experienced a fair degree of stability in recent years, although at the cost of limited freedom. Society is relatively open and increased economic wealth has led to materialism and secularism, although a new tolerance towards Islam has people returning to the mosques.

Daristan is a signatory to the United Nations Declaration of Human Rights and as such has religious freedom written into its constitution. Although the attitude of the authorities toward the church and conversion has varied considerably over the years, in the last few years there has been a small measure of religious tolerance.

Despite almost 150 years of Christian missionary work, there has been very little fruit. There has been occasional growth in the indigenous church, but this has invariably receded. It is only in the last five years that significant growth has occurred and appears to be sustained. The factors affecting this growth are the focus of this paper.

Church History to the Late 1990s

Long ago the church in this region was strong and well-established. However, decline set in and eventually Muslim armies seized power with relatively little opposition. From that time forward there was virtually no successful Christian witness in the region.

Christian missionaries first went back to Daristan in the nineteenth century, but there was very little fruit until almost the very end of the twentieth century. The church never measured more than a few tens of believers, despite a window of opportunity after the Second World War when the work was virtually unopposed. Christian evangelism has not been encouraged, and those coming to faith have experienced significant social opposition and also intermittent state opposition. However, even during clampdowns believers have been relatively well treated by the authorities, and none have been imprisoned or experienced severe physical abuse.

There was some growth in the church some years ago, but this petered out through a mixture of internal division over doctrinal matters and infiltration by informers. The result was that in the early 1990s there were perhaps less than fifty Daristanis in the country who would name themselves as believers in Jesus, of whom less than ten would ever meet together. There was, however, a lot of sowing by many people in many different ways. Many people invested time in relationships. Literature was handed out. There were radio broadcasts and the advent of Christian satellite TV. Every year there would be news of a very few decisions to follow Christ; but, although at different times new groups started meeting, there was very little overall growth. This changed toward the end of the 1990s with some key people coming to faith and a significant number of people being baptized, paving the way for things to come.

New Hope for Daristan

At that time God gave the workers in Daristan fresh hope and vision for a project called *New Hope!* It started with one worker walking on the beach, who came to a small trickle of water in a narrow channel dug through the sand from a small pool to the sea. He returned to the same spot just a few minutes later and the trickle had literally become a wide river that could not be crossed. The Lord seemed to impress on his mind that this was a prophetic picture of living water gushing through the country. God was promising to pour out his Holy Spirit in an uncontrollable flood. However, the key to this was that there needed to be that first small breakthrough—the small channel—to start the flood.

From this came the idea for *a year of concentrated effort* aimed at achieving a breakthrough. This was much more than just "a year of prayer." It aimed to combine a huge prayer movement *with* evangelism, discipleship, and training. All the agencies in the country without exception supported the project and acknowledged that God was behind it. During the year, hundreds of churches and networks around the world prayed for Daristan with material (including video, information booklet, and prayer diaries) translated into several languages. Many prayer teams visited the country. Teaching weekends were organized once a month that brought together almost all the known believers in the country to teach them to "be church."

It was during the special weekend gatherings in the winter that the most significant growth occurred. These weekends were based around food, fellowship, worship, and instruction from various visiting culturally related teachers focusing on the cost of discipleship and on the body of Christ. There were over twenty believers present at the first weekend. By the second weekend there were over thirty, and some believers reported that they were beginning to meet together in their own towns. At the third weekend there were over forty-five present, and several of these had not even been Christians the month previously! The remarkable thing was that MBBs were bringing their own friends and family, who were then coming to faith.

Post *New Hope!*

When *New Hope!* began, it was estimated that over 100 new believers were baptized and several new groups were started. Today workers and church leaders reckon that there are at least 300 believers, 150–200 of whom are actively involved in the life of the church, which continues to meet in twelve small groups around the country, although the majority are in the capital. The church is led entirely by local leaders who have formed a sort of council to coordinate the functioning of the church nationally.

Analysis

God has done wonderful things in Daristan. However, it is important to bear in mind that:

1.   There are many factors at play, and it would be unwise to isolate any one factor as being "the key."

2.   People see things from different perspectives according to their role, gifts, feelings, and preferences. It is very difficult to be truly objective, especially when working from within the story.

3.   Such events are always built on a foundation of years of God being at work in different ways. Many others had toiled and sown in Daristan over the twentieth century.

4.   There are no quick, easy answers to seeing the kingdom come amongst Muslims. We need to remain dependent on God rather than on our own schemes.

Types of People Coming to Faith

Mainly Young. Most of those who have come to faith over the last five years are young people, with a high proportion of students. However, this was not to the exclusion of older people (including one notable character in his seventies) and indeed, in some instances, whole families.

Equal Numbers of Males and Females. There also seems to have been an almost equal number of males and females coming to faith, although there has been some regional variation.

From Most Social Classes. There was a cross section of society coming to faith, with the probable exception of the very rich. Professionals, manual laborers, students, and unemployed have all been represented.

Mainly Urban. There was also a cross section of urban and rural responses, although most of the church groups have formed in the more cosmopolitan cities. Believers in rural areas have faced significantly more opposition from both the authorities and society. Very few groups of believers have come together and survived in rural areas.

Mainly from a Nonconservative Background. There were relatively few people who came to faith from a strict Islamic background. Although Daristan is predominantly Sunni Muslim, there is a high degree of nominalism, and until recently only a minority would be considered devout in their Islamic observance. The majority of those coming to faith were from a nominal or secular background where Islam provided little more than a cultural identity. Some were even professing atheists or communists. In other words many, though not all, who came to faith did so from a nonconservative Muslim background.

Ways that People Have Come to Faith

People came to faith in many different ways, of course. The following, ending with the most common, were some of the most important.

Demonic Encounter. Only one lady (and consequently her husband) came to faith through a power encounter, when she was set free through prayer in Jesus' name from fear, nightmares, and demonic visitations brought on by involvement with curses and charms at a saint's shrine.

Dreams. Several people reported having dreams of Jesus as part of the process of coming to faith, either at the outset of their journey or as part of the process alongside other factors. Interestingly, the local believers feel that the percentage of people who have had significant dreams is high.

Unplanned Meetings. More came to faith through unplanned meetings. For instance, two Christians met a young man sitting under a tree reading a Bible who subsequently came to faith. Other Christians made a point of spending time in the Catholic cathedral and met several people who went there seeking to find out about Christianity. Others were picked up by Christian workers, while hitchhiking.

Radio, TV, and Correspondence Follow-up. Follow-up of radio and TV correspondence contacts was an important avenue in coming to faith. Many of the stations cooperated with Christian workers in order for contacts to be followed up. Names and addresses were shared amongst the agencies for visiting. This was probably the largest single tool in seeing people come to faith outside of the main urban areas.

Expatriate-Local Relationships. There were up to 100 expatriate Christian workers with the aim of sharing their faith with locals. Many relationships were formed and there were a good number of instances where these relationships led to people coming to faith, often through bringing them into contact with a group of worshiping believers.

Bold Witness by Nationals. By far the most important factor was local believers sharing their faith with family, friends, and contacts. Prior to this time most local believers had been fearful of doing so, and the national church had been cautious about new people coming into their gatherings. This fear was broken during the year of *New Hope!* as people quite naturally started inviting their friends to come along and see what was happening.

Factors in People Coming to Faith in Daristan

Bold Witness of Local Believers. The year of *New Hope!* was a turning point in seeing local believers becoming bold evangelists. This came about for several reasons. Firstly, it must be assumed that the great intensity of prayer for the country at that time had an effect and increased their boldness. Secondly, there were key young local leaders who set an example of fearless openness and proclamation, some being frequently questioned by the authorities. Thirdly, there was teaching on persecution and the cost of following Jesus. Lastly, the believers were taught to learn the paragraph in their constitution that ascribes them freedom of conscience and belief in line with the UN Declaration of Human Rights, to which Daristan is a signatory. Many local believers were able to recite this to the police when they were being questioned!

Public Meetings. Local believers held monthly public meetings using one of the international church buildings in the city. All the different groups—mainly consisting of locals but also some expatriates—were invited to attend and there would be worship, teaching, fellowship, and a meal. People were encouraged to bring their friends, and even enquirers off the street were welcomed. The authorities were aware of these meetings, presumably attended them, and also seemed to indicate that they were happier when believers met openly in church buildings rather than secretly in houses. The Christians also had a stand selling legally imported Bibles at an international book fair in the city.

Intentional Planning for Growth. The catalyst for this bold witness was at the beginning of *New Hope!* when a series of teaching weekends were held. As many believers as possible were gathered together from around the country for a weekend of worship, fellowship, and teaching. Many experienced Christian community for the first time, as there was an intentional modeling of church life. These weekends were designed to prepare the believers to receive new believers and to "become church" together in the expectation that God would answer prayer and bring many people to salvation. This was exactly what happened. Some came to the second weekend with reports that they had begun to have similar meetings in their own town. By the third weekend some were bringing their friends along.

Cooperation and Unity. All this was done against a backdrop of cooperation and unity between the different agencies. Everyone was involved in helping to pull together *New Hope!*, teaching weekends, and prayer initiatives. It was significant that all the gifts (from Ephesians 4) were evident in different degrees and the people were prepared to work together. There were apostles (those gifted in establishing churches), prophets (those who were able to see the situation and speak God's word into it), evangelists (those gifted in explaining the gospel to others), pastors (those good at caring for others), and teachers (those good at equipping and discipling others).

Prayer. Although *New Hope!* was always more than just "a year of prayer," prayer was undoubtedly the foundation. There was much united prayer, both in the country and around the world. From the beginning, churches and networks were offered the materials and challenged to pray. A video was made explaining the project, giving background information, and providing prayer points. There was a handbook, monthly prayer diaries, and then weekly e-mails. All of these were translated into nine different languages and distributed worldwide. Prayer meetings were organized in the country and over thirty short-term teams visited the country to pray.

The Social and Political Context. The social and political context was relatively open during this period. While the authorities took an active interest in what was happening and frequently questioned people, they did not seriously try to stop what was happening. Also, while many families opposed members becoming believers and sometimes threw them out of their homes, the prevailing attitude of society at the time was one of increasing tolerance. Sadly, this may no longer be the case with political events in the Middle East hardening attitudes towards the West.

The God Factor. However, the greatest factor was that it was God's plan at God's time and that men and women merely got in line with what he was doing. It came about through a prophetic word, and at every stage things just seemed to "take off." While there was a lot of human work and effort involved, God was obviously moving by his Spirit.

Some Cautionary Notes and Lessons to Learn

Plateau Period. The rate of growth in Daristan has slowed, although it has not been reversed. This plateau could be seen as a time of consolidation or may be due to other factors, such as a shortage of leaders, inadequate discipleship, or the departure of key expatriate workers.

Transition to Local Leadership. The leadership of the local church is now totally in the hands of local believers. Only a few expatriate workers are involved, most working outside of the church to see new groups established. The transition to local leadership is obviously a key necessity for seeing an indigenous church established. However, transitions can be made too quickly under pressure to be seen to have an "indigenous" movement. Shared leadership may result in more maturity and stability at a time when instilling solid discipleship is vital.

Dissipation of Energy on Structures. It is very easy in a situation of church growth for a lot of time and energy to be spent on organizing church structures to the detriment of both speed of growth and depth of discipleship. It is very natural for local believers to want to copy Western models of church life. However, it would be much better if the emerging church can form its own structures over time without the baggage that expatriates (and their videos, teaching materials, etc.) often bring with them.

Need for Discipleship, Not Just "Conversion." When a lot of people start coming to faith, it is essential that they do not just "pray the prayer" but are firmly grounded and discipled in their new faith. This was a weakness at times in Daristan. Some evangelists were happy with getting people to "pray the prayer"; at a later stage these people were sometimes resistant to discipleship and transformed lifestyles, as this had not been clearly presented as part of the cost of new birth. Having said this, there have also been many, many solid conversions where discipleship and growth are happening.

Outside Influences Can Often Be Unintentionally Destructive. Sometimes short-term teams of visiting Christian background believers and teachers with strong theological convictions can be a negative influence on new believers and the developing church, leading to destructive disunity. In particular, those who spoke against charismatic issues caused a lot of division and infighting. Foreign money can also quickly cause resentment, greed, suspicion, and mistrust—not to mention an unhealthy reliance on outside support. The local church today is pursuing a positive policy of trying to be self-sufficient within the country, which is to be strongly encouraged.

No Cookie Cutter Solutions. Finally, it must be emphasized again that this was very much God's plan and God's work. A year of prayer is not the answer to breakthrough everywhere. Recently there have been other prayer projects organized for other Muslim countries, which is well and good. However, God could equally well use another method to bring about results that do not resemble the above experience at all. The important thing is to be asking God for his unique key into every situation. Our tendency is always to latch on to a method or best practice and to fail to latch on to God. Perhaps the reason that God uses different methods in different places is to keep us dependent on him and not on human schemes. There are no cookie cutter solutions.

CHAPTER 20

THE BEAUTY OF JESUS AS AN EVANGELISTIC FACTOR

ABRAHAM DURÁN

Our team spent more than ten years serving a non-Arab people located in the Middle East and Central Asia. By God's unmerited mercy, they have seen a church of several hundred members coming to Jesus. Most of these Muslim background believers (MBBs) came to the Lord through a local team that our team trained and envisioned.

I want to mention seven factors that were effective in this particular case and may be important to consider in the evangelization of Muslims. In our very limited and localized experience we saw people coming to Christ when:

1. They were ready for the gospel.

2. Their prejudices were destroyed.

3. We built upon what they knew.

4. They saw the beauty of Jesus.

5. We told them the truth about Jesus.

6. They saw the manifestation of the kingdom of God.

7. They realized there was a community to support them.

They Were Ready for the Gospel

The Bible gives clear indication that God has special times to make things happen. In Genesis 15, the Lord told Abraham that his descendents were going to be captive for four hundred years. Then at the proper time he raised up Moses to free the captives. In Mark 1:15 Jesus announced, "The time is fulfilled, and the kingdom of God has come near" (NRSV). In Galatians 4:4 it is, "But when the fullness of time had come, God sent his Son, born of a woman, born under the law" (NRSV). Paul sees his call to life and ministry in similar terms, "But when God, who had set me apart before I was born and called me through his grace, was pleased to reveal his Son to me." (Galatians 1:15–16 NRSV).

We know that the Holy Spirit prevented Paul from taking the gospel to the Roman province of Asia and led him instead to Europe (Acts 16:6–10), where he had a difficult but wonderful ministry. Later, the way opened for him in Asia with much fruit (Acts 19:10).

I am not sure how this works. There is strong theological debate as to why God, "who desires everyone to be saved and to come to the knowledge of the truth" (1 Timothy 2:4 NRSV) would wait for "the right time" (1 Timothy 2:6 NRSV) to do something crucial in the salvation plan.

I am not proposing the strong fatalistic approach of some elders in William Carey's church who declared, "If God wants to save the heathen, he can do it without us." I am not proposing a moratorium on the lands that seem difficult today. On the contrary, there is strong indication in Scripture that these propitious times are related to prayer or remarkable answers to prayer. This is self-evident: "The Israelites groaned under their slavery, and cried out. Out of the slavery their cry for help rose up to God. God heard their groaning, and God remembered his covenant with Abraham, Isaac, and Jacob" (Exodus 2:23–24 NRSV).

What I am sure of is that a hundred years ago it was not possible for most converts in my people group to stay with their families. The influence of Muslim community leaders was stronger than blood ties, and family members were the first to kill "apostates." Other factors were involved: Culture and faith were intermingled and new followers of Jesus were often encouraged to renounce neutral aspects of their culture. Nationalism and modernization definitively weakened the hold and authority of Islamic leaders in our community.

We responded to the Lord's invitation and tried to go to this people group for two years, but we had to wait and pray. We entered the city only when it was obviously the right time.

Their Prejudices Were Destroyed

The team followed the people group approach. It was impossible to live lives simultaneously pleasing to our people group, the small CBB (Christian background believers) community, secular foreigners, other Christian workers, and other people groups in the city. We made a strong effort to belong to the people of our particular adopted group. Donald Larson wrote, "When we examine those who fail [to be successful language learners] we often find that they do not see themselves as outsiders, or if they do, do not really care whether or not they are acceptable to insiders."[1]

We made every effort possible, by God's grace, to belong to our adopted people group. We learned what their profiles were for an ideal man and woman, and we tried to fulfill those standards. We tried to walk, behave, eat, drink, talk, share, keep silence, sleep, and relate in ways that our people group considered right, proper, and ideal. We did not make our achievement or lack of achievement of this the measure of our self-worth, striving instead to please Christ alone, but pleasing him by trying to please everyone "for Christ's sake." Not every team member could do this; some had to return home or needed continuous support from the team to stay.

We focused upon one people group, and did everything that would not contradict the Lord's will to avoid being stumbling blocks for them. We heard unbelievers commenting to other people how we became one with them, defending our reputation before people who did not know us and even openly contradicting statements of religious leaders against us.

Of course we were not perfect or always consistent, but God's grace worked both in helping us to destroy prejudices about how Christians behave as well as helping people to forget our mistakes and see our successful efforts to be like them. We strove to dispel their prejudices against the reliability of the Bible and about the meaning of Christian beliefs. We never initiated apologetic discussions, but we responded as appropriate, bringing conversations back to issues about truth, sin, love, and Jesus' personality.

People cannot see the beauty of Jesus if they can only see our ugliness.

We Built upon What They Knew

No one particular level of contextualization is useful for every society, but it is important to use some form of contextualization. In most cases, it is not good to try to present the gospel as something completely new—from an unknown prophet. We found many Muslims who love Jesus, even if they think that they cannot be his followers, and who even found him to be the most interesting character in the Qur'an, or the first great revolutionary, or who are attracted by his doctrine of peace. Usually it is useful to start with the name and facts that they know about this intriguing figure.

Muslims can better see the beauty of Jesus if the word we use for *Jesus* helps them to know that we are talking about one of *their* prophets, not one of the prophets of the Christians.

They Saw the Beauty of Jesus

We tried to lead people to Jesus by attracting them to his personality and teachings. The key word is *attraction*. Once misunderstandings and prejudices began to be destroyed, and building strongly on ideas accepted by all Muslims about Jesus, we presented the beauty of Christ's teachings about God, human beings, society, religious leaders, and God's kingdom before we talked to them about who Jesus is.

This we learned from the Master himself, who spoke to the first disciples about many things before he taught about himself. When he finally did so, he started with a question: "Who do you think I am?"

The words of Jesus have their greatest power when they convince us not rationally but experientially. Jesus talks about the important things in life: things like God, human nature, sin, family, lust, and greed. We believe him not because he convinces us intellectually but because his teaching "rings true"—it resonates with our experience. We often do not understand what he says. Very often he goes against what seems logical. His way is completely at odds with the way of the strong and the wise (aren't we all trying to be strong and wise?); but we believe him, because repeatedly, against all odds, "it works." We think we are good, and discover that we are unable to keep "the law" or noble "New Year" or "new life" resolutions consistently. We are sure we can fix society with more education, and our best projects end in chaos. We insist that the revolution will solve the problems, and it multiplies them. We affirm that we can manage wealth and power, and they become our masters. We know that we can change the world if religion is in power, and religion in power turns people into rebels and saints into actors and monsters.

So the ways of Jesus become attractive because they agree with our experience. We talk to that inner part of our Muslim friends that says "amen" to the teachings of Jesus. We do not try to defeat them in an argument; we talk to their hearts from our shared humanity.

We do not focus only on the attractiveness of the Lord's teachings, but also on his personality. The Lord is a friend to the friendless, a provider for the poor and needy, a healer for the sick, a loving father for children, a helper of widows, a lifter of the untouchable, a rescuer of discarded and despised people, a champion against religious hypocrites and rich exploiters.

He can be a hero for certain kinds of people: the spiritual beggars, the mourners, the meek (but also, paradoxically, those who seek justice), the merciful (but also those who cannot tolerate sin in their lives), the peacemakers, and even those persecuted for doing the right thing. We introduced him to them as the hero they were looking for, the one who did what they only wished they could do.

Our aim is that Jesus would have the same effect on Muslims that he had on the twelve who confessed, "Master, to whom shall we go? Only you have the words that give eternal life," and on the guards returning, empty-handed, after being sent to apprehend him: "We never heard anyone like him."

We aim towards the effect that caused practical and conservative Jews to say in their hearts: "I don't understand what he is talking about—it sounds gross and offensive, it is not according to what I've been taught since I was little—but I know I can trust the man. He knows what he is doing." We want them to be attracted to the person of Jesus before they are presented the doctrine about Jesus. We've seen Muslims, who believed everything orthodox Muslims are taught to think about Jesus, turn into radical followers of Jesus once they agree that they are sinners and cannot change themselves or society. When they do so, suddenly they have no major problems with Jesus as Savior, Son of God, or even God. They know experientially that his word about other things is the lone true voice. Why shouldn't they trust him in the things he says about himself? Only then will we present in Jesus' own words his extravagant claims.

We Told Them the Truth about Jesus

Once they were attracted to him, we concentrated on talking about Jesus and the essential role he has in the kingdom of God, the future of the world, and their own salvation. Using the story of Pilate, we encouraged them to make a decision of committing themselves to Jesus if they believe he is the salvation of the world, or to otherwise reject him. We explained that there is no neutral moral ground between believing in Jesus and his words and rejecting them.

By this stage, most are already committed to Jesus and believe his words to be true. This in itself is a miracle of grace, but for the first generation of believers it was not synonymous to believe him as the truth and to openly become his followers.

They Saw the Manifestation of the Kingdom of God

It is not enough to talk about the kingdom of God; it must be demonstrated. The Bible says that the kingdom of God is demonstrated in power, not in words. More specifically, it says that the kingdom is characterized by righteousness, peace, and joy and is manifested by the expulsion of evil spirits (Romans 14:17; Luke 11:20).

The first generation of believers, who came to the Lord directly through the expatriate workers in all cases, experienced the manifestation of the kingdom of God. In the first place, the team demonstrated the kingdom of God through good works: living in joy through suffering, showing peace in times of turmoil, taking the side of justice, serving the poor, healing the sick, educating the ignorant, providing for the needy. However, remarkable answers to prayer brought the reality of the kingdom of heaven before the eyes of their friends—sometimes as dreams, visions, healings, and prophecy. Not everyone who experienced the reality of the kingdom in this way became believers. Some even today would ask team members to pray for them when they are sick but would not give their lives to Jesus.

These phenomena still occur regularly but less frequently now that local believers do most of the evangelism, although remarkable healings still happen regularly. Not every prayer on behalf of sick unbelieving friends was answered, yet our Muslim friends did not have problems with God not answering our prayers. They still wanted us to pray again if they were sick.

To see the beauty of Jesus, they needed to see his compassion and care for them in taking the side of justice, sacrificial service, divine guidance, and works of power. Most Muslims are born into a community where they play, study, and suffer together, and in the end they expect to die there. Thus, from the beginning, we emphasized that to be born again in the kingdom of God is about relations, community, and mission—not merely about a "personal relationship" with God.

They Realized There Was a Community to Support Them

The people among whom we lived did everything together and considered the good of the family or community above the good of the individual. While encouraging and working hard to keep all MBBs living with their family (and succeeding in most cases), we also, in a very deep way, became family for the first believers. This was extremely demanding but indispensable. How were they going to believe in the God of love whom we profess if we are less loving than they, or if we did not show love in ways they could understand in their culture?

We encouraged them to share as much as they could about God or Christ with trustworthy friends, family, and neighbors. We explained to them that to be born in the kingdom of God is to be born with a mission—they had the privileged position of stopping the curse on their community and ushering in times of blessing. We told them about people of their own nation who followed Christ a hundred years before them. These believers were not a model for community, but still their spiritual descendants could feel unity with those who lived so long ago.

We also talked to them about other believers as they were coming to Christ (without telling them their names), and we encouraged them to meet as soon as they were ready. We arranged meetings in our home in which they were able to find out that they both were believers; they spent time together, became friends, and discovered that the other person was also a follower of Jesus.

Importantly, we also gave them the freedom to share Christ with others, celebrate as a community, and be bold about the Lord. We demonstrated that we were going to be there with them in the hard times, supporting them, and that same attitude passed on to the church. They never received criticism or were left alone in their problems because of boldness about their relationship with Jesus. In almost all cases, we were able to stay behind the scenes, but they knew that we were ready to take a very public stand if the situation demanded it.

A Patient, Community Approach

The beauty of Jesus is shown in community. The church is his body and his temple in this world. For Muslims to see the beauty of Jesus, they need to see a community committed to him and to each other—a community walking in love, goodness, peace, and joy; a community of people who paradoxically show power and weakness; a community of struggling but overcoming people just like them. They need to see that, even if they are forsaken and rejected by their physical families, they will be embraced in the loving arms of Jesus, manifested in flesh and bone in his church.

Jesus did not arrive from heaven as an adult and say to the monotheistic, legalistic Jews: "I am God Almighty fresh from heaven; and if you, right now, will repent and put your trust in my atoning sacrifice, you will be saved." If we want to share the good news of the gospel with our monotheistic, legalistic Muslim friends we must follow his example—a gradual approach that will lead people to discern the truth and beauty of Jesus' personality, teachings, and life, motivating them to be his followers.

SECTION 4
Concluding Reflections

CHAPTER 21

LOOKING BACK: A PERSONAL REFLECTION

HELEN STEADMAN

One of the privileges of increasing age is the ability to look back over several decades and to trace the hand of God at work on a broad canvas.

I was first alerted to the needs of the Muslim world during my student days in the early 1960s when I read *Torch for Islam*, the challenging biography of George Harris. He served for many years in northwest China without seeing any visible fruit. However, the needs of the immense university student population of Japan soon took first place in my thoughts and prayers as I prepared to serve God in that land. It was only when, several years later, I found myself redirected by God to the student world of Indonesia that the challenge of reaching Muslims for Jesus came back into focus.

The first substantial turnings to Christ among Indonesian Muslims took place in Java in the nineteenth century, leading to the formation of the East and Central Java Christian churches and the much smaller Pasundan church in West Java.[1] However, these ethnic churches adopted many of the outward forms of the Western church and so distanced themselves from the Muslim majority.

I arrived in Indonesia in the late 1960s in the wake of a second great turning to Christ that followed the abortive Communist coup on September 30, 1965. While the greatest number of these new Christians came from a background of traditional religions, there were also substantial turnings among the Javanese, often as a result of disillusionment at the ruthless treatment of suspected Communists by Muslim youth. As I heard story after story of baptisms in the villages of Central Java, how I longed and prayed for a similar movement of the Spirit of God amongst the Muslim peoples of the area where I was based, including almost half of the students to whom I taught science. However, the student Christian group in the university where I was serving was focusing on the urgent need for follow-up among the thousands of new Christians from traditional religious backgrounds. Thus our attempts at outreach to our Muslim colleagues and neighbors were both sporadic and somewhat halfhearted. Why leave the ripe harvest fields in the animistic villages to go to those who showed so little apparent interest in the gospel?

It took the death from cancer of a Muslim colleague to stir me to a deeper concern. He was a good man, and yet he had died without Christ. I had had a number of opportunities to share the good news of Jesus with him, but I had let these slip by from a sense of personal inadequacy and from a fear of misunderstanding. I realized in a new way that God would hold me responsible for my failure. Thus it was with a fresh sense of urgency that I tried to use to the full every opportunity that God gave. In particular, it was a privilege to be allowed to prepare a substantial number of Muslim background believers (MBBs) for baptism, even if most of these were Javanese folk Muslims or women who were planning to marry Christian men.

A move to an almost totally Islamic area of Indonesia gave a new edge to the vision for outreach. It was exciting to find four Indonesian friends who shared the same vision and to spend the following years seeking to reach out to our Muslim neighbors through a whole range of approaches, including Bible correspondence courses, social development projects, and training programs for the tiny group of Christians on campus. However, almost all the members of the small Christian community in the area were newcomers like us, and most believed that evangelism should focus on nominal Christians only. Surely it would be both unwise and dangerous to reach out to our Muslim neighbors! Far better to keep a low profile and pray for a rapid transfer back to a more open area of the country!

Sadly, this attitude was still the norm amongst most Indonesian Christians. Although the steady trickle of MBBs into the Christian church never dried up, it was only the few who were deeply concerned to reach the Muslim majority. These were still the days when it was assumed that all MBBs would join one of the existing churches, all of which were regarded as "centers of Western religion" by our Muslim friends because of their largely noncontextualized outward forms.

The early 1980s brought a move to Java and the privilege of working for a short period alongside a senior MBB church member whom God was using to reach out to Muslims. As an experienced and respected quranic teacher before he turned to Christ, he was quietly sharing the gospel with a steady stream of Muslims who came to his home, as well as writing apologetic literature. Together we visited a number of churches in the capital city, sharing our vision for outreach. However, once again the response was disappointing. Wasn't there enough to do in the Christian community? Shouldn't "care of the sheep and lambs" take priority over other ministry?

A further move east took me to an area where the local congregation of which I was part had around two thousand regular adult members and adherents, over 25 percent of whom were MBBs. Thus we rejoiced to see a steady stream of relatives and friends coming to Christ and joining the church. However, we were still doing very little to actively cross barriers with the gospel and we had not even thought of lowering some of these barriers by using a contextualized approach!

Leaving Indonesia in the mid-1980s gave me the opportunity of observing firsthand what God was doing among Muslims in other parts of East Asia. In countries where there was a relatively strong Christian church, separated by ethnic and linguistic barriers from its Muslim neighbors, the situation seemed to parallel that in Indonesia, usually without even the steady flow of people that we had been privileged to see coming to Christ each year.

Then it seemed that God's time had come. A growing evidence of interest in and prayer for the Muslim world followed the fall of the Communist governments in country after country of Eastern Europe. This growing interest, which was as evident in parts of Asia as it was in the West, was matched by a new desire among Southeast Asian Christians to learn how to share the gospel with their Muslim neighbors. In country after country, local Christians deliberately moved into Muslim areas and sought to share the love of God in Jesus Christ by both life and lip. In some, but by no means all, cases expatriate workers stimulated these initiatives. New contextualized approaches were adopted and slowly small house fellowships of MBBs started to emerge.

With already a large number of MBBs in church membership, Indonesia proved to be particularly ripe for this new low-key approach. Thus it was a privilege to be able to return to Indonesia five years ago to teach missiology in a small theological seminary, at the same time working alongside an Indonesian group supporting local workers in a number of Muslim areas of the country.

As I reflect on many years of active ministry, there seem to me to be a number of things that are important to remember in the context of the growing worldwide focus on the Muslim world:

1. **The ministry in which we are engaged is God's work and not ours.** He it is who calls, equips, and enables as we seek to share the richness of Christ with our Muslim friends. While it appears that it is God's time for a significant increase in the number of MBBs

worldwide, God is sovereign, and it is he who will choose the time for this longed-for breakthrough in each country.

I fear that we are sometimes too caught up with our strategies and methods, sometimes promoted in a competitive spirit as *the* strategy that God is going to use to build his kingdom. Yet it is clear from reports coming in from different parts of the world that God is in fact using a wide range of methods and approaches to bring both individuals and groups to Jesus.

2. **God's work began before we were around!** Without the faithful sowing of the seed over many decades, we would not be seeing the response that we are being privileged to see today. How we thank God for his many, often nameless, servants who served with commitment and zeal without seeing any fruit.

3. **God's primary instrument for bringing the good news of Jesus to those still outside the kingdom is still the local church.** It is distressing to hear our postgraduate students, who are themselves active in outreach to unreached people groups, speak of the arrogance of some expatriate workers who are unwilling to listen to advice from local colleagues. While I recognize that the life of the local church members in predominantly Muslim areas may not always commend the gospel to our non-Christian friends, and while I appreciate the desire to plant contextualized congregations or see insider movements develop, I do not believe that these factors justify us totally bypassing local believers. We are called to pray and work in direct or indirect partnership with those in whose country we are visitors. It is usually they, and not us, who bear the brunt of any negative reaction to our ministry.

4. **In the light of the painful history of Christian-Muslim relationships, we need to ensure that we reach the whole person with the whole gospel in a way that demonstrates the all-surpassing**

love of Jesus. Too often Muslims have heard our words but seen them contradicted by our lives. Too frequently our ulterior motives have been evident, as we offer practical help with apparent strings attached. I am continually challenged by the fact that Jesus loved his enemies, as well as his friends, right to the end. How willing are we to spend and be spent in the service of our Muslim friends, even if we are never able to write wonderful prayer letters about mass turnings to Christ? How prepared are we to suffer for the Lord's sake and thus demonstrate that love which is "stronger than death"? I sometimes detect a disturbing element of triumphalism in our speaking and writing that seems far removed from the Spirit of Jesus.

5. **We must keep the Scriptures at the center of our ministry, whatever methods God may lead us to use.** It is only as we regularly evaluate all our words and deeds in the light of God's revealed Word that we will be kept from the ever-present threat of distortion and error. Likewise we need to help MBBs to experience the work of the Holy Spirit as he guides them "into all truth." How easy it is to see the inconsistencies in the lives of others and yet be blind to areas of our own lives and ministries that are a contradiction of biblical truth!

6. **We cannot, and must not, separate coming to faith from discipleship and becoming part of the body of Christ.** As the Lord leads us to adopt new approaches—insider movements, CPMs, contextualized fellowships, and so on—we need to be even more creative in finding ways of enabling MBBs to experience the power of the gospel to break down centuries-long barriers, as the Spirit of God brings them into fellowship with the one, worldwide body of Christ.

So I conclude these brief reflections with a deep sense of gratitude to God who has allowed me to serve for almost four decades in a predominantly Muslim area of the world. And I look to the future with great anticipation of all that God is going to do in the days ahead. To his name alone be all the glory!

CHAPTER 22

CONCLUSION: LOOKING AHEAD

DAVID SMITH

Reviewing these papers is for me, in a sense, like standing on holy ground. Here we read the chapters of people from many different countries telling us how they and their friends and compatriots have become disciples of Jesus. We hear one story after another of how God has found his way into the lives of individuals, families, and communities. We are reminded by Jean-Marie Gaudeul that "each human conscience is a holy temple where the Lord meets his children and draws them to himself" (chapter 7). I feel like Moses at the burning bush and want to take the shoes off my feet.

Those who gathered for the consultation where these papers were first presented wanted to reflect and discuss, and to analyze what these stories might mean for the worldwide mission of the church today. It has been my opportunity and privilege to read these papers and reflect on them in a more leisurely way. What follows, therefore, is a personal attempt to draw some conclusions and make suggestions about possible ways to move forward.

Some Conclusions about the Process Itself

The questionnaire developed by Dudley Woodberry (chapter 2 and the appendix) has clearly proved to be a highly significant way of eliciting information from a wide variety of different contexts. Answering the questions must have been a valuable experience for the hundreds who have taken part, since it must have forced them to reflect on their experience and ask themselves questions which might never have occurred to them before as being significant.

I very much hope that the evaluation of the responses that have come in and will continue to come in will be just as thorough and painstaking as the process of preparing the questions and gathering the replies. This evaluation probably needs to be done by a group and not just an individual, since all of us inevitably filter everything that we read and miss important messages which might be picked up by others. Here is an opportunity for continuing interaction between new believers, evangelists, teachers, and scholars of different kinds. All of this needs to be seen as an ongoing process, with believers from new situations being asked to answer the questionnaire. And as the process continues in the coming years, the questionnaire itself may need to be refined and developed in different ways, perhaps probing more deeply in certain areas and sometimes asking new sets of questions.

Three Significant Factors Which *All* Christians Need to Know

When teaching Christians over a number of years about relating to Muslims, I have often pointed out three major factors in the experience of those who have become disciples of Jesus. In reading these chapters, I have been relieved to find that this simple message isn't too wide of the mark. I suspect, therefore, that it needs to be an important part of any program of education and training for Christians. *Every* Christian in *all* our churches needs to know that in almost every case of Muslims coming to faith in Jesus at least two—and sometimes all three—of the following three factors have been at work.

Muslim Converts Have Seen and Experienced Sacrificial Love Shown by Christians

In these chapters we have seen one example after another of Muslims who have been impressed and attracted by the lives of the Christians they have observed. The quality of their lives and in particular their sacrificial love have made a deep impression. Writing in a West African context, for example, about interaction that took place over many years, Lowell de Jong observes that

> One key factor was close contact with Christians over a long period of time. . . . Our acts of compassion (projects, assistance to the poor, patience in the face of harassment, etc.) unsettled . . . many Fulbe's perceptions of Christians. How was it that these "pagans" who did not know Allah correctly could act like such good Muslims? Why was God's favor on them, predestining them for righteous acts, when they were not Muslims? (chapter 17)

For some in Central Asia we find that "when disappointed and hopeless, they see love between the Christian brothers and sisters, and they are interested to hear about Christ" (chapter 12). Christel Eric states powerfully the priority of relationships over apologetics when she writes: "My main focus in reaching out to Muslim women is not so much how can I *convince* the person, but how I can truly *love* her" (chapter 11).

Muslim Converts Have Read Some Portion of Scripture

In his chapter on the role of Scripture in Muslims coming to Christ, David Maranz observes this about Muslim conversions: "In most, the role of the Bible or some passages of Scripture were central to conversion. How could it be otherwise?" He quotes words of Robert Brow to summarize the importance of this factor: "When Muslims actually get to read the Bible, they find it presents a vast compelling picture. Getting people to read the Bible for themselves is a high priority" (chapter 5).

We could hardly ask for a clearer statement of the need to make the text of Scripture available as widely as possible through every available medium.

Muslim Converts Have Experienced a Special Manifestation of the Power of Christ

Almost every chapter speaks of individuals who, through dreams, visions, or healings, have experienced the power of God mediated through Jesus. Mary McVicker, for example, writes that "*experiencing* Jesus is the primary ingredient for Muslim women coming to faith in South Asia. . . . When women have access to God's Word, combined with supernatural revelation like visions or feeling the presence of Jesus, seeing an act of God confirms biblical truth, and this *experiential knowledge* guides them to faith" (chapter 10).

This is such a constant theme that we are forced to conclude that the Spirit of God, in seeking to gain entrance into people's lives, seems *at certain stages* to bypass the intellect to bring them face to face with the living Christ. When they see Jesus in a dream or witness a healing in the name of Jesus, they *experience his power* even before they fully *understand his identity*. It may be only later that they come to understand more fully who Jesus is and how precisely he has overcome the powers of evil.

Some Lessons about How Christians Should Be Praying

If, as Dan McVey suggests, "prayer is the primary tool of evangelism" (chapter 15), how precisely should Christians be praying?

For many years I have seen the prayer of the early church recorded in Acts 4:23–31 as a model of how Christians in the Muslim world should be praying about their witness. After their release from prison, the apostles

Peter and John meet with the church and together raise their voices in united prayer. They begin by acknowledging God as Creator and as the sovereign Lord of creation and of history and then go on to pray: "Now, Lord, consider their threats . . . " (Acts 4:29). Many chapters in this book show that in most situations the threat to Muslims who want to follow Christ—the threat of rejection, verbal and physical abuse, banishment from the family and the community, and even sometimes murder—is very real. Although the Law of Apostasy is not actually part of the law of most Islamic countries, the concept is still deeply ingrained in the minds of Muslims. This prayer of the early church begins by recognizing the seriousness of the issues at stake.

What the first Christians actually pray for, however, is highly in-structive. Instead of praying for protection and deliverance, they make only one request for themselves: " . . . and enable your servants to speak your word with great boldness." (Acts 4:29). They ask God to deliver them from fear, giving them courage and boldness to communicate the message about Jesus as fully as they can. Then, recognizing their own powerlessness in a difficult situation, they ask God to act in his sovereign power by touching the lives of the people around them: "Stretch out your hand to heal and perform miraculous signs and wonders through the name of your holy servant Jesus" (Acts 4:30). God's answer to the prayer is immediate and dramatic: "After they prayed, the place where they were meeting was shaken. And they were all filled with the Holy Spirit and spoke the word of God boldly" (Acts 4:31).

The chapter on Daristan shows how Christians became bolder as a result of their praying and witnessing. "By far the most important factor," we are told, "was local believers sharing their faith with family, friends, and contacts. Prior to this time most local believers had been fearful of doing so, and the national church had been cautious about new people coming into their gatherings. This fear was broken" (chapter 19). We find today, therefore, that when Christians pray in the same terms as the early church did, they develop a new sense of expectancy and will not be surprised when they find that God has touched peoples' lives.

Work That Remains to Be Done

Reading these papers makes one very aware of many significant developments in the last twenty or thirty years. But there can be no room for complacency, since there are so many areas where important lessons need to be learned in order to make our Christian witness stronger and clearer. What follows, therefore, is my own personal suggestion of ten areas in which important work remains to be done. They are not listed in order of priority, and are not offered in a spirit of criticism. This is simply my attempt to dream dreams and to ask: If this is what has already happened and is still happening before our eyes, what *could happen* and what *might still happen*? If we can put some of these lessons into practice more effectively, *how much more* could we witness in the coming years?

Focusing on Discipleship

While all of these chapters concentrate on the process of Muslims coming to faith in Jesus, many of them also touch on what is involved in discipling new believers. Some Christian workers would say that if the task of bringing people to an initial commitment is hard, the process of enabling them to grow and develop as believers who are integrated into some kind of Christian fellowship is often even harder. If we put time and energy into developing and sharing resources for evangelism, therefore, perhaps we need to put just as much energy into developing and sharing resources for discipleship.

Several writers here recognize that not all of those who come to a real faith continue in their discipleship, and some return to their Islamic faith and community. The research carried out by Patrick Sookhdeo of the Barnabas Trust some years ago suggested that the proportion of new believers who return to Islam is remarkably high. Could it be, therefore, that alongside the analysis of the testimonies of those who have come to faith there needs to be a more rigorous and honest study of the reasons why many do not continue in their Christian faith? Many of the reasons are no doubt obvious and are reflected in these chapters: pressure from the family and the Muslim community, economic hardship, difficulties within the Christian community, and the emotional strain involved in finding a new identity. Perhaps this should not be surprising, since the New Testament contains many examples of disciples who fall away in one way or another. But if we can admit that it may sometimes be *our* failings that make them go back, we might have to rethink much of our practice and our proclamation.

Developing a Theology of Suffering

Writing in the Central Asian context, Hasan Abdulahugli states the simple truth, demonstrated all over the world, that persecution is normal. "When someone comes to faith in Christ, they are immediately persecuted" (chapter 12). Dudley Woodberry, in his survey, notes the importance of "biblical teaching on the role of suffering" alongside "ministries of healing and power" (chapter 2). And Evelyne Reisacher is very honest about her awareness of the enduring pain felt by women:

During this research, something puzzled me. I know these women well, and the joy that they have to follow Jesus. I have observed their zeal, their commitment, and their deep bond with God over the years; yet I found that these women expressed more difficulties, concern, and heavy-heartedness than joy. Perhaps they knew me well enough to feel confident to share deep concerns spontaneously. To someone less close to them, they might have revealed another mood. Or maybe the issues they mentioned are still unresolved and painful. (chapter 9)

291

I remember hearing Kenneth Cragg speaking many years ago in Cairo about the significance of Peter's first reaction to the announcement that Jesus would have to suffer (Mark 8:27–38). He suggested that Peter's reaction of horror, which says in effect, "If you are the Christ of God, how is it possible that you could have to *suffer*?" could be very close to the traditional thinking of Muslims: "How is it conceivable that Almighty God could allow his prophet and apostle on earth to suffer and die in such a humiliating way?" It may be, therefore, that Peter's first epistle, written around thirty years after the crucifixion to prepare the scattered Christians in Asia Minor for increased persecution from the authorities, is especially appropriate for reflecting on the response to suffering among believers from a Muslim background. Peter has come to understand the divine logic that demands that Jesus had to suffer, and the corollary that his disciples also are bound to suffer: "Christ suffered for you, leaving you an example, that you should follow in his steps" (1 Peter 2:21).

Further confirmation of the special significance of 1 Peter in this context has recently come to me from a rather unexpected source—a summary of a recent doctoral thesis on this letter:

> The present study aims to show that the author's overarching concern, in response to the persecutions faced by these young churches, is with the formation of Christian character, which is chiefly evinced in growing active dependence upon God and growing moral integrity. The author's seemingly paradoxical response to the sufferings of his addressees is the repeated command to "do good." In this, the author reveals that his deepest concern is with the *moral* challenges that arise out of the pain of social ostracism. Temptations to retaliation, assimilation or isolating themselves threaten Christian convictions and praxis, and the author's aim in confronting these temptations is to en-

courage these Christians to maintain their distinctive lifestyle, from which their persecutions arise, and in so doing to facilitate Christian character formation. . . . He seeks to turn persecution into an opportunity for growth in Christian character instead of an occasion for despondency.[1]

A theology of suffering will need this kind of biblical starting point, and at the same time to be informed by the kind of reflection that took place at a consultation held in Nigeria in July 1999 under the title "Suffering and Power in Christian-Muslim Relations: The Political Challenge of Islam Today and Its Implications for the Church in Education and Mission."[2]

Practicing Appropriate Contextualization

Lowell de Jong's chapters on the Fulbe include a fine summary of the vision of contextualization: "Our primal vision was to see the gospel well up from deep inside Fulbe culture, deeply embedded inside Fulbe hearts both theologically and philosophically" (chapter 16). Edward Evans (chapter 13) quotes a question from Kenneth Cragg which sums up one of the basic motives of everyone who shares this kind of vision: "What . . . can be done to encourage in Islam the truth that becoming a Christian is not ceasing to belong with Muslim need, Muslim thought and Muslim kin?"

Dan McVey describes the positive impact of a serious attempt to contextualize Christian belief and practice in context: "The infusion of Christian faith and life into the rituals of naming ceremonies, funerals, weddings, communal labor, and festivals such as harvest and those dedicated to expressions of loyalty to chiefs has gone far in opening the doors for proclamation" (chapter 15). And Lowell de Jong describes the approach of those who have rejected the model of "extraction" in favor of the model of "embedding":

I walk with our new believers as they wrestle with the gospel, apply it to their lives, and communicate it to their peers. They are taking me down paths little visited in my mind and walk with Christ. I can do little more than walk with them, observe them, and keep their feet anchored in the Bible. They must take the lead and set the agenda. I am confident that they, filled with the Spirit, will in time plant the gospel deeply in Fulbe culture, more effectively and more profoundly than Islam was implanted some 400 years ago. And out of this movement of the Spirit, the church will emerge. (chapter 16)

All this should be an incentive to explore further the different possibilities of contextualization. There are clearly many different approaches which are being adopted in different contexts. At one end of the spectrum are those who encourage new believers to integrate as fully as possible into existing churches. At the other end are those who encourage them to stay within their families, communities, and even within the mosque, doing so in the name of Jesus. Many would defend some of the more extreme positions partly because they minimize persecution and partly because they make it possible for a wider circle of people to be influenced. Whatever positions are taken along this spectrum, the debate about the limits of contextualization needs to continue.[3]

Exploring Ecclesiological Issues

Evangelical Christians do not often get excited about the doctrine of the church, preferring to get on with the practical job of "planting churches." What has often happened, therefore, is that if they are working in an area where there are no existing churches, they introduce something like the church order of the denominations from which they themselves come.

Several chapters in this book suggest that the situation now may well be changing, since they contain examples of situations where new models are being explored. The chapter on Central Asia, for example, underlines the importance of small house groups and the kind of elders described in the New Testament (chapter 12). In Daristan we see the gradual evolution of appropriate models in which church structures develop naturally—not imposed by missionaries. It is "much better if the emerging church can form its own structures over time without the baggage that expatriates (and their videos, teaching materials, etc.) often bring with them" (chapter 19). And from the Fulbe context de Jong emphasizes the need for genuine patience in this process: "Following Muslim example, should not missionaries give new believers 'the reins' by permitting them to remain as an informal Bible study and prayer group, for years if necessary—giving them time to contextualize and develop a church at their own pace and time for natural, culturally acceptable leadership to emerge?" (chapter 16).

If these models are seen to work over an extended period of time in certain situations, somewhere along the line further questions will need to be faced. How, for example, should they celebrate the Lord's Supper, and how should they baptize? How should the different groups in one place, area, or country relate to each other? How open and public can they be, and should they at any stage seek some kind of recognition from the authorities? How will they relate to believers in other countries and to the worldwide church? Whether we like it or not, answering these questions will force us to reflect seriously on our doctrine of the church and to study the first few centuries of the church's history.

Working on a Theology of Islam

"Good theology," says Jim Tebbe, "does not always produce good mission, but no theology or bad theology will certainly produce bad mission" (chapter 6). One fundamental theological question which needs to be faced at every stage concerns the way we think about Islam. How do the missionaries think about the nature of Islam? And how do new believers come to think about the religion in which they have been nurtured? Do they think of it as something totally misguided and which they need to repudiate, or simply as something inadequate and defective because it has not led them to see the fuller revelation of God in Christ? Questions of this kind are raised by Lowell de Jong's honest reflection on the development of his thinking as a Christian missionary among Muslims:

> In my earlier years I respected Islam before the people, and would use verses from the Qur'an to support my point of view, but in my heart I thought of Islam as Enemy Number One. My basic heart attitude was at odds with the stated goal of my ministry: to embed Jesus into the Muslim Fulbe worldview and belief system. However, in order to embed Jesus into a world-view and belief system, one must be willing to enter therein, walk along with that worldview and belief system as far as is biblically possible, and bring Jesus as the answer to the issues within it. I am not proposing that missionaries become neo-Muslims. Rather, in restudying Islam with a renewed attitude during the past two years, I am realizing that Christianity and qur'anic Islam can indeed walk a long way together. Islam can be viewed as a resource which can be employed in the cause of Christ. (chapter 17)

What we see reflected here is a gradual transformation of attitudes that has taken place in the mind of a group of missionaries over a period of many years. They set out on their ministry with very negative views about Islam, but are forced to change some of their ideas not for tactical reasons but rather because of their study of the Qur'an and their deep and ongoing engagement with enquirers and new believers.

Christians working among Muslims may therefore need to wrestle much more seriously with these two approaches to Islam which exist uneasily side by side. On the one hand there are those who believe (and sometimes even say to Muslims) that Islam is a religion inspired by

Satan, and that the God of Islam is "totally different" from the God of Christianity. On the other hand there are those who, while recognizing all the ways in which Islam seems to deny fundamental elements of the gospel, want to build on all the genuine common ground that there is and who insist that Muslims and Christians are seeking to worship the same Being, even though their concepts and experience of that Being may be different. We are not likely to be able to resolve these issues overnight. But de Jong's testimony shows very clearly that the way that Christians *relate to Muslims* is bound to be affected profoundly by what they *think about Islam.*

Adapting Our Apologetic

Dudley Woodberry's questionnaire enquires about the variety of ways in which Muslims have encountered presentations of the gospel, and one of these questions is directly related to the role of apologetics: "Were there any Christian beliefs or teachings which made it difficult for you to become a Christian or which are still difficult?" I wonder, however, whether we might need to ask several further questions to discover the different stages by which Muslims come to question traditional Islamic ideas about the Trinity, the deity of Christ, the crucifixion, and the integrity of the Bible. How helpful did they find the answers given by Christians? And as they gradually come to see God, Jesus, and the Bible in a new light, do they want to express their new beliefs in precisely the way that the Christians have described them? Were they totally convinced, for example, by the explanations they were given about Jesus being "the Son of God" and about the meaning of the crucifixion? Having come to see Jesus as "more than a prophet," do they use the same language that the Christians used earlier with them, or are they developing new ways of explaining the message which make more sense to Muslims?

Many generations of missionaries have been brought up on Carl Pfander's *Balance of Truth*, which was originally written in 1829 and later revised and translated into many different languages. The fact that it was reprinted in English as recently as 1986 suggests that it has stood the test of time. At the same time there is today a growing awareness of the limitations of some aspects of Pfander's approach. In teaching about these subjects over a number of years I have found Jean-Marie Gaudeul's *Encounters and Clashes: Islam and Christianity in History*[4] an invaluable resource for enabling students to understand the variety of approaches that have been used in debate between Christians and Muslims from the beginning to the present day.

I would suggest that there are four areas in particular where we may need to be asking questions about our apologetic approaches:

- Is it ever appropriate for Christians to attack Muslim beliefs and practices? Is it ever right to say anything critical about Muhammad?

- Is there a clear distinction between polemics and apologetics, and if so where do we draw the line between them?

- Is it possible to have genuine theological dialogue with Muslims?

- How valuable are public debates, and what are the most productive ways that they should be staged?

Instead of using all the same well-worn arguments, we may need to explore fresh ways of commending the faith, making more use of the experience of new believers.

Understanding the Different Kinds of Islam and Muslims

What is Islam? How are we to understand the enormous variety in the expressions of Islam reflected in these chapters? Some of the basic textbooks on Islam written by Christians describe something that is clear and precise, but bears little resemblance to the faith and practice of the Muslims whose experience is described in these chapters. Chapter 12, for example, describes a situation in which nominal Muslims experiencing new political freedom after decades under atheistic communism become much more interested in their Islamic faith. Lowell de Jong's chapters on the Fulbe give a very helpful description of what Islam is like in many parts of Africa after 400 years of development: "Islam has been integrated into Fulbe culture to form a mature, stable entity: what we might call Fulbe Islam. . . . The result is a very African Islam . . . a very Fulbe, but essentially Muslim, Islam" (chapter 16).

Does this suggest that we need to give much more thought to the way we describe Islam? Woodberry's questionnaire asks the simple question: "To what category of Islam did you belong? (Sunni, Shi'a, Sufi, Folk)." I wonder, however, whether we might need to ask a lot more questions than this about the kind of Islam from which these new believers have come. I would be interested to find out what proportion of the new believers, for example, were committed, practicing Muslims, and how many were merely nominal. Are Shi'ites generally more open to the gospel than Sunnis? If the more pietistic Muslims find in Christ the fulfillment of their spiritual longings, how many who have come to faith have been very committed politically and driven by a strong sense of justice? How much of what we observe is related to "Islam" and how much to local culture? If we recognize the enormous differences between different cultural and political contexts, should we not also recognize the significant differences between men and women, as Evelyne Reisacher does in her account of believers of North African origin (chapter 9)? The enormous differences among Muslims is leading many to be much more cautious over generalizations about "Islam," as if it is something monolithic that can easily be described, and to speak far more about "Muslims" than about "Islam."

Addressing Political Issues

Some chapters refer to factors in the political context which played some part in people coming to faith. Dudley Woodberry, for example, points out that political upheavals in Iran and Pakistan led to increased openness to the gospel (chapter 2). The creation of the new sovereign republics in the former Soviet Union has created a greater openness to the Christian message (chapter 12). And the effects of 9/11 are noted in Pakistan (chapter 13). Andreas Maurer describes how in the context of South Africa "a person is motivated for sociopolitical reasons to change his/her religious allegiance" (chapter 8). We learn that in Central Asia: "More than a decade after the fall of communism and state-sponsored atheism, the vast majority of nominal Muslims here are seeking God with renewed zeal. Many are turning to a revitalized commitment to stricter Islamic practice. . . . However . . . life is difficult and Central Asian Muslims are increasingly open to the gospel" (chapter 12).

Because of the example of Muhammad in engaging in *hijrah* (the flight of Muhammad and his followers from Mecca to Medina in 622) in order to establish the first Islamic community in Medina, it is hardly surprising that Islam appears to be a very political religion. Western, "Christian" imperialism brought almost all the Muslim world under its control for more than a century; and although the earlier forms of imperialism ended around the middle of the twentieth century, new forms of imperialism—cultural, economic, and political—live on in almost all the situations of conflict between Muslims and non-Muslims. I therefore wonder whether more attention needs to be paid to political issues in our dialogue with those who have come to faith. There are only two questions in the questionnaire that touch on political issues: "Are you a Christian because of the influence of any of the following: Political circumstances? Economic circumstances?" And "Were there social or political influences which made it difficult for you to become a Christian or remain a Christian?" I suspect, however, that these questions may not be worded clearly enough to elicit the information we may need to have about the importance of the bigger political issues.

It may be appropriate to raise in this context the question of the American-led occupation of Iraq and the effect it is likely to have on Christian-Muslim relations in the future. The declared motives for the American and British invasion of Iraq in May 2003 were the removal of Saddam Hussein from power and the prevention of attacks with weapons of mass destruction. Most observers would add, however, that other important motives included the desire to safeguard oil supplies for the West, to protect Israel, and to reshape the Middle East in accordance with American interests. The violent attacks on Christian churches in Iraq demonstrate that Christians in Iraq are associated in the minds of Muslim extremists with the so-called "Christian West" that is waging war on the Muslim East. An American Christian scholar of Islam who has worked for many years in the Arab world told me recently that he believed that nothing had done more damage to Christian-Muslims relations since the start of the First Crusade in 1096 than the recent war in Iraq. If we live in the proverbial global village, we shouldn't be surprised if these events continue for many decades to come to have a profound effect on the ordinary Muslim's perception of "Christians" and "Christianity."

Challenging Christian Zionism

Many recent studies suggest that Western (and particularly American) one-sided support for the state of Israel has been *a* major—if not *the* major—factor in the anger of Muslims towards the West. Many missionaries, especially in the Arab world, testify to the fact that the enthusiastic support of Israel given by many evangelical Christians (especially in the United States) is a major stumbling block for the gospel. The message from Muslims seems to be: "If you Christians are supporting—for theological reasons—something that seems to us to be fundamentally unjust, how can you expect us to even open our minds to consider your message?"

I therefore find myself puzzling over the gap between the testimonies recorded here in these pages and the testimonies of missionaries. Are we to conclude that, for those Muslims who have become disciples of Jesus, Zionism and Israel have never been the major concern that we have been told they are for most Muslims? Is it that the vast majority of these Muslims have never been very interested in political issues? Or is it that there is nothing in the questionnaire itself (or the other studies) that would elicit a response expressing concern about this issue in the minds of Muslims? I'm surprised, in fact, that the question "Were there social or political influences which made it difficult for you to become a Christian or to remain a Christian?" does not include the issue of Zionism and Israel as one possible answer.

Many Christians believe that Christian support for Israel continues to be a major factor influencing Muslims against Christianity, and that many in this position remain hardened against the gospel. Could it not be that a more evenhanded approach to the Israeli-Palestinian conflict among Christians might lead to a much greater openness to the gospel among Muslims? If Muslims could see individual Christians *and* what they perceive as "the Christian West" hungering and thirsting after righteousness/justice and being genuine peacemakers between Israel and the Palestinians, might they be much more open to considering the gospel?

Studying Conversion to *Islam*

Beyond the question of conversion *from* Islam *to* Christianity, should we not also be paying at least some attention to conversion *from* Christianity *to* Islam? Writing about Pakistan, Edward Evans points out that more convert from Christianity to Islam than from Islam to Christianity. And in the South African context Andreas Maurer notes: "It should be acknowledged that conversion moves both ways. . . . Christians need . . .

to see conversion as not just a one-way but a two-way movement. . . . The conversion door swings both ways." He states very clearly that one major factor for those who converted to Islam was their rejection of the racist policies of apartheid, which for many years were undergirded by Christian teaching, and acknowledges that "five out of ten converts from Christianity to Islam indicated that the sociopolitical situation in South Africa was a reason for them to convert to Islam" (chapter 8).

When some convert to Islam because of their desire to be part of a close-knit community, Christians need to be challenged about the kind of community they are modeling in their churches and fellowships. If some convert because they are attracted to the simplicity of Islamic theology, should Christians be asking themselves whether they are prepared to take Islamic categories more seriously and express their faith and life in ways that are less offensive to Muslims? And if a number (especially in the West) are attracted by Sufism, does this not suggest that Christians should give much more attention to the study and practice of Christian spirituality? In our excitement over those who have come to faith in Christ, some sober reflection of movement the other way could lead to some valuable soul-searching.

Conclusion

Having begun with Moses at the burning bush and his awareness that he was standing on holy ground (Exodus 3:5), I end with Joshua and his vision that "very much of the land still remains to be possessed" (Joshua 13:1 NIV; NRSV reads: "There are still very large areas of land to be taken over"). I am not thinking of territorial conquest, of course, but rather of individuals, families, and whole communities coming into the kingdom of God as disciples of Jesus. Every chapter in this book speaks of significant developments and advances in the progress of the gospel among Muslims, for which we will want to be thankful. But if we can build on what has been achieved and learned in recent decades, who knows *how much more land there might be to be possessed?*

APPENDIX

If you would like to participate in the ongoing survey referred to in the chapter by Dudley Woodberry, please return completed copies of this form to him at <dudley@fuller.edu> or at:

Fuller Theological Seminary
School of Intercultural Studies
Pasadena, CA 91182
USA

You may also contact him at that address to request this form in Microsoft Word format for easier reproduction and use.

———

Your Spiritual Journey

Questionnaire

Please help us understand the spiritual journey which various people have taken as they have come to believe in Jesus Christ by answering the following questions about your own journey or that of another person that you know well.

1. Where did you live when you first became interested in becoming a believer in Jesus Christ?

_____ City _____ Town _____ Village

2. How long did you live there?

_____ 0–1 year _____ 1–2 years _____ 3–5 years _____ 5+ years

3. Where do you live now?

_____ City _____ Town _____ Village

4. How long have you lived there?

_____ 0–1 year _____ 1–2 years _____ 3–5 years _____ 5+ years

5. What country do you live in? _____

6. To what ethnic group do you belong? _____

7. To what category of Islam did you belong?

_____ Sunni _____ Shi'a _____ Sufi _____ Folk

_____ Other

Comments:

_____

_____

Did any of the following contribute to your conversion?			No	Some	Much
20	Literature (books, tracts, Bible por-tions, etc.)?	Before Conversion			
21		At Conversion			
22		After Conversion			
23	Radio?	Before Conversion			
24		At Conversion			
25		After Conversion			
26	TV or video?	Before Conversion			
27		At Conversion			
28		After Conversion			
29	Bible study group?	Before Conversion			
30		At Conversion			
31		After Conversion			
32	Bible correspon-dence course?	Before Conversion			
33		At Conversion			
34		After Conversion			
35	Medical program (hospital, clinic, etc.)?	Before Conversion			
36		At Conversion			
37		After Conversion			
38	Educational program (Christian school, college, literacy program, etc.)?	Before Conversion			
39		At Conversion			
40		After Conversion			

41	Relief or develop-ment program?	Before Conversion			
42		At Conversion			
43		After Conversion			
44	Personal witness by one or more people?	Before Conversion			
45		At Conversion			
46		After Conversion			
47	Large evangelistic meetings or rallies?	Before Conversion			
48		At Conversion			
49		After Conversion			
50	Theological debate or dialogue with Christians?	Before Conversion			
51		At Conversion			
52		After Conversion			
53	Audio cassettes?	Before Conversion			
54		At Conversion			
55		After Conversion			

Comments:

_____

_____

_____

Are you a Christian because of the influence of any of the following?			No	Some	Much
56	Political circumstances?	Before Conversion			
57		At Conversion			
58		After Conversion			

59	Economic circumstances?	Before Conversion			
60		At Conversion			
61		After Conversion			

Comments:

_____

_____

_____

Were there certain experiences which influenced you towards faith in Christ?			No	Some	Much
62	Observing the life-style of a particular Christian or group of Christians?	Before Conversion			
63		At Conversion			
64		After Conversion			
65	Healing from illness?	Before Conversion			
66		At Conversion			
67		After Conversion			
68	Visions or dreams?	Before Conversion			
69		At Conversion			
70		After Conversion			
71	Answered prayer?	Before Conversion			
72		At Conversion			
73		After Conversion			
74	Miracles or observing the power of Christ in a specific situation?	Before Conversion			
75		At Conversion			
76		After Conversion			

77	Dissatisfaction with Muslims or Islam?	Before Conversion			
78		At Conversion			
79		After Conversion			

Comments:

_____

_____

_____

Were there any Christian beliefs or teachings which made it difficult for you to become a Christian or which are still difficult?			No	Some	Much
107	The Christian doctrine of the Trinity?	Before Conversion			
108		At Conversion			
109		After Conversion			
110	The Incarnation of Jesus as the Son of God?	Before Conversion			
111		At Conversion			
112		After Conversion			

Comments:

_____

_____

_____

Were there social or political influences which made it difficult for you to become a Christian or remain a Christian?			No	Some	Much
113	Pressure from Muslim family members?	Before Conversion			
114		At Conversion			
115		After Conversion			
116	Pressure from the Muslim community?	Before Conversion			
117		At Conversion			
118		After Conversion			
119	Conversion forbidden by law?	Before Conversion			
120		At Conversion			
121		After Conversion			
122	The Christian church did not welcome you or worshiped in ways that are foreign?	Before Conversion			
123		At Conversion			
124		After Conversion			

Comments:

_____

_____

_____

Did you have any of the following ideas about Christianity which made it difficult to become a Christian or to remain a Christian?			No	Some	Much
125	Christianity is a Western religion?	Before Conversion			
126		At Conversion			
127		After Conversion			
128	Christianity has persecuted or exploited Muslims?	Before Conversion			
129		At Conversion			
130		After Conversion			
131	Christians have a secular lifestyle, low morality, etc.?	Before Conversion			
132		At Conversion			
133		After Conversion			

Comments:

_____

_____

_____

To your knowledge, do you regard any of the following factors as important to your experience as a Christian?			No	Some	Much
134	There was already a Christian church in this area?	Before Conversion			
135		At Conversion			
136		After Conversion			
137	The forms of worship in the church were ones with which I could feel comfortable?	Before Conversion			
138		At Conversion			
139		After Conversion			

140	Other Christians made me feel welcome in their fellowship?	Before Conversion			
141		At Conversion			
142		After Conversion			

Comments:

_____

_____

_____

143 Are you male or female?

_____ Male ___ Female

ENDNOTES

CHAPTER 1

1. Surah 1:6, Matthew 7:14.

2. Greg Livingstone, *Planting Churches in Muslim Cities* (Grand Rapids: Baker, 1993), 154.

3. Stanley H. Skreslet, "Doctoral Dissertations on Mission: Ten-Year Update, 1992–2001," *International Bulletin of Missionary Research* 27, no. 3 (July 2003).

4. Richard Peace, *Conversion in the New Testament: Paul and the Twelve* (Grand Rapids: Eerdmans), 286.

5. Andrew F. Walls, "Converts or Proselytes? The Crisis over Conversion in the Early Church," *International Bulletin of Missionary Research* 28, no. 1 (January 2004).

CHAPTER 2

1. Avery T. Willis Jr., *Indonesian Revival: Why Two Million Came to Christ* (Pasadena: William Carey Library, 1977).

CHAPTER 3

1. Phenomenology, in a simple sense, can be defined as "what people think is going on." Ontology is "what is really going on," and in particular as seen by God.

CHAPTER 4

1. Clifford Geertz, *Islam Observed: Religious Development in Morocco and Indonesia* (Chicago: University of Chicago Press, 1971), 4. "Antipodes" refers to the opposite ends of the earth.

2. James F. Engel and H. Wilbert Norton, *What's Gone Wrong with the Harvest?* (Grand Rapids: Zondervan, 1975), <www.newwway.org/engel/>. See also "An Interpersonal Communication Model: The Engel Scale Explained" at <www.gospelcom.net/guide/resources/tellitoften.php>.

3. Viggo Søgaard, *Media in Church and Mission: Communicating the Gospel* (Pasadena: William Carey Library, 1993). Søgaard's added dimension highlights changed attitude toward God and the gospel.

4. Paul C. Vitz, *Psychology as Religion: The Cult of Self-Worship* (Grand Rapids: Eerdmans, 1977, 1986), 10.

5. Gustave Edmund von Grunebaum, "The Cultural Function of the Dream as Illustrated by Classical Islam," in *The Dream and Human Societies*, ed. Gustave Edmund von Grunebaum and Roger Caillois (Berkeley: University of California Press, 1966), 3–21.

6. Hannes Wiher, *Shame and Guilt: A Key to Cross-Cultural Ministry* (Bonn: Edition IWG, Mission Academics, Band 10, Verlag für Kultur und Wissenschaft, 2003), 367. This quotation makes reference in the original to Robert Priest, "Missionary Elenctics: Conscience and Culture," *Missiology* XXII: 291–306.

7. Andrew Walls, "Converts or Proselytes? The Crisis over Conversion in the Early Church," *International Bulletin of Missionary Research* (January 2004): 2–6.

8. Paul Hiebert, *Anthropological Reflections on Missiological Issues* (Grand Rapids: Baker, 1994), chap. 6.

9. Harvie M. Conn, "The Muslim Convert and His Culture," in *The Gospel and Islam,* ed. Don McCurry (MARC: Monrovia, CA, 1979), 103–104.

10. Karl Georg Kuhn, *Theological Dictionary of the New Testament*, Vol. VI, trans. and ed. by Geoffrey W. Bromiley (Grand Rapids: Eerdmans, 1975), 727–44; and Ulrich Becker, *New International Dictionary of New Testament Theology*, Vol. 1, ed. by Colin Brown (Grand Rapids: Zondervan, 1986), 359–62.

11. Walls, "Converts or Proselytes?" 6.

12. Lewis R. Rambo, *Understanding Religious Conversion* (New Haven, CT: Yale University Press, 1993), 42.

13. David Britt, "From Homogeneity to Congruence: A Church-Community Model," *Urban Mission* 8, no. 3 (January 1991): 27–41.

14. Gabriël Jansen, "Reaching Moroccans in Amsterdam (the Netherlands) with the Gospel," (master's thesis, Tyndale Theological Seminary, Bad Hoevedorp, the Netherlands, 2000), 130.

15. David Greenlee, "Christian Conversion from Islam: Social, Cultural, Communication, and Supernatural Factors in the Process of Conversion and Faithful Church Participation," PhD diss., (Trinity International University, Deerfield, IL, 1996).

16. Or Hindu, as reported by Herbert E. Hoefer, *Churchless Christianity* (Pasadena: William Carey Library, 1991, 2001).

17. See Joshua Massey, "God's Amazing Diversity in Drawing Muslims to Christ," *International Journal of Frontier Missions* 17, no. 1 (spring 2000): 3–14.

18. For a detailed discussion see Rick Love, *Muslims, Magic and the Kingdom of God* (Pasadena: William Carey Library, 2000).

19. Søgaard, *Media in Church and Mission*.

20. Donald Smith, *Creating Understanding* (Grand Rapids: Zondervan, 1992), 142–43.

21. Donald G. Bloesch, "Conversion," in *Evangelical Dictionary of Theology*, ed. Walter A. Elwell (Carlisle, UK: Paternoster, and Grand Rapids: Baker Books, 1994).

CHAPTER 5

1. *The International Standard Bible Encyclopedia*, 1956, s.v. "conversion."

2. The sources of testimonies used in this paper were the following sites: <www.answeringislam.org>, <www.arabicbible.com>, <www.exmuslim.com>, <www.the-good-way.com>, and <www.thegoodnews.org>.

3. J. Dudley Woodberry and Russell G. Shubin, "Muslims Tell: Why I Chose Jesus," *Mission Frontiers* (March 2001), cited on <www.brow.on.ca/Articles/MuslimCh.htm>.

4. Paul-Gordon Chandler, "Mazhar Mallouhi: Gandhi's Living Christian Legacy in the Muslim World," *International Bulletin of Missionary Research* 27, no. 2 (April 2003): 54–59.

CHAPTER 6

1. Byron L. Haines and Frank L. Cooley, eds., *Christians and Muslims Together: An Exploration by Presbyterians* (Philadelphia: Geneva Press, 1987), 102.

2. Colin Chapman, *Cross and Crescent: Responding to the Challenge of Islam* (Leicester, UK: Inter-Varsity, 1995), 76. Emphasis in original.

3. Kenneth Cragg, "Temple Gairdner's Legacy," *International Bulletin of Missionary Research* 5 (1981); 165

4. Edward J. Hughes, *Wilfred Cantwell Smith: A Theology for the World* (London: SCM, 1986), 194–95.

5. Wilfred Cantwell Smith, *Faith and Belief* (Princeton: Princeton University Press, 1979), 247.

6. René Latourelle, SJ, *Theology of Revelation*, Vol. 1 (New York: Alba House, 1966), 148, 171–72. Wolfhart Pannenberg, *Systematic Theology*, Vol. 1, trans. Geoffrey W. Bromiley (Grand Rapids: Eerdmans, 1991), 217–19.

7. Edward A. Dowey Jr., *A Commentary on the Confession of 1967 and an Introduction to "The Book of Confessions"* (Philadelphia: Westminster, 1968), 239.

8. Benjamin Breckinridge Warfield, *The Inspiration and Authority of the Bible,* ed. Samuel G. Craig (Philadelphia: Presbyterian and Reformed, 1948), 101.

9. Ibid.

10. R. C. Zaehner, "Why Not Islam?" in *Religious Studies* 11 (1975): 177.

11. For fuller treatment on atonement and Christ as prophet, priest, and king in Cragg, see Jim Tebbe, "Christian Scriptures in Muslim Culture in the Work of Kenneth Cragg" (A thesis submitted for the degree of Doctor of Philosophy, Department of Religious Studies, St. John's College, Nottingham, Open University, August, 1997) 243–51.

12. Albert Kenneth Cragg, *The Lively Credentials of God* (London: Darton, Longman and Todd, 1995), 72.

13. Albert Kenneth Cragg, *The Call of the Minaret* (Maryknoll, NY: Orbis, 1985), 289.

14. Albert Kenneth Cragg, *Returning to Mount Hira': Islam in Contemporary Themes* (London: Bellew Publishing, 1994), 72.

15. Ibid.

16. Albert Kenneth Cragg, *What Decided Christianity* (Worthing, UK: Churchman, 1989), 35.

CHAPTER 7

1. J. M. Gaudeul, *Called from Islam to Christ: Why Muslims become Christians* (London: Monarch Books, 1999).

2. On this subject, one could read R. Levy, *The Social Structure of Islam* (Cambridge: Cambridge University Press, 1927, 1965).

3. Here we only translate some of the names used to describe God in Islam: rahmân, rahîm, ghafûr, ghaffâr, `afûw, halîm, karîm.

4. Here again we use the same list of divine names, in particular: `adl, wâsi`, basîr, samî`, `alîm, hakam, muhsî, muntaqim.

CHAPTER 8

1. This article is an edited version of a paper which originally appeared in *Missionalia*, the Journal of the Southern African Missiological Society, 30, no. 2 (August 2002), and is used by permission.

2. Jean-Marie Gaudeul, *Called from Islam to Christ: Why Muslims become Christians* (London: Monarch Books, 1999).

3. J. Al-Sain, *Ich Kämpfte für Allah: Eine Frau auf der Such nach der Wahrheit* (Wuppertal: Brockhaus, 2000).

4. I give an outline of various missiological approaches to conversion in chapter two of my dissertation, "In Search of a New Life: Conversion Motives of Christians and Muslims" (Pretoria, South Africa: UNISA, 1999).

5. W. Kauuova, *Religious Pluralism: A Challenge to the Church in Southern Africa* (Pochefstroom, South Africa: North-West University, 1997), p. i.

6. J. N. J. Kritzinger, "A Contextual Christian Theology of Religions," *Missionalia* 19 (1991): 217ff.

7. Ibid., 227. Kritzinger refers to Ron Nicolson, "Religious Pluralism and the New South Africa: Dove of Peace or a Dead Duck? *Journal for the Study of Religion*. Vol. 4 (No.1, March), 67-82.

8. Ibid., 228. Kritzinger's arguments are based on two publications of the World Conference on Religion and Peace in South Africa (WCRP-SA 1988; 1991).

9. David J. Bosch, *Transforming Mission: Paradigm Shifts in Theology of Mission* (New York: Orbis, 1991), 483–88.

10. Kritzinger, "Contextual Christian Theology," 225.

11. All references to Rambo associated with this diagram are from L. R. Rambo, *Understanding Religious Conversion* (New Haven, CT: Yale University, 1993), 13–14.

12. Charles H. Kraft, *Christianity in Culture: A Study in Dynamic Biblical Theologizing in Cross-Cultural Perspective* (New York: Orbis, 1979), 329.

13. Cf. Walter Conn, *Christian Conversion: A Developmental Interpretation of Autonomy and Surrender* (New York: Paulist Press, 1986), 7.

14. J. Lofland and N. Skonovd, "Conversion Motifs," *Journal for the Scientific Study of Religion* 20 (1981): 373–385.

15. Rambo, *Understanding Religious Conversion*, 14ff.

16. See chapters two and three of my dissertation, "In Search of a New Life: Conversion Motives of Christians and Muslims," pp. 36–132, and in dialogue with the findings of my interviews see chapters five and six, pp. 157–203. I regard all five of these motives as of equal importance and treated them impartially in my research. In other words, the sequence in which they are arranged has no significance.

17. G. J. Van Butselaar, "Christian Conversion in Rwanda: The Motivations," *International Bulletin of Missionary Research* 5 (1981): 111–113. Van Butselaar calls this the "spiritual" motive for conversion. However, the meaning he attaches to it is very similar to Rambo's description of the "intellectual" motive (*Understanding Religious Conversion*, p. 14).

18. Rambo, *Understanding Religious Conversion*, p. 15; cf. Lofland and Skonovd, "Conversion Motifs."

19. A. P. Cowie, ed., *Oxford Advanced Learner's Dictionary*, 4th ed., (Oxford: Oxford University Press, 1989), 896.

20. William James, *The Varieties of Religious Experience* (New York: Viking Press, 1902).

21. J. H. Kroeger, "Naming the Conversion We Seek," *Missiology* 3 (1996): 371.

22. Cowie, *Oxford Advanced Learner's Dictionary*, 1291.

23. C. Raschke, "Revelation and Conversion: A Semantic Appraisal," *Anglican Theological Review* 60 (1978): 425.

24. C. V. McKinney, "Conversion to Christianity: A Bajju Case Study," *Missiology* 22: 149.

25. Warren S. Brown and C. Caetano, "Conversion, Cognition, and Neuropsychology," in *Handbook of Conversion*, ed. H. N. Malony and S. Southard (Birmingham, AL: Religious Education Press, 1992), 152.

26. Ibid, 149–52.

27. J. Lofland and R. Stark, "Becoming a World Saver: A Theory of Conversion to a Deviant Perspective," *American Sociological Review* 30 (1965): 862–875.

28. Van Butselaar, "Christian Conversion in Rwanda," 113.

29. Thomas Robbins, *Cults, Converts and Charisma: The Sociology of New Religious Movements* (London: Sage Publications, 1988) 69.

30. Van Butselaar, "Christian Conversion in Rwanda," 112.

31. J. N. J. Kritzinger, "Islam as Rival of the Gospel in Africa," *Missionalia* 8 (1980): 95.

32. Van Butselaar, "Christian Conversion in Rwanda," 113. The similarities between Van Butselaar's study and mine are probably due to the fact that both were conducted in Africa (Rwanda and South Africa, respectively).

33. A.H. Maslow, *Motivation and Personality* (New York: Harper & Row, 1970), 17.

34. I discuss these combinations in chapters five and six of my dissertation, where I analyze the twenty conversion narratives with the help of my analytical grid ("In Search of a New Life," pp. 157–203).

35. Cf. L. Poston, "Becoming a Muslim in the Christian West: A Profile of Conversion to a Minority Religion," *Institute of Muslim Minority Affairs* 12 (1991), 159–169.

36. The apartheid system in South Africa, which caused widespread suffering in black communities, was justified by means of Christian theology. This caused many black Christians to become disillusioned with Christianity, and some converted to Islam as a result of this.

37. Rambo, *Understanding Religious Conversion*, 41.

38. Walter Conn *Christian Conversion: A Developmental Interpretation of Autonomy and Surrender* (New York: Paulist Press, 1986) 7.

39. This small group should function in the context of a holistic understanding of conversion; i.e., by taking seriously all the needs and motivations that move people to change their religious allegiance, and by providing care for converts who move towards and away from Christianity.

40. Many Christians would say that this is going too far, namely to assist people who want to leave the faith community. I disagree with this argument. By assisting a person I mean that I would provide that person with literature about the other religion, I would accompany them to visit people of the other faith, allow them to get information before making a decision, etc. In actual fact I would say that through this process both parties benefit. In my experience, by displaying a caring and loving attitude certain people reconsidered the situation and did not convert to the other faith. This might also have been the case in the life of convert "C7" (see Maurer, "In Search of a New Life," pp. 174–75), had a Christian person helped her to make a thorough investigation of both faiths before taking a decision towards Islam.

CHAPTER 9

1. A. Yusuf Ali, *The Holy Qur'an: Text, Translation and Commentary* (Islamic Foundation, 1975).

2. Ibid.

3. Maudoodi, Maulana Abul A'ala, *The Laws of Marriage and Divorce in Islam*, 2nd ed. (Safa, Kuwait: Islamic Book Publishers, 1987).

4. Sahih Bukhari, Hadith 4692 of *Mishkat al-Musabih*.

CHAPTER 10

1. While the *Oxford American Dictionary and Language Guide* defines experience as "an event regarded as affecting one (*an unpleasant experience*)" or "the fact or process of being so affected (*learned by*

experience)," when I participate with, listen to, interact with, and observe Muslim women in South Asia, I discover another perspective of experience. Experience is in the midst of everyday life and connects to the very core of one's being, touching needs, emotions, senses, wonderings, queries, and longings. It replies to the unspoken of the heart, mind, and spirit. Experience flows deep into the inner being and validates her identity, affirms her belonging, and stretches her to further depths of understanding.

2.   Bilquis Sheikh, *I Dared to Call Him Father* (Pune, India: Word of Life Publications, 1980, and Lincoln, VA: Chosen Books, 1978), 35, 41.

3.   A. P. J. Abdul Kalam, *Wings of Fire: An Autobiography* (Hyderabad: Universities Press (India) Private Limited, 1999), p. v.

4.   In the Bible, many women encounter Jesus. Women *experience* Jesus through healing and deliverance (Mark 5:25–34; Luke 4:38–39; 13:10–13ff), through miracles (Luke 7:12–17; John 2:1–11; 11:30–45), as his disciples (Luke 8:1–3), from acceptance and forgiveness (Luke 7:36–50; John 4:1–42; 8:1–11), and through learning theology in the midst of tragedy (John 11:17–29).

5.   The origins of this influential model are traced to Claude E. Shannon and W. Weaver, *The Mathematical Theory of Communication* (Urbana: University of Illinois Press, 1949), trying to fully and accurately transmit messages through the phone lines while employees of the American Bell Telephone Company.

6.   J. O. Terry, *God and Woman: A Handbook with 40 Story Lessons* [each volume] *in Chronological Order for Storying the Good News to a Primarily Oral Culture: Muslim Women's Worldview*, Vols. 1, 2 (Chennai, India: Mission Educational Books, 2002).

7.   A. H., *Producing Mature Fruit* (Makati City, Philippines: CSM Publishing, 1999).

8.   Why are stories powerful? Entering into the story, its context and its telling, one experiences the fullness of the unfolding story and its meaning begins to emerge and linger and replay. For story as a method, the temptation is to emphasize the content—concentrating on the message and its cognitive processes (the facts, logic, and arguments enclosed in the story)—rather than the experience of the story itself, which is the core of the woman's processing that enables her to understand truth. Where stories engage women in the experience, the door opens. "Stories

meet our need to be actively involved in learning through discovery."
Quoted from Miriam Adeney, *Daughters of Islam: Building Bridges with Muslim Women* (Downers Grove: InterVarsity Press, 2002), 151.

9. Girija Khanna and Mariamma A. Varghese, *Indian Women Today* (New Delhi: Vikas Publishing House, 1978), 2. Manu was a lawmaker of the Smrita period (200 BC–200 AD) who impacted the future status of Indian women through his social codes and sanctions. He championed women's freedom to safeguard their position and preserve the family structure.

10. Khanna and Varghese, *Indian Women*, 50.

11. An example is "Piranima's healing room," operated by a Christian woman named Amma, in a residential neighborhood on the campus of Osmania University in Hyderabad, South India. (*Piranima* is a title of respect given to a woman married to a *murshid* or *pir* [Sufi religious teacher and guide].) Patients often come because they hear about Amma's great "*muhabbat* and *shakti*" (love and spiritual power). Joyce Flueckiger, "Storytelling in the Rhetoric of a Muslim Female Healer in South India," *The Bulletin of the Henry Martyn Institute of Islamic Studies* 13:1, 2 (1994), pp. 57, 59.

12. A. H., "Discipleship of Muslim Background Believers through Chronological Bible Storying," in *Ministry to Muslim Women: Longing to Call Them Sisters*, Fran Love and Jeleta Eckheart, eds. (Pasadena: William Carey Library, 2000), 149.

13. Finnegan, *Communicating: The Multiple Modes of Human Interconnection* (London: Routledge, 2002)] pp. xvi, 6. Finnegan's theoretical approach of "the active dimension of human interconnectedness" relies on pioneer of bodily communication Ray L. Birdwhistell's conception of communication; see the *International Encyclopedia of the Social Sciences*, Vol. 3, D. L. Sills, ed., s.v. "Communication" (New York: Macmillan and Free Press, 1968), 25, 26.

14. Kathleen Nicholls, *Asian Arts and Christian Hope* (New Delhi: Select Books, 1983), and Miriam Adeney, *Daughters of Islam*, model how the Christian communicates to create a multisensory environment. For example, Nicholls identifies redemptive qualities of *Urdu* poetry—relished across the Indian subcontinent—and Adeney exhorts Christian artists and writers to use their talent to communicate the gospel.

15. Sheikh, *I Dared to Call Him Father*, 36–37.

16. Ibid., 44–45.

17. Phil Parshall and Julie Parshall, *Lifting the Veil: The World of Muslim Women* (Waynesboro, GA: Gabriel Publishing, 2002), 226.

18. Flueckiger, "Storytelling," 63.

19. South Asian Muslim women who encounter Jesus through physical manifestations tend to be less educated and economically challenged, though *not* exclusively. They may be accustomed to relying on power beyond their own through the use of *tavis* (amulets), visits to the *dargah* (shrine) or similar power places like Piranima's healing room, and other folk practices; see Paul G. Hiebert, R. Daniel Shaw, and Tite Tienou, *Understanding Folk Religion: A Christian Response to Popular Beliefs and Practices* (Grand Rapids: Baker, 1999). It is even more essential, therefore, for Muslim women to experience the reality of Jesus in their daily lives and to know God's power for daily living.

20. There are a growing number of Muslim women in South Asia who have met with Jesus through knowledge and study combined *with* an experiential encounter. The truth is presented to them (they were challenged with clear presentations of the gospel, often repeated through relationship), but it is the multisensory experience that enables the women to understand and embrace the gospel. The women are primarily from educated homes and middle to upper class families.

21. As recounted in 2001 by Begum Bilquis' close friend, Mrs. Mitchell.

22. Shahida Lateef, *Muslim Women in India, Political and Private Realities: 1890s–1980s* (New Delhi: Kali for Women, 1990), 3.

23. Mrs. Mitchell wrote to me in 2001, "Over a period of several years we would go on vacation as a family, way up in the Himalayan mountains, north of the hospital. There God brought a nomadic people into our lives. Here is where God used songs in a powerful way to open the door to share the Gospel to around 25–30 people. When I was challenged by a young student present that my song did not agree with their Islamic faith, he was hushed by the matriarch of the clan with 'If those are the words of the song, there is nothing she can do about it.' I discovered later, that they passed on their history through songs and believed them to have authority. So the songs had more power than if I had just told them the story of the Gospel in words alone! Many memorized the song automatically and when we would return, they would learn new verses!"

24. One example is Sister Nikos, who uses everyday items in a Muslim woman's home so the one coming to faith can experience her faith in a real way and easily share with others. She explains the significance of the objects in the life and worship of the woman: "1) The [Indian] sweet is a sign of friendship and is also used when she is celebrating the worship of God. 2) The red rose speaks to her about love in general, excluding sensual love. So it may speak of the love of a mother for a child. A rose is used at a Muslim wedding and at other celebrations in their religion. The sweet and the rose represent God's friendship and love. 3) Muslims do not usually drink wine. I explain to them that for a Christian wine is symbolic of the blood of Jesus Christ shed for the covering and the re-mission of sin. Rose water, when sprinkled, symbolises purification from sin. 4) The unleavened bread in the life and worship of a Muslim means unadulterated living, i.e. pure, spotless, righteous lives. For a Christian, it speaks of the spotless body of Jesus Christ, crucified for us." Quoted from Nikos Ministries Newsletter (Birmingham, UK: 2001).

CHAPTER 13

1.   The best overall history of the people movement to Christianity is Frederick and Margaret Stock, *People Movements in the Punjab* (Pasa-dena: William Carey Library, 1975). For a sociological study of urban poor Christians a generation ago, see Pieter Streefland, *The Sweepers of Slaughterhouse: Conflict and Survival in a Karachi Neighbourhood* (The Netherlands: Van Gorcum, 1979).

2.   Seppo Syrjänen, *In Search of Meaning and Identity: Conversion to Christianity in Pakistani Muslim Culture* (Helsinki: Finnish Society for Missiology and Ecumenics, 1987). In addition (and more recently than my study), Warren Larson published his research on *Islamic Ideology and Fundamentalism in Pakistan: Climate of Conversion to Christian-ity?* (Lanham, Maryland: University Press of America, 1998).

3.   For example, Steven Masood, *Into The Light* (Eastbourne, UK: Kingsway, 1986); Thelma Sangster, *The Torn Veil: The Story of Sister Gulshan Esther* (Basingstoke, UK: Marshall, Morgan & Scott, 1984); Bilquis Sheikh, *I Dared to Call Him Father* (Eastbourne, UK: Kingsway, 1978); Ralph Wotton, *Jesus, More than a Prophet* (Leicester, UK: Inter-Varsity, 1980); Tamur Jan, *Ex-Muslims for Christ* (Birmingham, UK: The Crossbearers, 1980).

4.   Syrjänen, *In Search*, 177.

5. Syrjänen, *In Search*, 176.

6. Sheikh, *I Dared*, 71, 74, 76, 90.

7. Ann E. Mayer, *Islam and Human Rights: Tradition and Politics* (Boulder, CO: Westview Press, 1991), 63.

8. For in-depth studies by Muslim and non-Muslim authors, see M. S. el-Awa, *Punishment in Islamic Law: A Comparative Study* (Indianapolis: American Trust Publication, 1982); Mahmoud Ayoub, "Religious Freedom and the Law of Apostasy in Islam," *Islamochristiana* Vol. 20 (1994): 75–91; W. Heffening, article "Murtadd" in the *Encyclopaedia of Islam*, Second Edition (Leiden, Netherlands: Brill); Abul 'Ala Mawdudi, *The Punishment of the Apostate According to Islamic Law* (translation of *Murtadd ki Saza Islami Qanun men,* by Syed Silas Husain, Canada: publisher not given, c. 1995); A. Yusuf Ali, *The Holy Qur'an: Text, Translation and Commentary* (Leicester, UK: Islamic Foundation, 1975); T. W. Juynboll, article "Apostasy," in James Hastings, ed., *Encylopaedia of Religion and Ethics* Vol.1 (Edinburgh, 1967 edition); Mohammad A. Madani, *Verdict of Islamic Law on Blasphemy and Apostasy* (Lahore, Pakistan: Idara-e-Islamiat, 1994); Abdullahi Ahmed Al-Na'im, "The Islamic Law of Apostasy and Its Modern Applicability," in *Religion* Vol. 16 (1986): 197–221; Rudolph Peters and Gert de Vries, "Apostasy in Islam," in *Die Welt Des Islams* Vol. 17, Nos. 1–4 (1976–1977): 1–25; Samuel Zwemer, "The Law of Apostasy," in *The Moslem World* Vol. 14 (1924): 373–91.

9. This hadith is recorded by Ibn Abbas, and found in the collections of Bukhari, Nasa'i, al-Tirmidhi, and Abu Daood: quoted by Ayoub, p. 83, El-Awa, p. 52, etc.

10. A *hadd* offense is one where the penalty is specified in the Qur'an and which therefore leaves no leeway to the law courts to impose any other punishment. Examining the position of the Sunni law schools, Sidahmad concludes that apostasy is defined as *hadd* by Shafi'is and Malikis, and treated as *hadd* by Hanafis and Hanbalis; Muhammad A. Sidahmad, *The Hudud* (Malaysia: Perpustakaan Negara Malayion, 1995), 36–39.

11. Hanafi law as applied in the Indian subcontinent is codified in the *Hidaya,* translated by Charles Hamilton (1791 translation, reprinted in New Delhi: Kitab Bhavan, 1985); see p. 226ff.

12. Reported in *The News*, Lahore, Pakistan, August 7, 1998.

13. Mawdudi, *Punishment of the Apostate*, 49.

14. This murder took place in 1997. See the U.S. Department of State's *Country Reports on Human Rights Practices for 1997* (Washington: U.S. Government Printing Office, 1998), p. 1683.

15. Aslam Khan,, or "A/2"quoted in Syrjänen, *In Search*, 167.

16. In other legislation the British recognized the right of Muslims to convert, while in some cases seeking to restrict it. See Muhammad K. Masud, "Apostasy and Judicial Separation in British India," in *Islamic Legal Interpretation: Muftis and Their Fatwas*, ed. Masud, Merrick, and Power (Cambridge, MA: Harvard University Press, 1996).

17. Before the case was finalized, in 1992 Iqbal died in jail—almost certainly poisoned by prisoners or guards, who thus took the law into their own hands. See Naeem Shakir, "Fundamentalism, Enforcement of Shariah and Law on Blasphemy in Pakistan," in *Al-Mushir* Vol. 34, No. 4 (1992): 120ff.

18. Quoted in Edward Mortimer, *Faith and Power: The Politics of Islam* (UK: Faber & Faber, 1982), 208.

19. M. S. Masumi, "Review of S. A. Rahman's *Punishment of Apostasy in Islam*," in *Al-Mushir* Vol. II, No. 4 (1972): 310.

20. *Takbeer* magazine, 30.1.92.

21. Janet B. White, *Esther: Faithful Unto Death*, (no publisher given, ca. 1964) 25.

22. Sangster, *Torn Veil*, 146. For an anthropologist's viewpoint, see Alison Shaw, *A Pakistani Community in Britain* (Oxford: Blackwells, 1988).

23. Syrjänen, *In Search*, 112–13.

24. See his article in the *International Review of Mission*, 1983, 385–92.

25. Studies show the importance of *izzat* right across the range of Pakistan's varied ethnic groups. For instance, on the Punjabis see Zekiye Eglar, *A Punjabi Village in Pakistan* (Washington, D.C.: Columbia University Press, 1960); on the Baluchis see Stephen Pastner, article "Baluchi" in *Muslim Peoples: A World Ethnographic Survey*, ed. R. Weekes (Westport, CT: Greenwood Press, 1978); on the Pathans see Akbar Ahmed, *Pukhtun Economy and Society: Traditional Structure and Economic Development in a Tribal Society* (UK: Routledge, 1980), pp. 201ff., and Fredrik Barth, *Features of Person and Society in Swat* (UK:

Routledge, 1981); on the Sindhis see John Honigmann, article "Sindi" in *Muslim Peoples: A World Ethnographic Survey*, ed. R. Weekes (Westport, CT: Greenwood Press, 1978).

26. Patras Yusuf, "The Principle of *Izzat:* Its Role in the Spiritual Formation of Punjabi Religious *[sic]*," in *Al-Mushir* 22, no. 1 (1980): 20.

27. Sheikh, *I Dared*, 78.

28. Ahmed, *Pukhtun Economy and Society*, 201ff.

29. I attempted to arrive at a "typical" figure for each category by assigning points (A=6, B=5 . . . down to F=1) and taking the mean. This method, though rather artificial and not to be taken too seriously, yielded the "mean categories of treatment" as follows: Lower class 2.8 (slightly milder than category D), Middle classes taken together 3.4 (between D and C), and Upper class 4.0 (category C).

30. Cragg, *The Call of The Minaret*, quoted in Phil Parshall, *Beyond the Mosque* (Grand Rapids: Baker, 1985) 180.

CHAPTER 14

1. An unreached people group (UPG) means a group of at least 10,000 people in which Christians number less than 1 percent.

2. Most of these churches are comprised of nonindigenous people.

3. George Hunter III, *The Contagious Congregation: Frontiers in Evangelism and Church Growth* (Nashville: Abingdon, 1979), 37.

CHAPTER 15

1. This, and the following place names, are pseudonyms to protect the true identities and locations of the believers.

2. William J. Saal, *Reaching Muslims for Christ* (Chicago: Moody Press, 1991), 90–91.

3. James P. Dretke, *A Christian Approach to Muslims: Reflections from West Africa* (Pasadena: William Carey Library, 1979), 177.

4. John Robb, "Overcoming Resistance Through Prayer," in *Reaching the Resistant. Barriers and Bridges for Mission,* J. Dudley Woodbury, ed. (Pasadena: William Carey Library, 1998), 180–92.

5. Among the Jijimbas, the "dang" is the clan to which each citizen belongs. These clan lineages are based on one's family relationships

counted back to the fourth grandfather on the father's side, resulting in social identity with not so much regard for direct relationships. The "yingnima," or extended family, is not so broad in definition, but is also often typified by loose connections among the family members and applies more accurately to dwellers of the same household, whether by birth, adoption, marriage, or even friendship.

6. Paul Neeley and Sue Hall, "Praising the High King of Heaven," in Ethnomusicology: Articles on Music in Missions, <www.worship-arts-network.com>.

CHAPTER 16

1. The Fulbe (pronounced *fulbay*) are nomadic cattle herders and Muslims, and are known by several names. Fulbe, or technically *Fulɓe* (singular is *Pullo*), is what the Fulbe call themselves. In English they are also frequently called Fulani, which appears to have originated in Nigeria with the British. The French call them Peul. In Senegal they are referred to as Fula, and many other ethnic groups in West Africa know them by some variant of this name. Their language is known as Pulaar in Senegal and Guinea but in all other countries is known as Fulfulde. There are more than 20 million Fulbe in West Africa, mostly scattered across the Sahel (but occasionally further south) from Senegal in the west to Central African Republic in the east. Significant population concentrations are found in Senegal, Guinea, Mali, Burkina Faso, Niger, and Nigeria. There are six major dialects, some of which are more or less mutually intelligible but require separate Bible translations.

2. See J. Spencer Trimingham, *A History of Islam in West Africa*, for a thorough study of the spread of Islam in West Africa.

3. Though Islam introduced a new eschatology, the underlying worldview of the popular Islam that was brought across the Sahara Desert, especially in its Sufi forms, dovetailed nicely with the animistic worldview of the Fulbe, especially at the level of animistic science where day-to-day problems are solved.

4. Malcolm Hunter, for years a missionary to nomads with SIM International, was once told by a nomad, "When you can put your church on a camel, I will become a Christian." We know this can be done, but why don't we do it?

5. From the beginning I had attempted to identify myself as a marabout of the *Linjiila* (New Testament). At first, when we were still learning

how to live in a Fulbe village and our language skills were limited, I could not be a very impressive marabout. In time I was able to somewhat flesh out this identity, but have often felt that I could have developed this more extensively and consistently.

6. Works consulted in preparation of this paper included Elias Fouad Accad, *Building Bridges: Christianity and Islam* (Colorado Springs: Navpress, 1997); Al-Ghazali, *Inner Dimensions of Islamic Worship,* trans. Muhtar Holland (Leicestershire, UK: The Islamic Foundation, 1992); Colin Chapman, *Cross and Crescent: Responding to the Challenge of Islam* (Leicester, UK: Inter-Varsity, 1995); Jean-Marie Gaudeul, *Called from Islam to Christ: Why Muslims become Christians* (London: Monarch Books, 1999); Tarif Khalidi, *The Muslim Jesus: Sayings and Stories in Islamic Literature* (Cambridge, MA: Harvard University Press, 2001); *Islamic Creeds: A Selection,* trans. J. Montgomery Watt (Edinburgh: Edinburgh University Press, 1994); and J. Dudley Woodberry, "Contextualization Among Muslims Reusing Common Pillars," *International Journal of Frontier Missions* 13, no. 4 (October–December 1996).

CHAPTER 17

1. Similar verses can be found in John 7:31; 12:11, 42. Also see 1 John 2:22–23; 4:2, 15; 5:1, 6–11, 20.

CHAPTER 18

1. David Garrison, *Church Planting Movements* (Richmond, Virginia and Wiesbaden, Germany: IMB, 1999).

2. In the "C-scale" of "Christ-centered communities" developed by John Travis, a "C-1" community of believers would use "outsider" language and likely have a large cultural gap with the Muslim community, while "C-5" refers to Christ-centered communities of "Messianic Muslims" who have accepted Jesus as Savior and Lord and have not adopted outside cultural practices and language. For a description and application of the C-scale, see Joshua Massey, "God's Amazing Diversity in Drawing Muslims to Christ," *International Journal of Frontier Missions* 17 (Spring 2000).

3. David Garrison, *Church Planting Movements,* <www.missions.com/Downloads/WordDocs/CPM%20Booklet.pdf>.

4. Donald A. McGavran, *The Bridges of God* (New York: Friendship Press, 1981), rev. ed.

5. Donald A. McGavran, "The Bridges of God" in *Perspectives on the World Christian Movement* (Pasadena: William Carey Library, 1999), 323–338.

6. For the material system, especially in physics, elementary particle physicists are often in debate with condensed matter physicists. For the elementary particle physicists, the detailed physical behavior and properties of each individual particle is very important. They presume that an entire macroscopic system can be understood by learning each elementary particle's behavior, as the macroscopic system consists of those particles. However, it is known that the behavior of a single particle is totally different when it is in a condensed matter system. The two groups of physicists actually have different approaches. While one is analytical, individualistic, and microscopic, the other is holistic (or statistical), collective, and macroscopic.

7. McGavran, *Bridges of God*.

8. This type of time dependence, called stretched-exponential, is observed most commonly in a system consisting of distributed clusters experiencing a reorientation process under a constrained condition.

9. Dean S. Gilliland, *Pauline Theology and Mission Practice* (Eugene, OR: Wipf and Stock Publishers, 1998), 88.

10. Wolfgang Simson, *Houses that Change the World* (Waynesboro, GA: Authentic, 1999), 276.

11. Garrison, *Church Planting Movements*.

12. Phil Parshall, "Danger! New Directions in Contextualization" in *Evangelical Missions Quarterly* (October 1998), 404–410.

13. Scott Woods, "A Biblical Look at C5 Muslim Evangelism" in *Evangelical Missions Quarterly*, 39 no. 2 (April 2003), 188–195.

CHAPTER 20

1. Donald Larson, *Guidelines for Barefoot Language Learning* (St. Paul, MN: CMS Publishing, 1984).

CHAPTER 21

1. See David Bentley-Taylor, *The Weathercock's Reward: Christian Progress in Muslim Java* (London: Overseas Missionary Fellowship, 1967), for an English version of the thrilling story of the founding and growth of the East Java Christian Church.

CHAPTER 22

1. J. de Waal Dryden, "Refined by Fire: Paraenetic Literary Strategies in 1 Peter," *Tyndale Bulletin* 55, no. 2 (2004): 317–20.

2. *Transformation*, 17, no. 1 (January–March 2000), the title and theme of the entire issue.

3. See, for example, the articles and responses on this theme by Phil Parshall and others in *Evangelical Missions Quarterly*, starting with his "Danger! New Directions in Contextualization," *EMQ* 34, no. 3 (October 1998) and most recently "Lifting the Fatwa," *EMQ* 39, no. 3 (July 2004).

4. Jean-Marie Gaudeul, *Encounters and Clashes: Islam and Christianity in History*, rev. ed., Vol. 1: *A Survey*; Vol. 2: *Texts* (Rome: Pontifical Institute for Arab and Islamic Studies, 1984).